"That Magnificent Army of Youth and Peace"

THE CIVILIAN CONSERVATION CORPS
IN NORTH CAROLINA, 1933-1942

By this all will know

Served his country well as a member of the

Civilian Conservation Corps

that magnificent Army of Youth and Peace that put into action the Awakening of the People to the facts of Conservation and Recreation; and that with all honors he completed his tour of Duty at _____

_____, on _____

Camp Superintendent.

Director of Emergency Conservation Work

Company Commander.

Director of the National Park Service

This certificate was issued by the Civilian Conservation Corps. It bears a dynamic conservation message. It was issued to members of "that magnificent Army of Youth and Peace." The recipient's name has been digitally removed. From the Mars Hill College Archives.

"That Magnificent Army of Youth and Peace"

The Civilian Conservation Corps in North Carolina, 1933-1942

HARLEY E. JOLLEY

Office of Archives and History
North Carolina Department of Cultural Resources
Raleigh
2007

North Carolina Department of Cultural Resources
Lisbeth C. Evans
Secretary

Office of Archives and History
Jeffrey J. Crow
Deputy Secretary

Division of Historical Resources
David L. S. Brook
Director

Historical Publications Section
Donna E. Kelly
Administrator

Front Cover: [*upper right*] from the Blue Ridge Parkway Archives (see p. 68); [*lower right*] from the National Archives (see p. 8); [*lower left*] from the North Carolina State Archives; [*upper left*] from the Mars Hill College Archives (see p. 103); [*center*] from the Great Smoky Mountains National Park Archives (see p. 52).

Back Cover: From the National Archives (see p. 106).

Printed by Edwards Brothers

Contents

Maps, Tables, and Illustrations

Foreword

In 2005, the Historical Publications Section contracted with Harley Jolley, retired professor at Mars Hills College, to produce a history of the Civilian Conservation Corps (CCC) in North Carolina. The section then contracted with Robert M. Topkins, former editor with the section, to copy edit and index the work. Dr. Jolley provided numerous photographs, replete with permissions for their use. Most were representative of the western part of the state, so additional images were gathered to represent the Piedmont and coastal region. In addition to distributing the images more equitably, their placement within the text, as well as their identification, was necessary. Because of its close proximity, the State Archives provided much-needed material for illustrations. Susan Trimble, with the HPS staff, did a magnificent job of laying everything out, Bill Owens, marketing specialist, helped design the cover, and Lisa Bailey applied her proofreading skills.

Because the majority of the research for the project was completed prior to the Internet, few online sources are cited. For subsequent material about the CCC in North Carolina, visit the website www.cccnorthcarolina.org.

The year 2008 marks the seventy-fifth anniversary of the establishment of the CCC. Dr. Jolley has done a remarkable job of telling the story of "that magnificent Army of Youth & Peace" and how much North Carolina owes those young men.

Donna E. Kelly, *Administrator*
Historical Publications Section

Preface

One of the rich, unheralded cultural legacies enjoyed by the people of North Carolina and the millions of visitors to the state is that contributed by the Civilian Conservation Corps between 1933 and 1942. The agency, born of the Great Depression and sired by President Franklin D. Roosevelt, was established as a means of rehabilitating a nation disastrously plagued by a relentless economic depression accompanied by widespread soil erosion so devastating that it threatened the very sustenance of America. Mass unemployment had become a way of life: 4 million unemployed in 1930, 8 million in 1931, and 12 million in 1937. In North Carolina alone, twenty-seven out of every one hundred persons were on relief in 1933. Moreover, an accomplice, wind and water erosion, had robbed the nation's soil of much of its fertility. One specialist declared that three billion tons of fertile soil were lost each year. To make matters worse, some five million of the nation's young people were out of work, away from homes, out on the railroads and highways, out on the prowl, and heartbreakingly out of hope.

To counter this horrendous waste of natural and human resources, Franklin D. Roosevelt, immediately upon becoming president, secured from Congress in 1933 passage of "An Act for the Relief of Unemployment Through the Performance of Useful Public Work and For Other Purposes." The law created the Civilian Conservation Corps (CCC) to employ single men ages eighteen through twenty-five.

Within a remarkably short time every state in the nation had conservation camps at work, laboring to salvage the land and to rehabilitate previously neglected young men. By the time the program was terminated in July 1942, thousands of North Carolinians had participated in and benefited from the CCC, both economically and culturally. Thousands of acres of ravaged land in North Carolina, including beach fronts, had been salvaged from erosion and rehabilitated. Many of the recreational resources that make North Carolina a leader in tourism—the Great Smoky Mountains National Park, the Blue Ridge Parkway, the Cape Hatteras National Seashore, national forests, state forests, and state parks—had been either built by or had felt the healing touch of the CCC. Moreover, thousands of young Tar Heels and their families had been introduced to a new comprehension of the worth of mankind, better health, an enhanced work ethic, self-discipline, improved self-esteem, a sense of community, a willingness to cooperate with others, accelerated educational ambitions, a keener sense of patriotism, and a deeper awareness of societal relationships.

The intent of this volume is to place in a historical perspective the physical labors and cultural contributions of the Civilian Conservation Corps in one state, North Carolina, so that readers might better comprehend not only what the CCC was but also why it was established, what it accomplished, and what it bequeathed to the state and its citizens.

Acknowledgments

Credit and appreciation are hereby extended to the Mars Hill College Faculty Development Committee for encouraging and partially funding the lengthy research that this project entailed. Also, warmest thanks and appreciation are extended to the highly courteous and useful reference staff at the National Archives (both in Washington, D.C., and Atlanta, Georgia) and to all the public librarians throughout North Carolina who so skillfully and graciously shared their diverse holdings. Special thanks are conveyed to Betty Burkett of the microfilm library at Appalachian State University in Boone for her outstanding knowledge and expert technical services.

Keenest appreciation is hereby expressed to Donna E. Kelly, administrator, Historical Publications Section, North Carolina Office of Archives and History, and her staff for so adeptly shepherding this material through the challenging intricacies of the publishing process. Heartfelt thanks are likewise extended to Ron Holland, recently retired director, Western Office of Archives and History, Asheville, and Nick Lanier, photographer with that office, for their unstinting support of this project and for designing and producing the still active CCC traveling exhibit. Significant funding toward publication of this work was provided by the Kulynych Family Foundation I.

Finally, to Mess Steward Frank L. Bridges, Superintendent G. B. Maneval, and Subaltern Richard E. Todd, three CCC comrades removed from the ranks by death but whose unflagging encouragement, unselfish sharing of agency memorabilia, and ongoing moral support made this volume possible, this account of their work is hereby dedicated.

1 "We Are Men of the CCC": Genesis

On a crisp and beautiful day in October 1933 a fine-looking group of young men, uniformly dressed in blue denim, marched briskly down a newly made mountain trail, enthusiastically lifting their voices in song:

> We are men of the CCC.
> We are as happy as can be.
> We work all day, sleep all night.
> We are all okay and feel all right.

But what is most remarkable about those men is that, just a very short time before, they and millions like them were

> Nobody's men;
> Unhappy as they could be;
> Were never working;
> Were doing little but sleeping;
> And even that was most uncertain.[1]

Such men were the innocent victims of the so-called Great Depression. At a time when they should have been in school, at work, or engaged in something constructive, they were chronically unemployed, absent from home and school, and, worst of all, out of hope. Authorities estimated that in 1933 from five to seven million young men between the ages of sixteen and twenty-five years old were unemployed, many of them for a number of months. To the great dismay of these men, the door of opportunity had never been visible, much less opened, to them. As one of those rescued by the Civilian Conservation Corps later recalled, "We were humanity uprooted. We were boxcar barnacles. We were knights of the highway."[2] A concerned observer described the plight of these men: "They were in the clutches of a vaguely understood and much feared transgressor of their rights. . . . Untaught, suffering,

groping. . . . Here is much fine human material, capable of being brought to the best standards of American manhood, that has been neglected throughout its life, often utterly so."[3]

Simultaneously, Mother Nature and an unrelenting god called The Economy were mercilessly presenting their due bills. In many parts of the nation, the landscape was a bleak testimony to the ravages that man's prodigality and insensitive stewardship had brought about. Author Thomas Wolfe's tearful description of his beloved North Carolina mountains is illustrative of the abysmal scene: "The great mountain slopes and forests had been ruinously detimbered. The farm soil on the hillsides had eroded and washed down. . . . It was evident that a huge compulsive greed had been at work. The whole region had been sucked and gutted, milked dry, denuded of its rich primeval treasures."[4]

The appalling sucking and gutting described by Wolfe was a common occurrence across the nation. An atrocious, ravenous appetite for more, more, more, and even more had wrought havoc with America's resources, both human and natural. Overgrazing and erosion had laid waste the great American West; the Plains States were victims of erosion by both wind and water. Meanwhile, floods on the Mississippi River annually flushed four hundred million tons of vital life-giving earth down the waterway. Spokesmen in the Tennessee Valley reported that a century of unchecked erosion had wiped out at least half of the producing capacity of that region. The state of Iowa was denuded with the loss of some thirty billion tons of its best soil. In Georgia it was reported that "Steward County is gone"—taken by erosion. The chronicler of this dismal tale informed the nation that it was losing three billion tons of good soil by erosion every year, an amount sufficient to "require a train of freight cars 475,000 miles long; enough to girdle the planet 19 times at the equator."[5] Hugh Hammond Bennett, a prominent soil conservationist in North Carolina, estimated that soil erosion was costing the United States at least four hundred billion dollars annually. He warned that unless the nation altered its ways, it was headed toward "geological suicide."[6]

Compounding all of these problems was a flight by farm families to America's industrial regions in the hope of escaping the seemingly endless cycle of renewed hope and bankruptcy. For all too many farmers, the last era of prosperity had been that of World War I, with its ravenous demand for farm products. The 1920s, however, had proven devastating for American agriculture. At the end of that decade the Great Depression arrived as the final plague, accompanied by the drying up of the land, bringing a severe curtailment of bank loans and a widespread loss of hope. Those who had fled to city factories soon found that those presumed oases had dried up, too. The advancing Depression threatened millions of Americans, with no quarter offered to any class, age, sex, or color—all were at risk. A sharecropper's son described the times most eloquently: "Those were hard days. Our family were sharecroppers. There just wasn't any money. [President Herbert] Hoover is the fellow who made it possible to trim your toenails without taking off your shoes."[7]

The devastating inclusiveness of the Great Depression is luridly amplified by the following sampling of historians' comments, which describe the heart-wrenching conditions that then existed in the United States:

In a single day in April [1932], an estimated one-fourth of Mississippi went to auction.

Over 9,000 American banks either went bankrupt or closed their doors to avoid bankruptcy between 1930 and 1933.

By 1933, Americans had virtually ceased making investments in productive enterprises.

By 1932 between 1 million and 2 million Americans were homeless wanderers, among them an estimated 25,000 families.

"No home, no work, no money," despaired a Pennsylvanian as he pled for a "human" way to dispose of his family in 1934.

In 1932 a wagon load of oats could not buy a four-dollar pair of Thom McAn shoes.

An average of 100,000 people lost their jobs every week in the first three years after the crash.

A million unemployed walked the streets of New York; over half a million roamed the streets of Chicago. In Cleveland half the working force had no jobs; in Toledo, more than three quarters were without work.

Wheat fell from $1.05 a bushel in 1929 to 39 cents in 1932, corn from 81 cents to 39 cents a bushel, cotton from 17 cents to 6 cents a pound.

Unemployment rose: 4 million in 1930, 8 million in 1931, 12 million in 1932.

Eleven children in that house. They've got no shoes, no pants. In the house, no chairs. My God. You go in there, you cry, that's all.

For urban and rural Americans alike, malnutrition and homelessness became a growing problem.[8]

To its great discomfort, North Carolina, too, was a major victim of the Great Depression. As of early 1933, twenty-seven of every one hundred of its citizens were on relief, with the mountain and coastal regions the hardest hit. A report from the Emergency Relief Administration in Raleigh

Prepared by Statistical Department

PER CENT OF POPULATION ON RELIEF BY COUNTIES
JANUARY, 1935

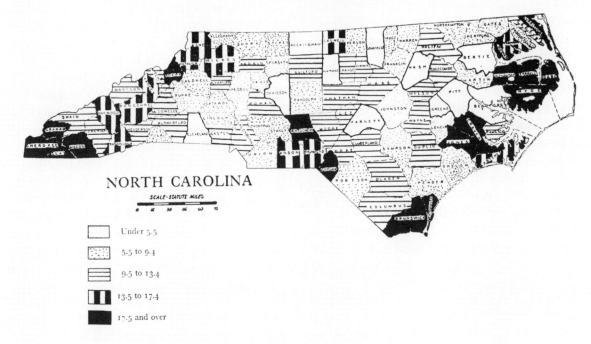

PER CENT OF POPULATION ON RELIEF BY COUNTIES
MAY, 1935

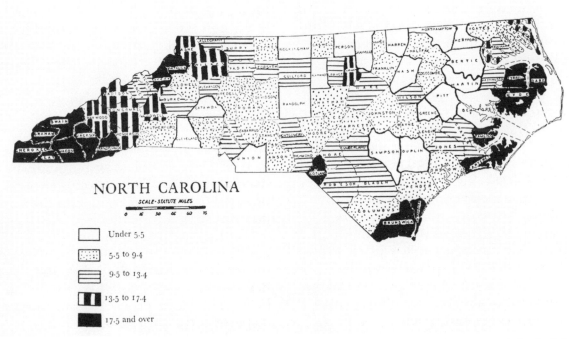

From J. S. Kirk et al., eds., *Emergency Relief in North Carolina: A Record of the Development and the Activities of the North Carolina Emergency Relief Administration, 1932-1935* (Raleigh: Emergency Relief Commission, 1936), 144.

all too vividly summarized the state's existing adverse economic conditions: "The mountains of North Carolina, justly famed for their scenic beauty, afford their inhabitants only the barest living, below all minimum standards of well-being."9 Long before the onset of the Depression, the economy of western North Carolina had become destitute, partially because of a failing market for mineral products but especially because of the depletion of timber resources. The economy of the Carolina tidewater country was likewise in the economic doldrums, the result of persistent adverse weather and a constantly declining fishing industry. Also suffering was the normally more prosperous industrial Piedmont, the victim of widespread closings of textile mills, fickle weather, and the vicarious effects of ever-worsening national economic conditions.10 One North Carolinian contending with the Depression expressed the dilemma this way: "We are like the drounding [sic] man, grabbing at everything that flotes [sic] by, trying to save what little we have."11

The need for some sort of drastic action was obvious, but the question of what sort of action, and whose responsibility such action might be, faced the American people. The answer lay in the nation's cultural legacy. The prevailing American philosophy pertaining to alleviating the woes of the needy sprang from the Poor Laws of England, which originated with King Henry VIII and his daughter, Queen Elizabeth I. Those laws charged local officials and churchwardens with identifying and providing for the poor. Nevertheless, relatives were deemed responsible for their needy kinfolk. Public work at taxpayers' expense was to be provided for those able to perform labor. Indeed, those able but unwilling to work were subject to punishment.12 In short, family, church, and local government were responsible for the welfare of the impoverished. Likewise, the stigma that branded the English poor as contemptible

failures in life's battles remained prevalent in American society when the Great Depression arrived.

Two previous attempts to change the prevailing concept of local responsibility and to substitute federal caretaking were given short shrift. In 1894, in the midst of a major economic depression, Jacob S. Coxey, an Ohio businessman, led a march of unemployed persons on the nation's capital, demanding federal relief. He urged the national government to enter into a multimillion-dollar road-building program, utilizing unemployed laborers. Coxey argued that such a project would provide work for the jobless, improve the nation's transportation system, and jump-start the entire economy. But he and his "army" were met by federal police, arrested for trespassing, and forced to disperse. President Grover Cleveland had not the slightest compunction in ordering that action. He fully realized that relief for those unfortunate souls was not his responsibility nor that of his government, but rather that of families, churches, or local governments. Thus Coxey's march on Washington was met by the mailed fist rather than a helping hand. In American society thereafter, "Coxey's Army" became a metaphor for an exercise in futility.13

A second march on Washington by unemployed persons seeking federal relief met a similar fate. In the spring of 1932 approximately fifteen thousand veterans of World War I, jobless and urgently in need of help, formed a "Bonus Expeditionary Force" and marched on the nation's capital. The men were seeking economic relief through the immediate payment of veteran's bonuses scheduled for payment in 1945. But when the beseeching former doughboys failed to heed President Herbert Hoover's order to disperse and return to their homes, he turned regular army troops under the command of Douglas MacArthur and Maj. George S. Patton Jr., armed with tanks, machine guns, bayonets, and tear

Louis Steadman was one of several Charlotte businessmen who made trucks available for gathering supplies to be distributed to the North Carolina contingent of the Bonus Army in Washington, D.C. From the *Charlotte Observer*, July 28, 1932.

gas, loose upon them. The troops torched and razed the veterans' makeshift camp and forcibly dispersed the men as members of an unruly mob. Hoover attempted to justify the harsh response by charging that the marchers were Communist rabble, not actual veterans, but the real reason for Hoover's directive was his fear that yielding to the marchers' demands would more than double the national deficit. Moreover, in his view, the marchers' financial woes were their own responsibility and neither his nor the federal government's. His attitude—so widely held in America—was implicit in his statement that "Victory over depression must be won by the resolution of our people to fight their own battles in their own communities."[14]

But, in the meantime, another army was mobilizing—a vast army of unemployed whose ranks by 1932 numbered in the millions and were increasing daily, to the chagrin of the Hoover administration. Indeed, President Hoover, adamant as ever about keeping the federal government out of the relief business, finally had to temper

his position. He had originally declared that "For the federal government to assume what has been local obligations would be to undermine the very basis of self-government," but as unemployment snowballed, reaching unprecedented levels of ten-plus million, he began to urge creation of federal work projects. Through his administration's Reconstruction Finance Corporation, the federal government made available $300 million that could be loaned to the states in providing temporary relief.[15] Unfortunately, little of the funding made its way to the needy. Hoover's too-little, too-late policies not only embittered the millions of unemployed but also guaranteed that his administration would go down to resounding defeat in the coming 1932 elections. Even so, the walls of tradition had been breached, if ever so slightly.

Nevertheless, no one listening to the speeches of Franklin D. Roosevelt, the man who ultimately succeeded Hoover as president, would have considered him a threat to the traditional concept of public relief.

Indeed, when faced with the relief issue as governor of New York, he staunchly categorized poor relief as "essentially a local function." In February 1932, while encouraging Sen. Robert Wagner to support emergency federal relief, Roosevelt cautioned that such a program "should not be regarded as a permanent government policy." Even when, as president, he signed the Unemployment Relief Act of May 12, 1933, designed to put millions of Americans to work on federal public works projects, he loudly affirmed that "The first obligation is on the locality."[16]

It is ironic that whereas Herbert Hoover drew political suicide from the wells of the Great Depression, Franklin Roosevelt drew forth the waters of political sustenance, giving his nation renewed hope and providing him with an unprecedented four terms in office—and an enormously expanded federal relief program. Indeed, the introductory segment of Roosevelt's pioneering March 21, 1933, message to Congress, which resulted in the passage of the Unemployment Relief Act, was prophetic of federal legislation that would indelibly alter and immeasurably increase the role of the national government as a relief agency:

> It is essential to our recovery program that measures immediately be enacted aimed at unemployment relief. A direct attack on this problem suggests three types of legislation.
>
> The first is the enrollment of workers now by the Federal Government for such public employment as can be quickly started and will not interfere with the demand for or the proper standards of normal employment.
>
> The second is grants to the States for relief work.
>
> The third extends to a broad public works labor-creating program.[17]

The second and third proposals were in reality little more than a continuation of programs previously instituted by the Hoover administration. But the first one enormously widened the gates of direct federal relief. Indeed it embodied Roosevelt's pioneering entry into massive nationwide federal relief—his now famous Civilian Conservation Corps. The March 21 message to Congress explicitly designated what Roosevelt desired as his first major attack upon unemployment: "I propose to create a civilian conservation corps to be used in simple work, not interfering with normal employment, and confining itself to forestry, the prevention of soil erosion, flood control, and similar projects."[18] Roosevelt's statement is deceptively simple. Behind it lay much animated discussion and brainstorming, many proposals and robust counterproposals. Like so much of the New Deal program, it was the by-product of numerous minds but was credited to the president. In later years Eleanor Roosevelt noted that the Civilian Conservation Corps was the New Deal initiative in which her husband took the greatest pride. "For years," she wrote, "Franklin had talked in desultory fashion about the value of out-of-doors work and knowledge for boys, and had always wanted to run a school at Hyde Park which would give young people a mixture of manual and intellectual exercise. I think these ideas were in the background of his mind when he began to plan the CCC."[19]

Many years later Secretary of the Interior Stewart L. Udall characterized Franklin D. Roosevelt as "both father and godfather of the CCC."[20] But numerous precedents antedated FDR's 1933 proposal. To cope with widespread unemployment while governor of New York, Roosevelt had instituted the Temporary Emergency Relief Administration, headed by Harry Hopkins, to employ thousands of needy people in reforestation and other conservation projects. In other states, such as Virginia, Wisconsin, Idaho, California, and Colorado, thousands of unemployed had been put to work on a variety of conservation projects. Moreover, the United States Forest Service, under the leadership of Chief Forester Robert Y. Stuart, had pioneered public works programs in the realm of reforestation and the improvement of stands of timber. Other forest-oriented authorities had projected notions of utilizing armies of the unemployed to promote conservation activities. Likewise in Europe numerous nations had established conservation-related work-relief programs. Bulgaria, Austria, Switzerland, France, Great Britain, and Germany, for example, had work-service camps aimed at relieving unemployment and promoting conservation.[21]

But Marguerite A. LeHand, private secretary to President Roosevelt, responding to a 1939 inquiry as to the origins of the CCC, provided the most likely scenario: "Essentially, the Civilian Conservation Corps idea is merely a combination of these two thoughts— (1) Putting people to work with public funds, and (2) conserving forests, water, and so on. As he [Roosevelt] looks back upon the origins of his measure to the Congress in the Spring of 1933 on unemployment relief in general, in which was included the proposal for the Civilian Conservation Corps, he cannot find that the idea for the . . . Corps was taken from any one source. It was rather the obvious conflux of the desire for conservation and the need for finding useful work for unemployed young men."[22]

Raymond Moley, one of Roosevelt's closest advisers at the beginning of the New Deal, supported this interpretation. He recalled that on March 24, 1933, twenty days after the inaugural, the president had outlined to him a plan for a "Civilian Conservation Corps." The proposal prompted Moley to recall the considerable attention created by an article published by Harvard professor William James in 1910. The article, titled "The Moral Equivalent of War," expressed James's horror at the unabating ruin wrought by war and proposed that as a counterweight to seemingly perpetual war, America's young men be conscripted not for military but for

national service in a "War against Nature." James suggested that a stint at activities such as road-building would have a salutary effect upon the nation's youth: "They would have paid their blood tax, done their part in the immemorial human warfare against nature; they would tread the earth more proudly."[23] But when Moley asked Roosevelt if he had taken any classes under James at Harvard, the president replied "no" and added that the only thing he remembered about the professor was his abundant beard.[24]

Nonetheless, the president's ideas and those of William James had much in common, as is suggested by the supporting evidence Roosevelt proffered to Congress when he proposed the CCC: "This enterprise is an established part of our national policy. It will conserve our precious natural resources. It will pay dividends to the present and future generations. It will make improvements in national and state domains which have been largely forgotten in the past few years of industrial development." Roosevelt followed this pragmatic statement with words quite reminiscent of William James: "More important, however, than the material gains, will be the moral and spiritual value of such work. The over-whelming majority of unemployed Americans who are now walking the streets and receiving private or public relief, would infinitely prefer to work. We can take a vast army of these unemployed out into healthful surroundings. We can eliminate to some extent at least the threat that enforced idleness brings to spiritual and moral stability."[25]

In proposing the CCC Roosevelt was speaking from the heart. His own beloved Hyde Park farm, victim of soil erosion, had become his proving ground for the positive value of reforestation and conservation. He sincerely believed that the forest was, in his words, "The most potent factor in maintaining Nature's delicate balance in the organic and inorganic worlds." He also

Franklin D. Roosevelt on a CCC inspection trip at Shenandoah National Park, Virginia, the first CCC camp in the United States, August 12, 1933. From the Records of the National Park Service, Record Group 79, National Archives.

called the forests the "lungs of our land, purifying our air and giving fresh strength to our people."[26]

Roosevelt was convinced that a pilgrimage into the wilderness to work with the land would rejuvenate the unemployed young people of America, as it traditionally had their pioneering forefathers. He ardently believed that "There is a merit for all of us in the ancient tale of the giant Antaeus, who, every time he touched his Mother Earth, arose with his strength renewed a hundred-fold."[27] Moreover, Roosevelt was a devout disciple of the Jeffersonian philosophy that diligent stewardship of the land was the key to national prosperity and the integrity of the individual. Thus, the opportunity to salvage both man and land motivated him to avidly devise, support, guide, and promote his most treasured political brainchild, the Civilian Conservation Corps.[28]

Roosevelt's explanation of why he proposed the agency dramatically

illuminates his basic humanitarianism: "Both to save a generation of upright and eager young men and to help save and restore our threatened resources, I had determined even before the Inauguration to take as many of these young men as we could off the city street corners and place them in the woods at healthful employment and sufficient wage so that their families might also be benefitted by the employment." After the president's innovative proposal had become a striking success, he gleefully recalled that there were legions of doubters. "They said, 'These boys from the cities do not want to go to camp. They do not want to go and live in tents. They never saw an ax. You can not get them to go, and if you do, they will run away the first night they are in camp.'" He remembered being ridiculed with "ribald laughter about planting trees, this crazy dream, this political gesture." But, nevertheless, he exclaimed, "Let's try it!"[29]

Trying it required an abundance of political jockeying. Adviser Raymond Moley urged Roosevelt to move cautiously and to devise a well-planned proposal that would merit congressional approval and simultaneously fend off diehard critics. The need for such a program was painfully obvious, but lingering doubts as to specifically how to create a nationwide work force without competing with employment in the private sector, stealing work contracts away from private enterprise, undercutting the prevailing wage scale, and becoming a laughingstock for lack of productivity quickly emerged.[30] The president, envisioning a forest-conservation army of a half-million young men, summoned several leaders to help brainstorm a viable program. Close personal advisers such as Moley and Louis M. Howe were augmented by the political officials most likely to be involved in implementing the project: Harold L. Ickes, secretary of the interior; Henry A. Wallace, secretary of agriculture; George Dern, secretary of war; and Frances Perkins, secretary of labor. The president quickly indicated what he desired each of these officials to do: the Department of Labor was to be the recruiting agent; the Department of War was to be the "conditioning" agent, offering physical conditioning, housing, clothing, food, and medical care and ensuring orderly conduct; and the Departments of Agriculture and the Interior, as well as War, were to be providers of acceptable jobs.[31]

Despite all the preliminary soul-searching and carefully crafted strategy, when Roosevelt's proposal for a civilian conservation corps—with enrollees earning one dollar a day for conservation work— came before Congress in late March 1933, a number of congressional and public critics bitterly lashed out. For example, champions of labor unions, alarmed over the army's role in the program, charged that such a corps would reduce national wages to a mere subsistence and would militarize labor itself. William Green, labor's chief spokesman, vilified the plan, declaring that "It smacks, as I see it, of fascism, of Hitlerism, of a form of sovietism." In testimony before Congress, Herbert Benjamin, a Communist, was even more condemnatory: "This bill undertakes to establish and legalize a form of force[d] labor," he charged.[32] Meanwhile, Norman Thomas, a socialist spokesman, charged that "such work-camps fit into the psychology of a Fascist, not a Socialist, state."[33] The older, more traditional view that denied any federal responsibility to the needy emerged in the form of a speech by Rep. Carroll L. Beedy of Maine, who warned his colleagues that approval of such a work corps would cause "the masses to believe that it is the Government's duty to put them on the payroll."[34]

In the end, the urgency of doing something positive for America's unemployed youth overrode such objections and brought speedy passage of the bill on March 31, 1933. The legislation, titled "An Act for the Relief of Unemployment Through the Performance of Useful Public Work and for Other Purposes," was easily one of the most important conservation measures Congress ever enacted. Indeed, it embodied the vanguard of federal relief activities that were to become increasingly comprehensive and permanent. The act authorized the president to put unemployed people to work on federal, state, and private lands when in the public interest. Moreover, it stipulated that such work was to be concentrated on the "prevention of forest fires, floods and soil erosion, plant pest and disease control, the construction, maintenance, or repair of paths, trails, and fire lanes, as well as any incidental conservation tasks."[35] The legislation also stipulated that "in employing citizens for the purpose of this Act no discrimination shall be made on account of race, color, or creed."[36]

As with so much of the early New Deal legislation, Congress then left the administrative details of the employment program to the president. He and his advisers quickly drew up operational guidelines.

With them came a display of Roosevelt's renowned political shrewdness. Remembering well the concerns loudly voiced by organized labor, he appointed a respected labor union official, Robert Fechner, to serve as director of the program, which was officially known as "Emergency Conservation Work," or "ECW." Not until 1937 was that title dropped in favor of "Civilian Conservation Corps," or "CCC."[37] At the same time, the president approved an advisory council for the new program, nominating representatives from the Departments of Labor, War, Agriculture, and the Interior to work with Fechner.[38]

Roosevelt, banking on congressional approval and seeking to employ as quickly as possible a minimum of a quarter-million young men, launched a peacetime mobilization of American manpower unparalleled in the nation's history. At Roosevelt's command, a startling chain of events meshed with uncommon efficiency and speed, activating immediate responses from the highest echelons of the federal government to the smallest and most remote counties in all the states. The Departments of Labor, War, Agriculture, and the Interior became, out of sheer necessity, major participants in a gigantic federal relief program that, perhaps coincidentally, implemented William James's vision of national conscription for a war "against nature." But Roosevelt, of course, saw it as a war *for* nature.

That war fostered a whole host of romanticized names for the president's conservation forces: "Roosevelt's tree army," "the forest soldiers," "the forest expeditionary force," and "Roosevelt's Robin Hoods." The president, however, saw the war as a new opening through which his nation could turn back the forces of adversity, poverty, illiteracy, and waste, both of human and natural resources. From his staff went mobilization orders that directly and immediately affected every state in the Union. North Carolina, to its great delight,

quickly found itself in the line of march. The Civilian Conservation Corps, for the ensuing nine years, became a vital ingredient in the quality of Tar Heel human life and in the well-being of the state's natural resources.

EMERGENCY CONSERVATION WORK

ROBERT FECHNER, DIRECTOR

COUNCIL

W. FRANK PERSONS, *Representing the Secretary of Labor*

DUNCAN K. MAJOR, Jr.,
    General, U. S. Army, Representing the Secretary of War

F. A. SILCOX, *Forest Service, Representing the Secretary of Agriculture*

ARNO B. CAMMERER,
    National Park Service, Representing the Secretary of the Interior

CCC Soil Erosion Work

The Same Area 4½ Months Later

CCC director Robert Fechner was keenly aware of the value of good press and public support. His office constantly printed brochures such as the one pictured here. From Records of the Forest Service, Record Group 95, National Archives.

$\mathscr{A}$ charming senior citizen with a reminiscent gleam in her eye recently recalled how she and her teenage girl friends arose bright and early on the morning of May 27, 1933, to ensure themselves frontline positions at the Hot Springs, North Carolina, railroad station. "We had learned," she said, "that the first group of CCC boys to be stationed in Hot Springs were coming in early that morning and we were determined to be there, all gussied up, to scout for a good-looking boyfriend." "I remember," she continued, blushing, "that I quickly spotted one and blurted out, loudly, 'that one's mine!'"[1]

Little did those girls know that the opportunity afforded them to conduct their scouting expedition was but a small vignette within a complex nationwide chain of events designed to implement as expeditiously as possible the recently enacted (March 31) law creating a national civilian conservation corps. With a degree of urgency rarely exhibited by the federal government, the Departments of Labor, War, Agriculture, and the Interior had immediately embarked on their respective tasks. The Department of Labor, charged with recruiting for the new corps, designated W. Frank Persons as "selection director."[2] Persons, keenly aware of the need for wise haste, quickly decided to recruit for the corps through existing state relief or welfare agencies rather than devising a totally new recruiting system. Persons's staff formulated a quota system based on population as determined by the 1930 census—one enrollee for every five hundred persons in a state. Under that formula, North Carolina's initial quota was 6,500 recruits as of April 1933; a month later the figure was increased to 7,650. (By comparison, New York City alone was granted a quota of 7,500 recruits.)[3]

State and local selecting agencies were charged with the responsibility of working out details of the selection process such as establishing local quotas within specified state proportions and transporting selectees to acceptance stations for examination by army personnel.[4] Early in the program, Mrs. Annie L. O'Berry, then head of North Carolina's Emergency Relief Administration, was designated director of selection for the state. To facilitate her tasks, Mrs. O'Berry simply assigned to local welfare departments, scattered throughout the state, the responsibility of following through on the entire selection process. For the duration of the program, the state's relief-welfare agencies performed their recruitment duties efficiently, consistently filling their quotas with no additional federal funding.[5]

Simultaneously, the War Department entered upon a challenging and unprecedented peacetime task. The United States Army, a small post-World War I force of only 140,000 men, including some 12,000 officers, was charged with providing medical examinations, transportation, housing, food, clothing, and discipline for a sudden deluge of 250,000 enrollees (over whom it would have very little military authority), and the army responded in splendid fashion.[6] The army, under the leadership of Gen. Douglas MacArthur, divided the United States into nine administrative regions to be known as "corps," each to be headed by a commanding general. North Carolina, along with South Carolina, Georgia,

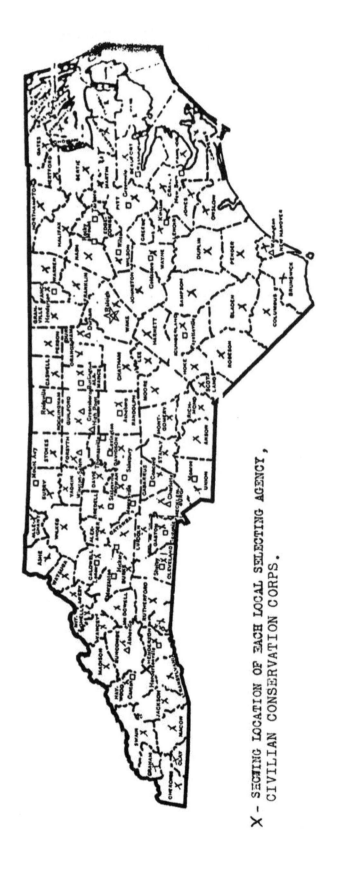

X - SECTING LOCATION OF EACH LOCAL SELECTING AGENCY,
CIVILIAN CONSERVATION CORPS.

INCORPORATED PLACES - POPULATION 1930

△ 30,000 TO 100,000

□ 5,000 TO 30,000

SCALE

50 0 50 MILES

The advent of the Civilian Conservation Corps in 1933 launched an administrative complex involving administrators, liaison personnel, and selecting agents, ranging from the Governor's Office to the local county welfare agent. Map from Records of the Civilian Conservation Corps, Record Group 35, National Archives.

Alabama, Tennessee, Mississippi, Louisiana, and Florida, became part of the "Fourth Corps," with headquarters in Atlanta.[7]

Another administrative feature devised by the army was the subdivision of each corps into "districts." North Carolina was divided into three such subdivisions: District A, with headquarters at Fort Bragg, serviced Buncombe and Madison counties and counties east of them; District B, with Fort McPherson, Georgia, as its headquarters, served such far western North Carolina counties as Macon, Transylvania, and Graham; and District C, headquartered at Fort Oglethorpe, Georgia, served the camps in Swain and Haywood counties assigned to the Great Smoky Mountains National Park.[8] All of these administrative mechanisms were vital elements in the army's plan for fulfilling as rapidly as possible its unusual peacetime mission. When its strategies for processing enrollees and placing them in work camps hit full stride, the nation was amazed at the speed with which the mobilization of civilians was carried out. General MacArthur remarked with great pride that the assignment "represented the greatest peace time demand ever made upon the army and constituted a task of character and proportions equivalent to the emergencies of war."[9]

North Carolina was uniquely qualified as a state in which both the Department of Agriculture (with its national forests) and the Department of the Interior (with its national parks) might successfully implement their plans to employ needy young people in conservation work. The Pisgah and Nantahala national forests, located in western North Carolina, had existed for less than twenty years and contained thousands of acres of woodlands that could benefit from the kind of hands-on care envisioned by conservation corps planners. The Great Smoky Mountains National Park, born almost simultaneously

with the Great Depression, likewise consisted of thousands of acres, many of which had been horribly mutilated by wanton timber operations. Moreover, forest land in the Great Smokies had been particularly hard-hit by a virus that had all but liquidated a once-mighty stand of American chestnut trees, leaving thousands of huge, skeletal eyesores standing throughout the park.[10] To heal such mutilations and ravages would require an army of laborers—workers that the budget of the national park system would never have been able to afford. Meanwhile, late in 1933, Congress, in pursuit of additional employment projects, approved initial construction of the Blue Ridge Parkway, a scenic corridor projected to link the Shenandoah National Park in southwestern Virginia with the Great Smoky Mountains National Park in western North Carolina.

Members of Congress quickly realized the economic and political value of attracting conservation corps projects to their respective states and districts. This revelation was not lost on North Carolina's congressional delegation. As early as March 23, 1933, Zebulon Weaver, who represented a western North Carolina district in the U.S. House of Representatives, was diligently wooing both Secretary of the Interior Harold L. Ickes and Secretary of Agriculture Henry A. Wallace, seeking to impress upon them that his district was ideally suited to host a number of work camps. Weaver emphasized that the Great Smoky Mountains National Park and the Pisgah and Nantahala national forests were situated reasonably close to large areas of unemployment in the heavily populated eastern cities and might readily provide instant employment for thousands.[11] Subsequently making a direct appeal to President Roosevelt, Weaver urged that North Carolina's national forests and national parks be "considered fully" when

Logging operations in the Black Mountains made the forest more susceptible to fire. The damaging fires that occurred gave growing concern to those who desired to protect the Mt. Mitchell area from further destruction. Photograph from Raymond Pulliam, "Destroying Mt. Mitchell," *American Forestry* XXI (February 1915): 89.

the proposed work camps were allocated among the states.[12] (Just to be on the safe side, Weaver proposed to the U.S. Department of Labor that several hundred workers be assigned the task of removing jetties in the French Broad River that had been placed there previously in hopes of improving navigation.)[13] Matching Weaver's diligence in seeking conservation corps projects for North Carolina was Sen. Robert Rice ("Our Bob") Reynolds. In parleys with labor department officials in Washington, Reynolds echoed

Zebulon Weaver's arguments concerning the multiple advantages his state possessed as potential host to numerous work camps; Reynolds also emphasized the state's moderate climate, which would permit year-round outdoor work.[14]

Behind the activities of congressional spokesmen lay requests from constituents avidly interested in having one or more work camps established in their respective locales. For example, civic and political leaders in Burke County dispatched telegrams to their representative and both U.S. senators, urging them to "EXERT YOUR INFLUENCE TO HAVE ESTABLISHED IN JONAS RIDGE SECTION OF BURKE COUNTY ONE OF THE GOVERNMENT REFORESTATION CAMPS. . . ."[15] Alert to Senator Reynolds's willingness to seek camps for his state, the Wilmington Chamber of Commerce urged him to "secure twenty Conservation Camps along the Inland Waterway from Norfolk to Jacksonville, *this winter.*" It was the chamber's hope that these "Conservation Camps may lead to a Regional Development like that of the Tennessee Valley. In any event, they will be of great material value to the South."[16]

In the meantime, Senator Reynolds conferred with Robert Y. Stuart, the chief U.S. forester, who assured the senator that North Carolina would be one of the first states authorized to recruit men for forest work and that the Great Smoky Mountains National Park would receive special consideration.[17] Reynolds followed this recruiting effort by securing an appointment with Secretary of Labor Frances Perkins, whom he urged to include North Carolina's scenic mountain ranges in her department's list of camp assignments. Secretary Perkins assured Reynolds that North Carolina would be well taken care of because complete reforestation of the Appalachian Mountain range was a vital component of President Roosevelt's

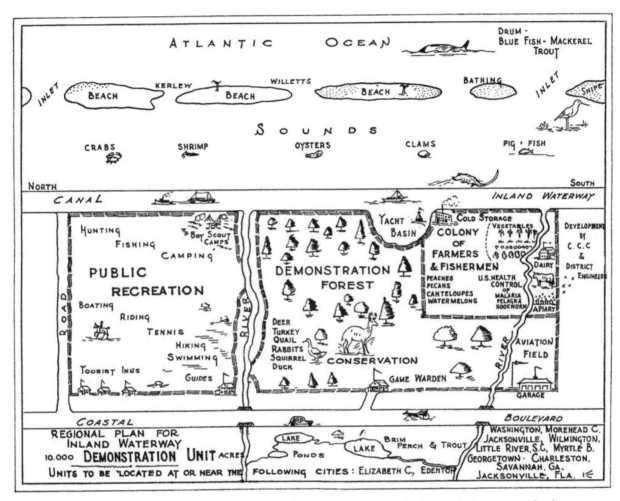

This plan shows CCC development along the "Inland Waterway" (*middle right*). It was attached to a memorandum from the Wilmington Chamber of Commerce to Sen. Robert Reynolds, ca. September 1933; from J. C. B. Ehringhaus, Governor's Papers, Box 50, State Archives, Office of Archives and History, Raleigh, N.C.

mammoth plan to develop the Tennessee Valley.[18]

Augmenting the endeavors of Weaver and Reynolds were the efforts of other members of North Carolina's congressional delegation, such as Rep. Alfred L. Bulwinkle of the state's Tenth District, which encompassed Charlotte, North Carolina's largest city. Seeking assurance that North Carolina would receive every possible benefit, he conferred with Robert Fechner and W. Frank Persons. Each, without hesitation, assured Bulwinkle that his district would receive camps, and Persons informed him that Charlotte would

most likely be one of the state's key mobilizing stations.[19]

It soon became evident that North Carolina was to be the beneficiary of diligent politicians, ardent planners, large federal landholdings within its borders, and a favorable climate and geographic location. As early as April 6, 1933, an Asheville newspaper announced that "WORK ON FOUR PISGAH CAMPS STARTS TODAY" and that six other camps had been allotted western North Carolina: on the Davidson River in Transylvania County, on Curtis Creek in McDowell County, outside of Hot Springs in Madison County, and in Mortimer, Caldwell County.[20]

Meanwhile, practically every newspaper in the state was eagerly following the progress of the conservation corps, and front-page headlines and editorials on the subject were common features. An editorial in the *Charlotte Observer* declared that President Roosevelt was never more a man of action than when he proposed the forestry program. "Under the Roosevelt Administration," the editor wrote, "the long-neglected forest parks in this particular area of the South are to come into their own, whereas, under former Administrations, they have been the last to receive attention of any kind, except promises that were never to be fulfilled."[21] In a considerably more enthusiastic tone, the editor of the *Franklin Press* characterized the "forestation plan" as "the most constructive project launched by the government since the building of the Panama Canal."[22] In an editorial titled "More for Our Money," the Shelby *Cleveland Star* pointed out that with the establishment of the conservation corps, the concept and practice of relief for the unemployed had undergone a major change: free handouts from relief agencies were now being replaced with the requirement that some sort of service be performed in return for the proffered aid. The "honor and morals of our unemployed," the editor continued, "are sustained when they are required to render a public service for help given them at public expense."[23]

Actual enrollment of conservation workers in North Carolina was announced on April 23, 1933, after Dr. Fred Morison, director of relief, Governor's Office of Relief, had received instructions on the procedure while attending a selection conference in the nation's capital and communicated that information to Nathan A. Gregg, North Carolina director of federal employment.[24] Building upon the cooperation of the state's news media,

a series of hastily arranged two-day workshops provided individual county relief agents with the necessary instructions and blank forms required to process applications. The instructions provided for a four-step selection procedure. First, local county welfare agencies would identify and select from existing relief rolls a sufficient number of young men to fill the county's quota. Second, those selected would be forwarded to designated examining stations, where the group would be turned over to the army for physical examinations. Third, those successfully completing that screening process would then be transported to a designated military unit— usually Fort Bragg—for two weeks of "conditioning," which included body-building exercises, light duty (non-fatiguing activities), inoculations, and taking a required oath. The fourth step in the process came at the end of the conditioning period, when the enrollees were transported, in cadres or in companies, to the camp that was to be their home for the ensuing six months.[25]

Each county had been assigned a specific quota. The precise number of applicants to be allotted was to be calculated using a combined formula of population and degree of destitution. The initial enrollment quota ranged from a high of 253 for Mecklenburg County to a low of 9 for Dare County.[26] With the quotas came a number of rules pertaining to eligibility, which were to serve as guidelines for the selecting agencies. For needy young men, the primary criteria required that the men be citizens of the United States; be between the ages of eighteen and twenty-five (later changed to seventeen and twenty-eight); be physically fit; be unmarried; be unemployed; be willing to accept payment of $30 per month, with $25 of that being sent home as an allotment to some dependent on the relief roll

The front of a recruiting poster. From Record Group 35, National Archives.

or in extreme need of financial assistance; and be a volunteer, but willing to remain in camp for a minimum of six months.[27]

As the quotas and rules concerning eligibility became public, local newspapers began commenting on them. The *Winston-Salem Journal,* for example, proclaimed that Forsyth County was entitled to "211 forestry jobs." A paper in Boone reported that 200 citizens of Watauga County had applied for the positions but that only 21 vacancies were available. A Marion journal had similar bad news for its readers: McDowell County had been allotted only 33 positions, whereas 408 needy young men had made application. In the Piedmont, Alamance County was not quite so disadvantaged: the Burlington *Daily Times-News* reported that 96 men had applied for the forestry positions, whereas the county quota was 61.[28] The Alamance County welfare office described a scene that was all too common throughout the state: "We were swamped by applicants. Many stood in line all morning waiting to be admitted into the recruiting office."[29] Wilkes County found itself in approximately the same unfortunate situation as McDowell, with 305 people seeking 46 positions.[30] Mecklenburg County shared equally adverse news: approximately 600 people applied for the county's 253 openings. Moreover, among those successful applicants, African Americans were

Each county was allotted an enrollment number based on the county's population. Swain County meets its quota of CCC enrollees, 1933. From the Great Smoky Mountains National Park Archives.

reported as "rare," with the accompanying explanation that they considered six months too long a time to be away from home.[31] Meanwhile in Caldwell County, Mrs. Cathleen W. Warren, superintendent of welfare work, declared that she was elated that her county had been assigned a quota of 44 because she had expected only about half that number. She confirmed the conditions prevalent in the Alamance County welfare office: "We have had a continuous stream of young men applying for work of any kind."[32]

A destitute barber in Raleigh wrote a letter to his relief agent asking him "to help me get this boy in camp." It reveals the humbling privations that came with hard times and perhaps helps to explain why there were so many applications for positions that paid only one dollar a day and necessitated being away from home:

I have a boy 18 years old last May 8th. He wants to get in the CC Camp and his mother and I would also like to get him in. I have a job in a barber shop, on the back chair & it being the back chair it doesn't pay anything hardly at all. I haven't drawn over $7.00 per week in 3 months & we have had lots of sickness, hospitle & Dr. & Drug [bills]. I can't pay and feed the children & wife and this Boy. Besides, I can't finance the children's schooling. Extra clothes & Book Rents and all and this Boy don't want to go unless he can look half-way decent. I have ben living in Raleigh 19 years & Have never ask any one to help me one cents worth. No way in the world. But now I am asking you people to help me get this boy in camp. Please, that will help us make the winter o.k. God knows that we are in kneed of this. I have tried all over town to get him a job. There is no jobs in town. If you don't believe what I say ask my Dr. & Druggist & Come & Inspect our cubbard & wardrobe. I know you will help me out in this some way. Many thanks. . . .[33]

Among the directives that relief agencies throughout North Carolina received from CCC officials in Washington was one that pertained to physical examinations. Each local agent was advised that immediately after selecting their candidates, they were to stand by for instructions relating to sending their selectees to the nearest army recruiting station. The four existing centers were situated in Charlotte, Asheville, Winston- Salem, and Raleigh, but for the sake of convenience five others—at Fort Bragg, Wilmington, Greensboro, New Bern, and Edenton—were added. Each center was to serve as a clearinghouse for satellite counties. For example, Charlotte was to serve Anson, Cabarrus, Cleveland, Gaston, Iredell, Lincoln, Mecklenburg, Richmond, Stanly, and Union counties.[34] As a follow-up, army physicians were scheduled to make a circuit of the various recruiting centers to examine specified numbers of recruits (usually about 120) each day. In accordance with that plan, Col. E. C. Waddill, chief of army recruiting in North Carolina, was dispatched to Asheville on May 9, 1933, to examine 673 recruits from Buncombe and the surrounding counties.[35]

A perhaps unwelcome accompaniment to the physical-examination process was the occasional rejection on the grounds of physical disability. The Department of War had hastily prescribed a series of minimum physical standards that applicants were required to meet. According to the standards, "The applicant must be able to see fairly well; have comparatively good hearing; his heart must be able to stand the stress of physical exertion; he must be

These enrollees from Mitchell County provide an excellent example of the clean-cut, budding young manhood that composed the Corps. Photo by Hugh Dellinger. From the Mars Hill College Archives.

intelligent enough to understand and carry out instructions relative to the work demanded; and must be able to transport himself by walking and perform manual labor requiring reasonably strong legs and feet."[36] Among the standard reasons for rejection on physical grounds was discovery in the applicant of a hernia, an ulcer, a venereal disease, a heart defect, leukemia, epilepsy, tuberculosis, circulatory failure, missing digits that would hinder work performance, or the indication of "idiocy."[37] Also to be rejected were any who had been convicted by a civil or military court of an offense punishable by death or imprisonment for more than one year; any person serving a current term of probation or parole because of a criminal conviction; civil law enforcement officials (such as justices of the peace, sheriffs, game wardens, and deputies); and any member of the National Guard.[38] To allow for an anticipated number of rejections, the county screening agencies usually selected a number of alternates to augment their regular quota. If the county had a health department, it was called upon to perform at least a cursory examination to prevent embarrassment at the army acceptance station.[39]

Along with physical requirements came another, more relevant one—one that selection boards were notified could not be included in any formal eligibility requirements but which was absolutely essential to the success or failure of the complete program: the caliber of the enrollee. The local selection agents were urged to select for "the forestry expedition force" only the very finest youth available— men who were clean-cut in appearance, purposeful, ambitious, willing to learn, willing to work, and preferably with Boy Scout experience.[40]

Throughout North Carolina, the process of enrollment moved steadily ahead. In Cleveland County 64 young men, including 1 African American, departed for work in the Pisgah National Forest.[41] In Alamance County 20 young men joined a caravan of trucks carrying a total of 103 enrollees from that locale to Greensboro for physicals; interestingly, the Alamance delegation was comprised of 11 white and 9 African American youths.[42] For virtually all of the more than seven thousand young Tar Heels who applied for service with the conservation corps, the experience included a number of "firsts"—first physical examination, first train ride, first inoculation, first time away from home, first time in company with a large number of strangers, first time eating army-style, and first time in uniform. From Burke County, young forest soldier Worth Franklin filed the following eyewitness report of his experiences as a conservation corps recruit:

We left Morganton Monday morning May 15th, about 7 o'clock, driven by William Avery in his school bus, arriving in Asheville about 9 o'clock. Out of a group of 55 men from Burke all passed the examination but four. These were replaced Monday afternoon. . . .

Monday night we were sent to a hotel for shelter and food. Most of the boys didn't get any sleep Monday night, as we knew we would be called at one o'clock Tuesday morning. We had breakfast at two o'clock and marched to the station with the boys from Transylvania, Swain, Graham, and Clay counties, a total of 112 white and 1 colored.

I was placed in charge of the three coaches attached to train No. 36, leaving Asheville at 4:15 a.m. . . . We were served lunch in the coaches at Greensboro, where we had a rest of one hour.

Arriving at Fort Bragg about 4:15 p.m., we were met by Captain Charles W. Glower, commanding officer of the 16th Field Artillery, who explained our duties and assigned us to tents. Six men were placed in each tent, where we had about two hours rest before "CHOW," the army slang for eats.[43]

Franklin subsequently wrote:

Wednesday morning we had our second examination and inoculation for smallpox and typhoid. All from Burke passed except two or three who will be replaced in the next few days. A few of the boys were a little sick for the first few days, due to the fact that some had never been away from home before, but I think they are getting along nicely now, after getting acquainted with the other boys. . . . We assure all the good people in Burke that we're working hard and doing everything within our power to make our work a success.[44]

To the home folks in Wake County went the welcome news from recruit E. L. Upchurch that "Raleigh's contingent of boys . . . are taking to camp life like ducks to water. . . . The food here is pretty good and we are all having a swell time. We expect to be in the mountains within the next few days. We are in the charge of Captain Venable of State College R.O.T.C."[45]

The *Charlotte Observer* became a vigilant observer of CCC activities. On one occasion it reported that a company of young men from Mecklenburg and nearby counties were enjoying their assignment to a camp situated in Transylvania County, at the foot of an immense stone escarpment known locally as John Rock. More particularly, the newspaper noted that the enrollees' appetites had improved markedly: "The first meal was served at dinner and every one was plenty ready for it. Right then and there the cooks decided they would have to double their food supply because the mountain air was taking effect." As to that mountain air, the paper had this to say: "During the afternoon all gave a hand in cleaning up the camp site and arranging for sleeping. After supper, everyone was ready to call it a day and turn in. It was very comfortable during the early part of the night, but by morning it seemed as though winter was back. Sunday morning more bedding was issued."[46]

A prevailing truth counteracted the occasional touch of homesickness and the sore arms resulting from inoculations: the young men were being afforded a rare opportunity to turn their lives toward a brighter future. As one of them expressed it: "It isn't the job. It isn't the money. It's getting away from a dreary rut. We couldn't do anything. We had no clothes to go to school. We can't go out with friends with no money. We can't go out with girls without money. For a year I just sat around. It isn't good for my body or my mind. Getting out in the air, away from failure[,] will let me come back with all bets off. I CAN START ALL OVER AGAIN."[47]

Another important experience shared by successful enrollees was the oath of enrollment, to which each was required to subscribe immediately after passing his physical examination. With the oath-taking came one final formality: the assigning of a serial number for purposes of identification. Each serial number was to be preceded by the letters "CC," followed by the number of the corps area in which the individual was enrolled and an additional identifying number. Thus, a North Carolina enrollee might typically receive a serial number reading "CC4-1234."[48] With these two final requirements satisfied, North Carolina's quota of needy young men were officially accorded membership in the conservation corps.

While an enormous amount of attention was being lavished on indigent Tar Heel youth, two surprisingly new dimensions were added to the CCC program: first, at President Roosevelt's behest, veterans of World War I were invited to become participants; and, second, in the interest of favorable working conditions, a number of local experienced men (LEMs) were assigned to the camps. Under the president's executive order, 25,000 veterans (10 percent of the projected youth enrollment) would be entitled to serve under the same provisions as the young men for whom the program was originally devised, with one important exception: the veterans would have to be segregated as a separate and distinct operation.[49] Thereafter, when CCC companies were being designated, two specific categories were used: "Veteran" for the military experienced and "Junior" for the younger, civilian men. Just as with "Juniors," a veterans quota was established for each state.

To promote good relations between camps and the neighboring community, local experienced men (commonly referred to as "LEMs") were hired to serve in such capacities as their skills warranted, e.g., trail boss. From the Mars Hill College Archives.

While veterans were being invited to enroll as a means of removing them from relief lists and honoring them for their patriotism, the second group of new participants, LEMs, were brought into the corps for a very different reason—because it was a culturally and politically astute thing to do. The program's director, Robert Fechner, wisely realized that it would be politically stupid to bring into a camp a flock of outsiders and thus usurp the local woodsman's territory. Thus he ordered that

in addition to young enrollees, a substantial number of unemployed men, married or unmarried, regardless of age, who resided in or near a camp's work area, had actual work experience, and were of a caliber suited to exercise wholesome leadership, be enrolled.

So it was that North Carolina was able to begin realizing what it had anticipated for several months: the actual establishment of the conservation camps, filled with eager workers, officers, and supervisors.

If change and variety are indeed the spice of life, the fortunate young men swept up by the first CCC enrollment in North Carolina, April-May 1933, must have imagined themselves in a most aromatic and exotic spice box. As one enrollee explained: "Above the constant murmur of voices and the metallic ring of surgical instruments, there came a combined but awed 'I do!' and history began for Company 405. *The Place*: a huge tent in Fort Bragg, North Carolina. *The Date*: May 5, 1933. On that date none of us knew exactly what we had sworn to but we all had a vague idea that an organization was being formed. It was."[1] Company 405 was a group of conservation corps employees headed for the mountains of North Carolina to perform pioneering forest conservation work for a minimum of six months. "From a life of loafing and fruitless search for any kind of work," the enrollee in the company continued, "we were suddenly thrown into a routine of work, sleep, eat, study, and play. To some of the company it was horrible, this working under the blazing sun. To others, it was a paradise of good food, a nice bed, and a cool shower."[2]

A great deal of thought and planning had gone into arranging for the "routine of work, sleep, eat, study, and play" that characterized CCC camp life in North Carolina. The basic question of just how many men would occupy each camp absorbed a considerable amount of time and consideration. Very early thinking projected camps of one hundred men each,

but economic and other practicalities suggested that two-hundred-man units would be preferable. The men who occupied each camp were termed a "company."[3] In a similar vein, there was the question of how to specifically designate each company. A solution was found in a twofold designation: by a numeral and a letter. The army quickly put into effect an official order under which a company's number would indicate its origin by corps area. Thus, blocks of numbers were assigned as follows: 101-199 to the First Corps, 201-299 to the Second Corps, 301-399 to the Third Corps, and so on through 901-999 to the Ninth Corps. As that numerical series became exhausted, a new series was devised by the simple expedient of adding 1,000 to each designated block of numbers—for example, 1101 for the First Corps. Numerals in the 2400 series, beginning with 2410, were set aside for companies comprised of veterans.[4]

Along with the numerical designations was an abbreviated name of the state to which the camp was assigned, as well as a letter of the alphabet that identified two other important elements: the supervising agency in charge of the camp's labor, and the work area or owner of the land on which the work was to take place. North Carolina camps included a wide array of supervising agencies and work areas. The alphabetical codes for the agencies in the state were as follows:

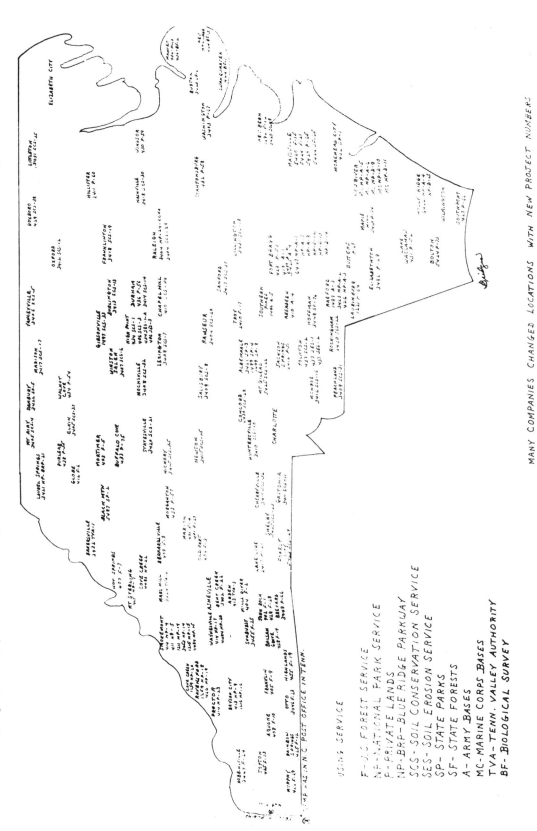

CCC CAMPS IN NORTH CAROLINA 1933-1942

This map, created by CCC alumnus Frank Bridges, shows the many locations of CCC camps throughout the state. From the Mars Hill College Archives.

"A" or "Army": military reservation
"BF": Bureau of Biological Survey,
    federal game refuge
"F": national forest
"NP": National Park Service
"P": private lands
"SF": state forest
"SCS": Soil Conservation Service
"SES": Soil Erosion Service
"SP": state park
"TVA": Tennessee Valley Authority[5]

The following camp designations demonstrate how the identification system functioned (and also suggest the wide diversity of work opportunities available to members of CCC companies):

NC A-1, Co. 410: camp on military reservation, Fort Bragg [various counties]

NC BF-1, Co. 424: camp for wildlife refuge, Swan Quarter, Hyde County

NC F-1, Co. 402: camp for national forest work, John Rock, Pisgah National Forest, Transylvania County

NC P-55, Co. 438: camp for rehabilitation of private lands, Purlear, Wilkes County

NC NP-4, Co. 414: camp for work in the Great Smoky Mountains National Park, Smokemont, Swain County

NC S-65, Co. 5424: camp for work in Hofmann State Forest, Jones County

NC SP-1, Co. 432: camp for rehabilitating Fort Macon State Park, Morehead City, Carteret County

NC TVA-2, Co. 3424: camp for Tennessee Valley Authority's soil erosion-control work, Mars Hill, Madison County[6]

Perhaps even more vital to the organization of the CCC companies than the number of enrollees or the method of specific designation was the matter of who was to control and administer the everyday life and work of each camp. The issue proved quite contentious, partially because the technical agencies charged with supervising the companies' work activities were extremely concerned about the role the army would play. Some officials of these agencies felt that once the Department of Labor had recruited and the army had conditioned new enrollees, the technical agencies should have the sole authority of assigning them. But, again, economics and practicality guided the final decision, which was that each camp would be jointly administered by the military and the civilian agency designated to supervise the camp's work activities. Specifically, the army's duties were to accept the men selected by the Department of Labor and the Veterans Administration; examine them physically and enroll qualified selectees into the CCC; command the corps, from enrollees' acceptance to final discharge, embracing all the functions of reconditioning, organization, administration, transportation, supply, sanitation, medical care, hospitalization, discipline, welfare, and education; construct work camps and all new installations necessary to carry out its foregoing duties; and furnish work details from work company to project superintendents.[7]

Implementing these regulations meant that each camp was a daily cooperative program between military and civilian administrators. The military operation usually consisted of a commanding officer, an adjutant, a supply officer, a camp physician, and a support staff that initially came from the army ranks but, as enrollees gained experience, increasingly from company ranks. The civilian contingent consisted of a project superintendent and his foreman, who were to lay out and supervise all aspects of work projects. Each new work day, at "work call," the military

Camp NC P-54, Walnut Cove. Note the remarkable variety of clothing and camp mascots. Note also the army corporal in the front row. By 1934 uniformity of clothing was standard practice, and army enlisted personnel had been replaced by enrollee leaders and assistant leaders. From the Mars Hill College Archives.

was to turn over all available enrollees to the civilian superintendent, who in turn was to convey them to the foreman for their daily work assignments.[8]

With the thorny question of control and administration of the conservation corps camps settled, establishing the camps could proceed apace. The historian of Camp NC F-9 Company 405, provides this description of the excitement that accompanied such an enterprise:

A single train, engine snorting and puffing, came chugging into Franklin, N.C., in the afternoon of May 24, 1933. Three cars erupted a horde of boys anxious to catch the first glimpse of their new home, and soon afterwards 100 members of Company 405, accompanied by four regular Army personnel and commanded by Captain R. H. Knapp of the 4th Field Artillery, were hard at work, erecting a camp out three miles from Franklin, then we appreciated Fort Bragg! From a comfortable and well organized Army post 105 men were thrown into a veritable wilderness overnight. To say the least it was a trying labor, building a camp for this number of men in a forest of underbrush, but such was Company 405's baptism and the boys took it with a grin, and to make a long story short, Camp NC F-9 was built.[9]

The excitement of establishing a camp was not confined to the CCC company. For more than a month, Macon County's newspaper, the *Franklin Press,* had been enthusiastically monitoring not only local efforts to secure the facility but also progress made in actually opening the camp.[10] On the day members of the incoming company arrived at the railroad depot in Franklin aboard a special train consisting of seven passenger coaches and three baggage cars—"the largest that had come over the line in many, many years"— the paper described the contingent as "A fine looking bunch of young men . . . thoroughly tanned. . . . Clad in army shirts, fishing hats, blue denim and khaki work pants and carrying dunny bags loaded with bedding and personal belongings, the boys looked like they were just starting out on a vacation camping trip. Jesting and jostling each other good-naturedly, they were happy over the prospect of working in the Nantahala Forest instead of staying home in Piedmont North Carolina vainly hunting for jobs that don't exist."[11]

Meanwhile, in McDowell County, the *Marion Progress* reported that a campsite had been approved for that vicinity. The paper noted that representatives of the army, Pisgah National Forest, and the State Board of Health had inspected likely sites for acceptable locations for conservation camps. Such a process was standard procedure for determining the site of all such facilities: representatives of the army, the agency charged with supervising the fieldwork, and a state sanitation engineer, acting upon a previously approved request for a camp location in a particular locale, collaborated to evaluate potential sites.[12] As the composition of the typical inspection committee suggests, health and sanitation, availability of water, and access to work sites were key factors in the question of whether to approve or reject a potential campsite. During the first six months of the program, 31 camps were approved in North Carolina,

including 14 for work on national forest lands, 11 for work on private lands, 1 for wildlife refuge activities, 4 for national parklands, and 1 for the army. The camps were spread across twenty-three counties, ranging from Cherokee in the far western part of the state to Hyde on the Atlantic coast.[13]

The newly established conservation camp, designated as Camp NC F-4, Company 401, Civilian Conservation Corps, was situated in McDowell County, seven miles above Lake Tahoma, northwest of Marion.[14] The first one hundred men to arrive at the camp were from Charlotte. They had been dispatched to Fort Bragg for conditioning on April 27, 1933, and upon their arrival at the McDowell County campsite at about 5:30 in the morning, May 20, found "nothing but a scanty-looking cornfield at the foot of many mountains" to welcome them.[15] Undeterred, the fresh recruits immediately began preparing their campsite: "Forty tents were quickly pitched, providing sleeping quarters. . . . A large pyramidal tent is used as a storehouse. A frame mess hall will be erected as soon as convenient. In the meantime, two field ranges under a wide tent fly make up the kitchen layout. Portable meals prepared by experienced cooks are served three times a day."[16]

In Swain County, four companies arrived at Bryson City in June 1933 aboard fourteen train cars to establish a conservation camp in the Great Smoky Mountains National Park. The enrollees formed the basis for the subsequent creation of NC NP-4, Company 414, Smokemont; NC NP-5, Company 411, Smokemont; NC NP-9, Company 413, Forney Creek, the pioneering camps in the North Carolina section of the park.[17] A Bryson City newspaper, grateful for the arrival of the men, cited a number of direct benefits the conservation camp would mean to Swain County: beautification of the nearby national park (a tourist

Camp Will Thomas (Camp NC NP-4), Company 414, Smokemont, was one of the pioneering camps in the Great Smoky Mountains National Park. Shown here is the camp's flagpole and company street. From the Great Smoky Mountains National Park Archives.

attraction for the county), the employment of 132 residents of the county who previously were on relief rolls, and direct dollar benefits in the form of money spent by the CCC companies to purchase provisions and other necessities from local merchants.[18] By August 1933 the farmers of Swain County had formed a farmers' cooperative market to cater to the needs of the three local CCC camps. The economic impact of that new market is suggested by one week's order from the camps, which consisted of 1,700 pounds of Irish potatoes; 20 dozen ears of fresh corn; 250 pounds of sweet potatoes; 100 pounds each of squash, turnips, tomatoes, and onions; 260 pounds of cabbage; a bushel of peppers; and 28 dozen carrots.[19]

A wide diversity of personal experiences is associated with the establishment of CCC camps throughout North Carolina. One enrollee offered his impressions of a national forest service campsite deep in the Great Smoky Mountains of Macon County: "We remained at Fort Bragg thirteen days, then we were told to get ready to leave for Aquone, North Carolina. An unheard of place, but also one that was so small you almost had to look twice to find it on a map. . . ." "We arrived at Andrews, N.C. (our railhead) Sunday morning and were conveyed to the camp site and what a sight! Nothing but briers, bushes, and snakes. But the surrounding scenery is unsurpassable. Towering three thousand feet above sea level, among the wonderful western North Carolina mountains, it is a spot ideally located for such a purpose."[20] At the same campsite, one chronicler later recalled that "a saw

Camp NC BF-1, Company 424, was established at Swan Quarter to prepare water resources and feeding grounds for migratory birds, such as swans and geese. From the *Official Annual*, Fourth Corps Area, 1936, Mars Hill College Archives.

mill was procured and logs were made into lumber for the purpose of erecting frames for tents and a mess hall. Soon enough lumber was ready to build the mess hall. Then there were floors and frames for tents. Soon the mess hall was completed. . . . [O]ur mess officer gave us a grand dinner (supper to you) the night of the opening of the mess hall, and ice cream, cake and etc., was really enjoyed by all."[21]

While trainloads of enrollees were pitching camp in the Great Smoky Mountains National Park, a similar group found itself in a most dissimilar situation. This was NC BF-1, Company 424, which offered the following account of its arrival at a camp in the coastal North Carolina county of Hyde: "On June 30, 1933, a company of one hundred and sixty-three men were brought to Belle Island, under the command of Royal L. Gervais, Captain, 4th Field Artillery. The men had to be transported from the Belhaven-Swan Quarter Highway by boat to Belle Island. The boats could not come ashore, so the men had to wade with their personal belongings on their back. Upon arrival there were many hardships to face. The camp site was covered with brush and trees, also with swarms of mosquitoes and plenty of snakes."[22]

By July 1933 the Morganton *News-Herald* was reporting that Burke County's appeal to its congressional delegation for a CCC camp (alluded to previously) had paid off. It advised readers that a six-acre tract located near the watersheds for the town of Morganton, the State Hospital for the Insane, and the North Carolina School for the Deaf had been secured by a rent-free lease. The announcement was a boon to local merchants: "The camp officers visited Town Manager W. I. Davis yesterday and conferred at length with persons submitting bids for ice, meats, milk, bread, and other foods to be on the camp menu. They will make daily visits to Morganton to obtain supplies, and a number of new trucks and automobiles have been purchased for camp use."[23]

While the citizens of Burke County were greeting new CCC arrivals for work in their beloved South Mountains, the residents of Hot Springs, Madison County, were hosting one hundred young enrollees fresh from the Fort Bragg conditioning camp—the initial members of NC F-7, Company 407. A local newspaper reported that the "boys appear to be happy and highly pleased with the local situation. The camp is located on what is known as the upper lawn of the old Mountain Park

All aspects of this camp—flower beds, U.S. flag, camp identification, attractive entrance, etc.—bespeak the pride most camps displayed in their efforts to create a home away from home. Photo by G. B. Maneval, June 1934. From the Mars Hill College Archives.

Hotel Wana Luna golf course." The camp's commanding officer and his charges, who had just spent two weeks at Fort Bragg under a blazing sun, were delighted to pitch camp among beautiful shade trees along the banks of a cool river.[24]

About this same time, the residents of Caldwell County became excited over the fruits of CCC-related lobbying by Sen. Robert R. Reynolds and Rep. Robert L. Doughton. The county received word that it had been assigned two camps: one at Mortimer (which became known as NC F-5, Company 403), and one at Globe (NC F-6, Company 412). The editor of a Lenoir newspaper captured the local mood: "It is a

rare occurrence when a presidential order affects the down-and-outs who know not where to turn for a meal, yet Caldwell county is preparing to feel the effects of President Roosevelt's reforestation project. . . ."[25] The camp at Mortimer was so unique in one respect that a local newspaper published a feature article titled, "Mortimer C.C.C. Men Boast of Ideal Camp Site to Official Newspaper in Washington, D.C." Instead of erecting a tent village, as practically all the rest of the camps did, the Mortimer facility began life in comfort and style, occupying an abandoned textile village. A former hotel in the complex became officers' quarters, and its dining room/kitchen facilities were readily adapted for use as a mess hall. The cottages at the abandoned mill village were likewise adapted and utilized as quarters for the enrollees. The young men assigned to the Mortimer camp were grateful for the relatively posh accommodations and the beauty of the surrounding workplace, the Pisgah National Forest. One of them remarked: "The majority consider it to be a treat or a resort and it seems to be an inspiration to each one in going about his work." He added, probably with tongue in cheek: "Our location here at Mortimer is comparatively ideal in many respects. First is the access to what we term civilization, only about 50 miles back in the Pisgah National Forest and an average of about 125 miles from every one's home."[26]

But the boys at Mortimer had no monopoly on unique quarters in North Carolina: veterans from the bonus march in Washington, D.C., were assigned the task of combating the evils of wind-and-wave erosion at Cape Hatteras and found themselves housed on barges floating in the Pamlico Sound.[27] A historian for NC NP-7, Company 415, Mount Sterling, Great Smoky Mountains National Park, related how he and his companions established their camp on the site of the former Crestmont Lumber Company, utilizing some of the old foundations and tapping into an old reservoir. (He included a dismal report on the conclusion of a difficult journey from Fort Bragg to Mount Sterling, May 26-27, 1933: "The baggage was unloaded and carried about one half a mile by hand amid a steady downpour of rain which continued throughout the day. The men were required to eat cold snacks until cooking facilities could be erected. Tents were pitched and construction of latrines, etc., were begun at once.")[28]

Still another group of young men, fresh from the farms of Craven, Pitt, and Wayne counties or the sidewalks of New Bern, Greenville, or Goldsboro, was arriving at Lake Waccamaw, Columbus County, in the southeastern part of North Carolina, to establish NC P-52, Company 437. A reporter assigned to cover the nascent camp had this to say: "There have been a lot of hazy ideas about these camps. Some of the boys and a lot of folks back home thought that this six-months enlistment period would be nothing more than an outing at Uncle Sam's expense. That illusion has already been blasted. There is hard work ahead, but the camp staff is being careful to go easy at first." The reporter added: "There is nothing military about the camp except the four officers and four enlisted men who make up its staff. There is no saluting, no bugle calls, no court martials, no kitchen police for punishment. Violators of the simple camp rules face dismissal. One lad who acted up the first night received this punishment. He was booed as he left camp."[29]

A short time later a camp was established at Jackson Springs, Moore County, on the site of a hotel that had originally stood on the site but had been destroyed by fire about two years earlier. The facility, known as NC P-51, Company 2412, was made up entirely of white veterans and was the first such camp to be established in North Carolina. With its opening came hope for the resumption of the moribund local turpentine industry in the Sandhills region of the state.[30] The Jackson Springs camp was quickly followed by a veterans' unit, Camp NC P-61, Company 2410, which was dispatched from Fort Bragg to Lake Lure, Rutherford County, to construct rock trails, fire towers, and related facilities.[31] Almost simultaneously, Camp NC P-60, Company 2411, a unit made up of African American veterans, was established at Hollister, Halifax County, to perform rehabilitation work on private lands.[32]

In an attempt to alter attitudes and to improve the economic standing of a sizable group of youthful victims of society, a number of young African American men from throughout North Carolina were sent to Fort Bragg for conditioning. Despite the fact that legislation creating the CCC had prohibited discrimination on account of race, color, or creed, the recruits were set apart immediately upon arrival at Fort Bragg and, at the end of their training period, assigned to racially segregated camps. One of the first companies of African American enrollees to be organized within the Fourth Corps was NC Army-4 (C), Company 410, created in June 1933. Following conditioning, the company was stationed on the Fort Bragg reservation to perform landscaping and similar work designed to convert a World War I-vintage post into a new and modern army installation. A second African American unit, NC Army-4 (C), Company 425, organized a few days earlier, was assigned to Rainbow Springs, Clay County, in the Nantahala National Forest. The company's historian later described his unit's unexpected trip to the North Carolina mountains:

We thought that we would be permitted to stay on the Gun Range at Fort Bragg which was quite near to the homes of many of us. Little did we then realize how fleeting was our stay to be in that place. On June 27, 1933, our camp commander received orders to take us to our new camp site in the far western part of the Old North State. Soon we were prepared for an all day trip by train to Murphy, N.C., where we were directed to board trucks for a 40-mile trip over the mountains to our physical camp site at Buck Creek, which appeared to us as a wilderness, in comparison to the camp we had left at Fort Bragg. We forgot our disappointment over leaving there, and set to the job of creating a camp on top of a swamp, and in seven days we had it transformed into a tented city.[33]

Meanwhile, a transformation of a different sort was taking place at selected sites throughout North Carolina: a few companies from the CCC's Second Corps area—New York, New Jersey, and Delaware—began to arrive for duty at North Carolina camps. Consternation, to put it mildly, was one of the dominant emotions experienced both by the new

Members of Camp NC F-12 (C), Company 425, at Camp Nathanael Greene, Rainbow Springs, N.C. From the *Official Annual*, Fourth Corps Area, 1936, Mars Hill College Archives.

arrivals and the denizens of the communities that received them. Lewis W. Green, a feature writer for the *Asheville Citizen*, neatly captured the cultural crosscurrents that resulted when a group of northerners were dispatched to Smokemont in the Great Smoky Mountains National Park as NC NP-14, Company 1211: "Into a strange and alien land came the hard-bitten toughs of the streets—the children of the depression. They were from New York and New Jersey, and it was 'Dose guys' and 'd'em guys' and 'youse guys'—and they were hard and cocky." Green further related how the northerners were "greeted" by their first sergeant, himself an emigré from Brooklyn, during orientation:

> "Tough guys, eh? Well, you are not in your own precinct now," he bawled at them. "You're in the Smoky Mountains. These people here don't take no crap. Don't try none of that stuff here. If you want your throat cut wide open, just mess with these mountain people and they'll accommodate you. You give 'em any stuff and we'll find you hanging from some lonesome pine tree the next day." "You ain't tough at all. . . . You're in their country and they don't take nothing from nobody." "And one more thing," he said, surveying his men. They were the Irish, the Jews, the Poles, the Italians, the Germans, all of Babel's rabble from the northern streets. "One more thing. To them you ain't nothing but a bunch of Wops, so be careful."[34]

Thus did the company acquire, retain, and pride itself on the name "Wop Brigade." Its sergeant later confided to the reporter that there were no actual hoods in the group but, rather, basically decent fellows from tough cities and with tough attitudes. But he also said that he knew in his heart that most of the lot had heard enough legends about southern mountaineers to fully believe his admonitions. Nevertheless, to help his charges adjust to their new surroundings, as well as to ward off possible adverse encounters, the sergeant made the rounds of the sheriffs' offices in Swain, Haywood, and Jackson counties, paving the way for non-hostile receptions in the event any of his northern wards went "visiting" during their off-duty hours. As it turned out, the biggest problem for the northern workers was the effect "good old mountain dew"—bootleg corn liquor—had upon them. A few wound up in local jails and were allowed to sleep off the effect and return to camp. Thereupon, the sergeant disciplined the miscreants with extra duty or restrictions to camp. Even so, community relations must have been especially favorable for some of the enrollees: the sergeant and three or more of his men married local women.[35]

The Wop Brigade and its sergeant figured prominently in a much-publicized visit by President Roosevelt to the Great Smoky Mountains National Park on September 2, 1940, to review the CCC troops and officially dedicate the park.

When the founder of the CCC, President Franklin D. Roosevelt, came to the Great Smoky Mountains National Park for its dedication, September 2, 1940, he had lunch with the enrollees who had participated in the dedication. From the Great Smoky Mountains National Park Archives.

During off-duty hours the brigade's sergeant had the habit of dressing in all-black western attire—black Stetson, black trousers, black shirt, and black boots. The grand and long-awaited ceremony, for which an enormous amount of planning had been conducted, took place at Newfound Gap, a point at which the Tennessee portion of the park abuts the North Carolina part. CCC boys from North Carolina were neatly attired in uniforms and arrayed in precise lines on their side of the gap. Tennessee's boys were similarly displayed on the other side. Brashly standing at the head of his unit, in full-black western regalia, was the Wop Brigade's sergeant. As later reported in a newspaper,

> The big black limousine bearing the great office-holder moved slowly along the long lines of men—all of one uniform save one man. There stood First Sergeant Johnson in his western get-up—as eye-stopping as Tom Mix would have been at the Versailles Conference.
>
> The official called for his driver to stop. His eyebrows were aloft and his mouth opened in an incredulous grin, a great long cigarette holder wiggling in agitation over a square chin.
>
> The official motioned to Johnson.
>
> "Come here, chappie," the man in the car said.
>
> Johnson stepped smartly forward. He had nothing to fear but fear itself.
>
> "What in hell are you supposed to be?" asked the elected official.
>
> "I'm supposed to be a C . . . C . . . C . . . boy," Johnson said, perfectly enunciating the C's and exaggerating the pauses between them.
>
> "Why do you pause so long between one C and the next?" asked the politician.
>
> "The Civilian . . . Conservation . . . Corps . . . ," said Johnson, emphasizing the "Civilian."
>
> The official roared with laughter. "Okay, I see your point. You're a civilian and you dress the way you want to?"
>
> Johnson nodded.
>
> "Do you have any food at your camp?"
>
> So it was that Johnson got in the car and they rode to the mess hall at Company 1211.[36]

The matter of the fairness of importing northerners into western North Carolina as CCC workers motivated the editor of a Waynesville newspaper to launch an inquiry under the title, "Is It Selfishness?" The editor questioned the wisdom of bringing in men from the streets of the North when hundreds of men in North Carolina, including those in Haywood County, were without work. He noted that his region had lost much taxable property when the Great Smoky Mountains National Park was given huge slices of the local mountains. "And then," he added, "to have men sent in from other sections of the nation to do the work is rather hard." Nevertheless, with the diplomacy of a skilled editor, he put the best possible face upon the question: "Perhaps it is selfishness on our part to even look at the matter in that light and without a doubt it is nothing but selfishness that has had a lot to do with the present condition of the world—so, here's to those who know best, our hearty cooperation and a more friendly feeling toward our unfortunate fellow men."[37]

"Hearty cooperation" and "a more friendly feeling" clearly were not the predominant feelings expressed by one Mr. Wright, a citizen of Laurinburg, North Carolina, when, about March 1935, the federal government dispatched a trainload of enrollees from New York City to that town to establish a CCC camp on a tract of land lying between his house and a local cemetery. Indeed, Wright hired a lawyer and brought legal proceedings to restrain the U.S. government from establishing "Thomas Flood, James Abate, Kalman Pasichizek, Rolando Valero, and others," totaling about two hundred, from establishing the prospective camp on the tract.[38] The suit proved unsuccessful, and the creation of the camp proceeded apace. As Wright got his first look at the young New Yorkers as they proceeded to pitch their tents next door to his house, the following scene transpired:

> Not in all his born days had Mr. Wright or anybody else seen such a helping hand out of the melting pot. It had everything in it, and none of it boded good to anybody.
>
> These fellows looked, to Mr. Wright, like they were caught in a trap and sent here. This one, and this one, and this other over here, and that fellow yonder—to be sure they were Jews. Anybody would know a Jew anywhere. But this one, now, he couldn't be a Jew. That long curly black hair—which breed was it that had hair like that? And dark skins? Yes, Eyetalians! That was it—Eyetalians. They had a lot of Eyetalians. More of them than anything else. This fellow, now, the one with the light hair and blue eyes—he must be what Mr. Wright vaguely thought of as an American.
>
> But no, no American would talk like that. And no American would answer to a name that sounded like somebody sneezing. Or at least it sounded that way to natives who had come, uncertainly, within looking distance. Somebody had, it sounded like, sneezed and the fellow with light hair and light eyes had answered like he had been spoken to . . . SASCIAKEK . . . no name to be shouted so it resounded against the tombstones of people who were called McNair, or Calhoun, or Blue, or McLaurin, or MacKinnon. But the tombstones didn't seem to mind.

As Wright watched and ruminated, he came to one highly satisfying conclusion: he would ignore the invaders because "They were worse than Yankees—they were foreigners. Moreover, they were from New York, and being from New York knew nothing but wicked night clubs, and belonged to gangs, and were probably armed with sawed-off shotguns and other paraphernalia of violence, and were about to begin a ruinous campaign of crime. It would be wors'n Sherman['s March]. Ten times worse."[39] Yet, because of superb leadership by the camp's staff and the town fathers of Laurinburg, a potentially explosive situation never materialized in

the quiet Scotland County seat. A short time later Mr. Wright came home to find a CCC boy, whose name had to be sneezed, sitting on his front porch with his daughter, who had no difficulty at all in pronouncing the lad's name.[40]

In the meantime, amid all the flurry surrounding the establishment of the camps, there came an unexpected but welcome new development: the introduction and adoption of names for the respective camps. An amazing number of names issued from a wide array of namesakes, including prominent local natural features, politicians, national heroes, famed African Americans, and renowned American military leaders. The following sampling reflects the sense of heritage, pride, empathy, and political astuteness embodied in the wide range of camp names as listed on the next page.[41]

The foregoing sampling of events laid the foundation for a program that continued until World War II rendered it impractical. In retrospect, the establishment of CCC camps in North Carolina resembled the flow of ocean tides: a high-cresting wave, swiftly sweeping across a beachhead, a major follow-up wave, a series of rolling billows, and then a receding of the tide until the beach lies serene and calm, as if all the preceding waves had been imaginary. The first six months of the CCC program in 1933 saw the high-cresting establishment of thirty-one camps; in 1934-1935 there came a second giant wave of new camps to fight soil erosion; and, consistently from 1933 to 1942, there was an ongoing shifting of camps, the abandonment of some whose tasks were accomplished, and the establishment of new camps for new projects. Then, as World War II approached, the tide began to recede and, by 1942, the process of abandonment of all camps was under way.

Camp Number	Company Number	Location	Name	Commemorating
TVA-2	3424	Mars Hill	Joe	Negro slave used as collateral in founding of Mars Hill College
SCS-1	434	High Point	Hugh Bennett	N.C.'s most famous soil conservationist
SCS-7	3408	Lexington	Jerrico	Jerry Boaze, former owner of land on which camp stood
NP-19	426	Near Cherokee	Round Bottom	Local geographic feature
SP-5	3422	Near Danbury	Mountain View	Magnificent view from camp
SCS-28	2430	Concord	Crispus Attucks	Only African American killed in Boston Massacre, 1770
SCS-32	3408	Mocksville	Daniel Boone	One of nation's most famous pioneers
F-10	408	Near Andrews	Winfield Scott	U.S. general prominent in Mexican and Civil Wars
F-14	428	Near Rosman	Balsam Grove	Beautiful stand of balsam trees surrounding camp
SCS-16	3416	Monroe	Old Hickory	Andrew Jackson
SCS-24	5423	Spindale	Post-Rogers	Untimely death of aviator Wiley Post and humorist Will Rogers in airplane crash
P-63	436	Manteo	Virginia Dare	Tribute to famed British "Lost Colony" and to first white child born in English America
SCS-14	3414	Durham	Carr	Julian S. Carr, Durham entrepreneur and philanthropist
SCS-29	3404	Near Raleigh	Carver	African American botanist George Washington Carver
F-12	425	Rainbow Springs	Nathanael Greene	Prominent Revolutionary War general
SCS-18	2431	Lillington	Avery	First soldier from Harnett County killed in World War I
F-13	435	Topton	Bob Reynolds	Sen. Robert R. Reynolds's support for CCC activities in western N.C.
NP-4	414	Near Bryson City	William H. Thomas	Efforts by Thomas, a white man, on behalf of Eastern Band of Cherokee Indians
F-7	407	Hot Springs	Alex Jones	To honor recently deceased fellow CCC officer
NP-5	411	Near Bryson City	Kephart Prong	Author Horace Kephart's ardent championing of Appalachian culture
P-22	3402	Near Asheville	Zeb Vance	N.C.'s beloved Civil War governor
SP-3	3421	Albemarle	Doughton	Congressman Robert L. Doughton's support for CCC activities in western N.C.
NP-24	446	Raleigh	Walter Hines Page	Prominent N.C. journalist and diplomat

"Let's Short-sheet Him!": Camp Life

From all walks of life, all classes of society, all sections of the state, thousands of North Carolina men, for all sorts of reasons, became members of the Civilian Conservation Corps and thereby committed a minimum of six months of their lives to an all-new, all-encompassing physical, emotional, and cultural experience—camp life and work with some two hundred other enrollees, practically all strangers to one another. One of them candidly revealed why he became an enrollee: "Pop had me join the CCC and I'll admit I hated the idea. However, things were bad at home, a dry spell had ruined the crops and Pop said I was just another mouth and no help at all, so I joined up."[1] Reflecting upon this all-too-common condition, the director of the CCC program, Robert Fechner, offered a most dismal picture of the youth he was in charge of salvaging: "During the early days of the depression, I was shocked to note the physical and mental condition of a big percentage of the young men entering the Corps. Products of a youth generation utterly neglected during the early depression years, these youngsters entered the CCC camps raw, thin, green, undernourished, diffident or sullen, quizzical, often defiant, and with little knowledge of normal sanitary rules of good living."[2]

Thousands of enrollees fitting this description began to pour into the camps. After observing the arrival of the first enrollees at the CCC camp located in the Great Smoky Mountains National Park, the park superintendent reported that despite two weeks of physical conditioning at army posts, the men's "real conditioning was ahead." The demands of laboring in the Great Smokies soon produced a rash of sore muscles and demands for frequent rest breaks. "A part of the enrollees," the superintendent noted, "had the impression that they were starting on a large picnic at which they would be clothed, fed, and cared for. The discovery that a certain amount of work was required came as a distinct shock. Those who persisted in their idea of a picnic and were not inclined to do their share of the work were informed that they were not welcome and were discharged along with others who had violated the few regulations governing the conduct of the personnel." Nevertheless, he likewise admitted that "Goldbrickers and malcontents were the exception rather than the rule; the vast majority were serious minded young men."[3] One fresh enrollee in NC NP-4, Company 414, headquartered at Smokemont in the Great Smokies, had this to say on the subject of those who failed to measure up to camp standards: "[W]e have some men who do not seem to be far-sighted enough to take advantage of their opportunities. They forget this CCC was established for their benefit. . . . In most organizations the undesirables are weeded out by those in authority but in this company they weed themselves out by deserting. In the majority of cases those men who 'go over the hill' are the type who enrolled in this organization with the idea of no work and a summer vacation in the mountains but when they found out there was work to be done they remembered business elsewhere."[4]

Every CCC camp was divided into two distinct sections, one called "company

TOP: The overhead staff at Camp Virginia Dare in Manteo, 1936.
BOTTOM: The cooks at Camp Virginia Dare in Manteo, 1936. Images from the camp annual, *High Tide*, of Company 436, page 21, Outer Banks History Center, Manteo, N.C.

overhead" and the other "work section." Moreover, in order to provide both supervision and labor for needed activities, three distinct groups of personnel were created: leaders, assistant leaders, and enrollees. Leaders were to receive $45 per month, assistant leaders $36, and enrollees the standard $30. The company overhead was, in essence the administrative branch of the camp, charged with absolute supervision of every detail of camp life. It consisted of an assigned military officer and a support staff chosen from the enrollees. A normal company of two hundred men would have had the following complement: a military staff consisting of a commanding officer, a supply officer, a mess officer, and a camp physician; and an enrollee staff consisting of five enrollee leaders, seven assistant leaders, and a number of unrated enrollees as deemed necessary. One of the five enrollee leaders was designated "senior leader" (the equivalent of the army's first sergeant); the other leaders served as storekeeper, mess steward, and first cooks. One of the assistant leaders served as company clerk; the others functioned as assistant cook, first-aid or medical assistant, assistant educational adviser, and chauffeur or mechanic.[5]

The ability, personality, and attitude of these men determined, to a major extent, the quality of life in a camp. If the senior leader was competent, the storekeeper ingenious, the mess steward diligent, and the cooks able, camp morale was most likely to be high. The mess steward and the cooks, in particular, were key factors in establishing, promoting, and maintaining a good camp. Similarly, the caliber of the military officers, their personality, concepts of command, and flexibility or inflexibility did much to shape camp life, positively or negatively. Martinets for commanding officers were rare. Most officers were well aware that they, too, were fortunate to be

employed and therefore labored on behalf of a successful camp.

The work section, as its name implied, was the portion of the camp's enrollment that five days a week was turned over to the agency charged with supervising work on all camp projects. The section generally had five leaders and nine assistant leaders. These men did in the field for the project superintendent what the overhead men did in camp for the commanding officer: took his orders and supervised the work details to which the camp had been assigned in a particular locale. The army had prescribed clear-cut regulations governing the number of hours the work section could labor: eight hours per day on Mondays through Fridays, with eight hours on Saturday of the same week as a make-up day resulting from weather conditions or other causes. The eight-hour day included a lunch hour and travel to and from work (not to exceed one hour).[6] The following table illustrates a more-or-less typical day's schedule at CCC camps:

6:00 A.M.	Reveille
6:00-6:30 A.M.	Shower, shave, preparation for day's events
6:30-6:45 A.M.	Calisthenics
7:00-7:30 A.M.	Breakfast
7:30-7:45 A.M.	Policing of barracks and grounds
7:45-8:00 A.M.	Work call/sick call
12:00 noon	Lunch
4:00 P.M.	Return to camp
5:00 P.M.	Retreat
5:30 P.M.	Dinner (in dress uniform)
6:00-9:45 P.M.	Free time/education classes
9:45 P.M.	Lights out[7]

The army was responsible for the design, layout, landscaping, safety, and all maintenance at each camp. As in most other aspects of the program, evolutionary changes occurred, many of them based on the necessity of improving the quality of camp life. The pioneering camps were little more than tent cities, created from recycled canvas tents of World War I vintage. Gradually tents disappeared, superseded by a variety of wooden structures, some of them cut and sawed on site. Within a year, however, the army had designed and was utilizing prefabricated units. It devised lightweight wooden panels that could be readily assembled to create a barrack, a mess hall, a recreational hall, officer quarters, or whatever was needed. (Moreover, the structures could just as easily be dismantled and reused at another site.) By 1936 prefabricated units were prescribed for all new camps or replacements, providing inexpensive, comfortable, easily maintained, weatherproof buildings for all camp purposes.[8]

That achievement in turn promoted a uniform basic schematic layout for each camp. Instead of the traditional army quadrangle, the standard CCC camp was in the shape of a "U," with some twenty-four buildings forming the entirety. The hollow portion of the "U" was open space, deliberately reserved for assembly and sports activities. Flanking the open space were administrative offices, officer quarters, utility buildings, a recreational hall, a mess hall, a bathhouse/latrine, a schoolhouse, an infirmary, and barracks (usually four). The buildings were generally painted (usually green or

This pioneering camp in the Great Smoky Mountains National Park was established May 25, 1933, using surplus tents from World War I to house enrollees. Image from the Great Smoky Mountains National Park Archives.

Camp John Rock (Camp NC F-14), Pisgah National Forest, 1936. This photo shows an example of camp layout and architectural style that existed prior to the adoption of standard prefabricated buildings. Image provided courtesy of Frank L. Bridges.

LEFT: This photo depicts a barracks scene from an early camp. Note the barracks bags, heating stove, and American flag. Footlockers soon replaced the barracks bags. The space around the stove was the social center in the winter months. Image by Frank L. Bridges. RIGHT: One of the great contributions of the CCC in the realm of rehabilitation was its emphasis on well-balanced, highly nutritious meals every day. Most enrollees encountered strange and unfamiliar offerings but thrived on them. Courtesy of Benny McGlammery. Images from the Mars Hill College Archives.

brown), but sometimes they were merely creosoted or tar-papered.[9]

The location of a campsite and the creativity of its overhead staff frequently determined whether or not a camp had electricity. A number of the North Carolina camps, such as the ones at Hot Springs, Lexington, and Winston-Salem, were located inside city limits and thus had ready access to electric power. On the other hand, some of the camps in the Great Smoky Mountains National Park and other isolated locations such as the Pisgah National Forest, had to devise and install their own power plants, sometimes involving innovative water-powered generators.[10] Location was likewise a determining factor in how a camp was heated. Most commonly, stoves fueled with either wood or coal were utilized. A barrack, accommodating as many as fifty enrollees, usually had two stoves, spaced equidistantly down a center aisle formed by twin rows of cots. The mess hall and the recreational hall were the two destinations most frequented on a daily basis. But the administrative building was the command post around which life revolved. It contained

offices for the overhead staff, including the military officers, the senior leader, and the company clerk. All orders pertaining to the conduct, activities, health, and safety of all camp residents flowed out of this office, which also hosted payday activities and disciplinary hearings.

Although commanding officers at each camp were responsible for disciplining those under their command, they were limited in the degree of discipline they could mete out. Among activities specifically prohibited at CCC camps were violations of federal, state, county, or local game laws; all forms of gambling; private ownership and operation of automobiles; and refusal to submit to vaccinations or inoculations or to accept medical or dental treatment considered necessary to remove a disability.[11] Moreover, company commanders were empowered to discharge enrollees for a variety of reasons, including completion of term of service, infraction of regulations, fraudulent or erroneous enrollment, physical disability resulting from one's own conduct (e.g., venereal disease), or marriage.[12]

Homesickness, practical jokes, pranks, teasing, and hazing were all part of camp life. "Let's short-sheet him!" was a very common idea, followed by the prank itself, as many a poor soul discovered after quietly slipping into the barrack after a night on the town. Another trick was the hoisting of the victim's bunk to the ceiling, to which it was fastened with baling wire. An even more devious act was to strip the victim's bed apart following morning inspection, making it appear that he would be disciplined for having had failed inspection. There was little that two enrollees couldn't conjure up to amuse themselves and to plague one of their own. It wasn't only the naive and slow-witted who were victimized; no one was immune, not even the superintendent.[13] One enrollee reflected on his experiences as a fresh newcomer in camp:

> The first few weeks in camp were hard on us boys; we were skinny and poor in health, as well as mentally depressed and homesick. . . . Normally and mentally the three C's have helped me a thousand-fold. Yet I almost missed all this because of the first few weeks in camp. The old timers, boys who had been in from one to two years, never bothered us, but the newer boys in camp sure put us new boys through the ropes. I hunted high and low one day for the key to the flag pole and also a pass for the latrine, obtainable only from the Commanding Officer. Some of the newcomers were so homesick that the kidding made them cry and all-in-all we were willing to call it quits. Some of us thought of going over the hill (deserting), but thought better of it and now are glad we did.[14]

Camp life presented multiple opportunities for social adjustment—some of them embarrassing, others major learning experiences. The commanding officer of Camp NC F-10 recalled what his enrollees encountered as they moved through conditioning camp at Fort Bragg and then on to their permanent assignment in the

mountains of North Carolina. The officer commanded a company of two hundred men, about equally divided between urbanites from the nearby cities and towns and country boys from the rural communities of western North Carolina. During their stint in conditioning camp, he said, "The city boys were smart, citywise, and well versed in the ways of city life and its conveniences. The mountain boys were naive, uninformed, and many had never been more than 10 miles from their home areas. Totally unacquainted with modern toilets, showers, latrine facilities, electricity, and the other taken-for-granted conveniences of the city, they were taunted, ridiculed, and were the subject of endless pranks by the city boys." But all of that changed drastically once the company arrived at its camp at Aquone, deep in the Great Smoky Mountains of Macon County: "When the owls hooted at night, and the rattlesnakes and copperhead snakes crawled and the dark closed in and the forest became an eerie, threatening jungle, the city boys cowed, and the mountain boys taunted them and played scary tricks. Now the shoe was on the other foot."[15]

Outright criminal or disorderly activity on the part of CCC enrollees, though rare, did occur on occasion. A young commander of Camp NC F-10, Company 408, an isolated camp in Macon County with few recreational opportunities, was party to one such uncommon incident. One Sunday morning he received a report of disorderly conduct in the tent of one of his local experienced men (LEMs), with whom he had previously had trouble. When he entered the tent, the commander found full and empty mason jars of "white lightning" scattered about, as well as playing cards and money, evidencing gambling in progress. He also observed "Hell in general being raised by boisterous LEMs and a few CCC enrollees." The commander immediately silenced the hilarity and ordered the offending culprits out of the tent and the LEMs out of camp. But one of the LEMs ran back into his tent, emerged with a pistol, and stuck it between the ribs of the commanding officer, saying: "You get the hell out of camp yourself or I'll send you out in a pine box. . . . Get going while going is good." The commander stood his ground, ejected the man from the camp, and had the Forest Service discharge him.[16]

A young superintendent for Camp NC F-27, Company 401, stationed in McDowell County, likewise encountered a major disciplinary problem—a near-mutiny by his truck drivers. By common agreement, truck drivers had as their major task the transportation of work crews to and from CCC projects. They were not required to perform any labor in the field, but, by unwritten agreement with their supervisors, they were to use each Saturday morning to service, lubricate, and wash their trucks, preparing them for inspection and use on the following Monday morning. Disgruntled about having to work on Saturdays, the drivers organized a protest movement, appointed a spokesman, and told the superintendent that they would no longer be cleaning up trucks on Saturdays. The superintendent later recalled his response to the challenge:

I told them that was fine with me, but until they did, there would be no meals served in the mess hall. I left the service area, went straight to the mess hall and locked both doors. I was very hot-headed in those days and I had no authority to do what I had just done. This would have been up to the camp commander. I went to his office and told him what I had just done. To save face for me, he went along with what I had done and waited to see if it was the right answer to the problem. In the meantime, word spread around the camp that the Superintendent had locked the mess hall and that no meals would be served until certain duties relative to the trucks had been performed. Then the spokesman for the truck drivers came to see me. We did not miss a meal.[17]

To alleviate conditions that produced such deleterious conduct, CCC administrators began very early to offer planned activities that would make available beneficial alternatives. Opportunities for education and particularly recreational activities such as baseball and boxing received greater emphasis and were initiated in the conditioning camps. Indeed, one of the first forms of outreach practiced by many camps was to invite members of local communities to participate in baseball games with enrollees stationed at the camps.[18] Moreover, CCC regulations directed each corps area commander to establish an athletic program throughout his area and to see that mass games and group athletics were developed to the highest degree, including the development of camp athletic talent.[19] Baseball, boxing, and basketball soon became popular off-hours activities in the camps, often producing intense rivalries between them. Many of the CCC players were quite talented. For example, enrollee Homer Biggers, who played baseball with Camp NC SCS-11, Company 3411, out of Gastonia, attracted the attention of Clark Griffith, owner of the Washington Senators, by hitting "two home runs out of Mr. G's ball park . . . a feat reserved, hitherto, for a few select members of the New York Yankees and Jimmy Foxx of the Boston [Red] Sox."[20]

Meanwhile, from various camps came news about additions of recreational facilities. At a camp in the Great Smoky Mountains of North Carolina, one newspaper reported, "A new baseball field is being constructed. There is already an indoor baseball diamond being used daily. Also there are preparations being made for tennis courts, volley ball courts, swimming pools, [a] boxing ring, and other athletic games."[21] As CCC camps were established and matured, a wide variety of sports facilities and activities became a routine part of camp life. Achievements in the

This baseball team from Camp White Lake, Elizabethtown, demonstrates the pride and esprit de corps that made competitive sports great morale builders. From the Mars Hill College Archives.

realm of sports contributed mightily to the sense of camp pride. For example, the basketball team at Camp Bob Reynolds (Camp NC F-13 of Topton in Cherokee County) won the championship of a tournament in which seventeen teams in western North Carolina competed.[22] Similarly, from Camp NC SCS-12 in Oxford came the exuberant announcement that its basketball team had captured a championship after winning sixteen of the eighteen games in which it had played—"a record to be proud of."[23]

Boxing, too, was a popular camp activity, and an aggressive rivalry for local, regional, corps-wide, and national championships soon developed. To compete in a sub-district Golden Gloves competition in 1940, Camp NC NP-19, headquartered at

Ravensford in the Great Smokies, fielded the following contenders:

Wallace "Sweetheart" Galloway, 129 pounds
William "Slow Motion" Kinser, 136 pounds
John "Pretty Boy" Matheny, 136 pounds
John "Butch" Jenkins, 140 pounds
Mont "Too Bad" Farmer, 145 pounds
Elmer "Popeye" Dowdle, 145 pounds
Clifford "Motion" Pressley, 145 pounds
Marshall "Breezy" McClannahan, 150 pounds
Clarence "Lockjaw" Israel, 169 pounds
Edger "Hawkshaw" Nichols, 170 pounds
Charles "Fat" Wilkie, 190 pounds.[24]

Boxing provided news of interest for local newspapers, particularly during holiday festivities. Just prior to the Fourth of July in 1933, a newspaper in Franklin proclaimed, on its front page, that "One of the big events of the day will be a boxing

TOP: Camp NC P-53 (C), Company 429, lightweight and heavyweight "mix it up" in Roxboro. BOTTOM: Boxers from NC SCS-14, stationed at Durham. Both images are from the *Official Annual*, Fourth Corps Area, 1936, Mars Hill College Archives.

program in the Courthouse, starting at 2 o'clock in the afternoon. 'Kid' Seay, of Franklin, is matched with 'Kid' Turner, a member of Franklin's Conservation Camp from Charlotte, in the main bout. Part of the proceeds will go to the Franklin Library Association."[25]

BOXING

AUGUST 26, 1936.
REC. HALL
ADM. $.10
21 ROUNDS

RED MURPHY	VS	JOE BUFF
145 Pounds	6 ROUNDS	140 Pounds
	For Welterweight Championship of F-14	

CHICKEN FRIESON	VS	PHIL ROGERS
122 Pounds	5 ROUNDS	115 Pounds
	For Bantamweight Championship of F 14	

JOE RABY	VS	BRUCE ROBERTS
155 Pounds	4 ROUNDS	155 Pounds
	For Middleweight Championship of F-14	

RED GLOVER	VS	C JONES
150 Pounds	3 ROUNDS	140 Pounds

RIP BOONE	VS	C DAVIS
135 Pounds	3 ROUNDS	140 Pounds

Due to the fact that the Company Fund cannot furnish any more monies, we have decided to charge a small admision of $ .10.
Every thing taken in will go to the Boxer.
Canteen Check will be excepted. Those wishing to go in on credit may do so.
Come on boy and enjoy Twenty One Rounds of good clean fighting.
Note the fighters for the Bantam Title have been training privately. Frieson is working out with Joe Buff and Rip Boone while I am training Rogers.
Also both have had a pretty good work out with Kid Cook of Ga

Frank L. Bridges, Promoter.

Among camp sports activities, boxing was easily one of the most popular and was highly competitive. Some enrollees became Golden Gloves champions. From the Mars Hill College Archives.

For the less aggressive-minded, there were other competitive games, including checkers:

> Jackson Springs, Oct. 18: Lee G. Galloway, of Rosman, has been officially crowned champion checker player of the CCC camp here, as well as the entire surrounding community.
>
> Mr. Galloway met all comers in the tournament just ended, both campers and town's people playing in the meet. Checkers are an outstanding part of the camp entertainment, and there are always plenty of challengers for Galloway or anyone else who feels superior.[26]

Camp NC Army-3, Company 1497 (Raeford), "strikes up the band." From the *Official Annual*, Fourth Corps Area, 1936, Mars Hill College Archives.

Another dimension of recreation at North Carolina's CCC camps involved music. Stringed instruments such as banjos and guitars were almost standard equipment. Group singing around the barrack stove or out on the lawn whiled away many a joyful hour. Some camp musicians became popular community entertainers. A string band from "Camp Granville" (Camp NC SCS-12, stationed at Oxford, Granville County) "played many meetings and farmer's [sic] conventions in the vicinity of the camp." Likewise, Camp NC SCS-20 in Ramseur boasted a "chorus of fifty singers. . . ."[27] Some camps were musically sophisticated enough to have their own drum-and-bugle corps. A CCC company stationed at Manteo gave its corps a somewhat vague review: "Our Drum and Bugles (particularly the bugles) have made a new era in our duties while in camp. We get up by them; we have formation by them; we eat by them; we have retreat by them; we go to classes by them; and we go to bed by them. After all that, we hear them practice about an hour every afternoon."[28]

Drum and bugle corps and retreat at Camp Virginia Dare (Camp NC P-63, Company 436) in Manteo, 1936. Image from the camp annual, *High Tide*, of Company 436, page 25.

Camp NC TVA-2, Company 3424 ("Camp Joe") included several musicians. The camp was named by its enrollees to honor a local slave who was used as collateral in the founding of Mars Hill College. Paradoxically, when the camp was changed over to veterans, they named it Camp Robert E. Lee. From the Mars Hill College Archives.

Surprisingly, in a few camps dramatics attracted a modest following. Perhaps a stimulant to that activity was the newly formed North Carolina Works Progress Administration (WPA) Federal Theatre Project, which offered to provide a director of dramatics to any CCC camp interested in producing plays. Among facilities that capitalized on that offer was Durham's Camp NC SCS-14, at which numerous plays were staged.[29] Assisting with dramatics at camps in the western part of North Carolina were the Federal Theatre Players of Atlanta, which among numerous other activities staged a drama titled, *Murder in the CCC Camp* on the evening of August 11, 1937, at Camp NC F-23, augmented by thirty members of Camp NC F-23, Company 3446, headquartered at Otto, Macon County.[30] Meanwhile, on the Carolina coast, the young men enrolled in Company 436 at "Camp Virginia Dare" (Camp NC BF-2) in Manteo were experiencing a dramatist's dream: they were invited to participate in the production of Paul Green's famed outdoor drama *The Lost Colony*. In a feature article cleverly titled "Feathers and War Paint: All in a Day's Work for the CCC," the Raleigh *News and Observer* reported that the entire camp responded by volunteering, serving as dancers, musicians, stage hands, and in other capacities, as needed, prompting a personal expression of thanks from Green himself.[31]

A recreational by-product of outdoor life for many of the CCC enrollees was their introduction to nature's wildlife. A member of one camp informed a local newspaper that it had started a company zoo that consisted of four snakes and a groundhog. "We have seen some bears up here," the young correspondent noted, "and most of the boys ran and hid."[32] The superintendent of a camp in McDowell County later recalled an amusing bear story:

Less than a mile away from camp was a federal game preserve. They had turned a large, female bear loose. She weighed about two hundred and fifty or three hundred pounds and was accustomed to being around people. The boys took up with her right away and fed her. They also taught her to sit up at a table and eat when we were outdoors. She would lie on her back and one of the CCC boys would put his hands on her front paws and his feet on her back paws. Then she would bounce him on her feet like a father playing with a small child.[33]

In a similar vein, the men from Camp NC P-62, Company 427, headquartered in Southport, brought alligators into camp as pets.[34] And, of course, snakes always got into the CCC act. Members of that same camp captured a rattlesnake five feet, eleven inches long, with nineteen rattles and a button.[35]

Far more appealing than snakes, bears, and alligators were the dances held at least once a month at most CCC camps. One such dance, hosted by Camp NC NP-4, Company 414, situated in the Great Smoky Mountains National Park, "opened in full swing" on the evening of November 17, 1933. "Where the ladies came from is still a mystery to many of the C.C.C. boys," a newspaper reported, "but they certainly turned out well. There were approximately 75 couples on the floor throughout the dance."[36] From Transylvania County came a similar report: "The first of a series of square dances was given at the Brevard CCC camp last Friday evening, with between 40 and 50 couples taking part."[37] In addition, as talking movies began to appear, a number of camps were made part of a circuit that provided workers with something to look forward to after a day's work in the field or forest. Some camps augmented movies with guest lecturers, such as Prof. S. P. Verner of Brevard

At Fort Bragg an enrollee at Camp NC Army-4 (C), Company 5425, and his dance partner perform the Lindy Hop. From the *Official Annual*, Fourth Corps Area, 1936, Mars Hill College Archives.

College, who spoke to the boys of Camp John Rock (Camp NC F-1, Company 402) on the subject of Central American customs and his personal experiences in the Panama Canal Zone while the canal was being constructed.[38]

Some camps came up with a "weekly smoker," held in the recreation hall. To encourage a favorable turnout, free cigarettes, candy, or other minor items were given to all who attended. At Camp NC BF-2, Company 436, in Manteo, a gifted female musician from the community often came to camp to play a piano as an

accompaniment to singing by the enrollees. Sometimes, at the conclusion of a smoker, some camp official or community spokesman would conduct a civics lesson, through which "a more comprehensive conception of true citizenship is gained each week."[39]

Strongly allied with recreational pastimes in camp were religious activities. Each corps area commander was responsible for oversight of all religious events within his corps. As a rule, a clergyman from the army or the reserves was assigned as corps area chaplain. In addition, chaplains were called from reserve to active duty, then each of them was assigned to eight specific camps and charged with supervising all spiritual undertakings at those camps. Besides carrying out the standard duties normally associated with chaplaincy, including conducting worship services and offering ministerial counseling, the chaplains were authorized to secure the services of such local volunteer clergy and religious agencies as they deemed necessary to fulfill their duties. Moreover, when circumstances warranted and no chaplain was available, local clergymen could be contracted to provide religious services and counseling for camps at the rate of $30 per month.[40] Both Protestant and Roman Catholic services were conducted regularly in most camps, often on week-nights, when most of the enrollees were in camp. Some units provided transportation to nearby churches when services were not available in camp.

A vital part of camp life was the bantering and joshing that were constant occupations of the men, both at work and at play. Indicative of such practices are the nicknames the enrollees hung on each other. Even the CCC itself came under attack, with "Canvas Covered Casanovas," "Confounded Comical Clowns," and "Civilization's Consumptive Corps" as some of the printable ones.[41] The old prosaic "Tom," "Dick," and "Harry" were quickly abandoned in favor of "Commodore," "Alley Oop," "Romeo," "Leap Year," "Burr Head," "Tangle Eyes," "Sweet William," "Madame So-and-So," "Lost John," "Dynamite," "Mud Turtle," "Pee Wee," "Wimpy," "Useless," "Sweetheart," "Slow Motion," "Pretty Boy," "Butch," "Breezie," "Lockjaw," "Red," "Lard Butt," "Flagpole," "Gander Legs," "Corn Willie," "Chink," "Wee Willie," "Fuzzy," "Popeye," "Pap," "Clark Gable," "Jelly Belly," "Shorty," "Babe," "Pool Shark," "Double Ugly," "Buffalo," "Doc," "BlackJack," "Granny," "Old Shag," "Love Bird," "Cat Fish," "Cueball," and on without end. One fellow in the Great Smokies earned his nickname, "Radio," because his mouth was always on. Another, in the Pisgah Forest region, acquired the name "Rainbow" because he was always to be found in the Davidson River trout-fishing.[42]

While life in camp for the young men may have been exciting and filled with new challenges, veterans often faced a different and more provocative task: survival—not only for themselves but for a wife and perhaps children left behind. One camp veteran with a wife and five children "enrolled in the CCC . . . [on] July 1, 1933, after a futile search for any sort of work that would enable him to remain with his family. He allotted all of his pay—$30 per month—to his wife so that she and the children would at least not go hungry and shelterless. For his own tobacco and toilet articles not furnished by the government, he washed clothes for other members of and did odd jobs around the camp, once establishing a cotton picking record on the Johnson farm near Lillington on a camp holiday."[43]

To present readers an allotment of $30—keeping $5 and sending $25 home— may sound like a miserable pittance, but in the economics of the early and mid-1930s a dollar enjoyed a most respectable purchasing power. In 1933, for example, chickens sold for 15 cents a pound; grade A eggs brought 22 cents a dozen; a man's broadcloth shirt sold for 49 cents; automobile tires were available at $6.39 each; peanut butter was marked 10 cents per pint; a box of washing powder sold for 5 cents, as did a cake of laundry soap; cast-iron cookstoves could be had at $18.00 each; living-room and bedroom suites were advertised at $45.00; a 24-pound bag of flour cost 78 cents; corn flakes were selling at 13 cents for two packages; women's broadcloth bloomers sold for 10 cents a pair and colored hose for 15 cents a pair; and men's Oxfords were available at $1.69 per pair. Unbelievably, numerous CCC enrollees purchased tailored suits through one of their entrepreneurial buddies for $25 to $50 each.[44] An enrollee from Durham later recalled how much purchasing power his five dollars had: "About the best thing I can remember was ordering a $5 worth of jelly beans from Sears and Roebuck. It was enough to fill up a foot-locker and still have some left over."[45]

In most camps the full complement to recreational activity was education. When it is recalled that 22 percent of all CCC enrollees had not progressed beyond the reading level of the average child who had completed the fourth grade, it is evident that all too many were illiterate. For example, when the parents of an enrollee from Granville County failed to hear from him, they asked the CCC selection board to find out why. The resulting investigation revealed that the son was unable to read or write and was apparently too embarrassed to ask someone to write home for him.[46] A variety of camp reports reveal that such illiteracy was not at all unusual. The facility at Oxford, Camp NC SCS-12, Company 3412, reported that twelve of its members could neither read nor write. The white veterans' camp at Bakersville, NC TVA-1,

Because of a shockingly high rate of illiteracy among early enrollees, it was decided to offer an educational opportunity in each camp. The type of courses offered varied widely, depending upon available instructors. From the Mars Hill College Archives.

Company 2432, had at least thirteen in the same category. Likewise, at New Bern, Camp NC F-15 (C), Company 5420, composed of young African Americans drawn from small fishing towns along the coast, determined that its two hundred members had, on average, a third-grade literacy level. Thirty of them could neither read nor write, and forty more were rated semiliterate.[47]

A classic example of the woeful lack of educational achievement among many enrollees appeared in *These Are Our Lives,* a publication resulting from a WPA Federal Writers' Project in North Carolina, Tennessee, and Georgia. One of the interviewees was a CCC boy dubbed "Weary Willie," who had this to say about his education: "I ain't never been much to school. Jist went to the second grade, that's all, excepting what I learned here in the CCC. I could have gone, I guess, but for some reason didn't keer nothing about it. Jist didn't want to go. I would have went if I wanted to. They didn't make me not go. We jist didn't none of us go. I got one brother that went to the second grade, too, and my sister she went to the first. Then she quit. We jist wasn't a family that liked school."[48]

Manus McCloskey, commanding general of District A, Fourth Corps Area, at Fort Bragg, not only was aware of the widespread shortcomings in educational attainment among his enrollees, but also established the first educational program in the entire CCC organization as a component of his first conditioning camp. The young men in his charge were taught "some of the fundamentals of life," including reading and writing.[49]

On the national level, W. Frank Persons, federal director of CCC selection, was probably the first person to advocate using the CCC to promote educational activities. Persons envisioned an educational adviser for each camp and academic ties to regional universities, especially through extension courses.[50] But both Robert Fechner, CCC director, and Maj. Gen. Douglas MacArthur, chief spokesman for the Department of War, were opposed, as were the Departments of Agriculture and the Interior, which contended that the purpose of emergency relief work was not education and that the enabling act that created the CCC did not mention it.[51] The army was adamantly opposed, fearing that if it opened the gates opposed, fearing that if it opened the gates to "educators," radicals and leftists would immediately infiltrate the camps and insidiously warp the program.[52] But as the enrollees poured into camp in those early days, it became more and more obvious that some sort of remedial education program was most essential. Fechner was besieged by a variety of advocates, ranging from foresters to university professors. In the end, both Fechner and MacArthur relented, but with the proviso that any educational program that might be adopted would be placed under army supervision. That arrangement was the way the matter worked out, and CCC regulations minced no words in declaring: "All general educational, avocational, and leisure time activities are the responsibility of the Army."[53]

Nevertheless, on November 22, 1933, the president approved a nationwide program for educating CCC enrollees under the guardianship of the nine army corps commanders. Under that program the National Office of Education selected an educational adviser for each corps area. It was that person's task to assist the corps commander in establishing an educational program for all camps under his command. In addition, an educational adviser was to be assigned to each camp, and an assistant leader from each camp's overhead was to assist him.[54] By June 1934 a full quota of 1,087 camp educational advisers (CEAs) had been selected. To achieve their goals, CCC educational advisers developed eight major activities: the removal of illiteracy, the correction of common school deficiencies, training on work projects, vocational instructions, cultural and general education, avocational and leisure-time training, development of character and citizenship, and job placement.[55]

A North Carolina beneficiary of the CCC-related educational program offered this testimony as to how the experiment had helped him:

Although not dressed in uniform, the educational adviser at Camp Virginia Dare is pictured with army personnel. From *High Tide*, page 7.

My name is Lanard Smith. I was born in Rutherford County, April 8, 1916. I have farmed most of my life. I worked in a store about three months and quit and came to the CCC. When I quit school I was in the third grade, but I hadn't learnt nothing. I have learnt more since I came here than I did at school. I have been in the CCC 31 months and have learned a lot. I would like to learn more if I could before I leave and I hope I can. I went to school here every night for five months and never mist [*sic*] a class but started going places at night and mist some classes. I thank the educational adviser for what he has done for me. When I came here I could not write my own name, but now I can write my name and read anything I want to.[56]

An enrollee in Company 5420 at an African American camp (NC F-15) near New Bern put the aim of CCC education much more succinctly: "To produce a CCC boy who can write a better letter home, return to his community a better citizen, and better equip himself with a vocational interest when his enrollment expires."[57] Manus McCloskey, commanding general for District A camps in North Carolina, insisted that every one of his forty-seven camps have woodworking classes, and he made sure the camps' shops were furnished with power equipment and tools to facilitate the instruction. He was reported to have said: "I want every one of those lads to be able to construct pig pens and cow sheds when they return to the farm."[58]

Much more than woodworking was offered, however. Courses in the educational program were gradually grouped into four categories: "Academic," which included courses offered at the elementary, high school, and college level; "Arts and Crafts," which included music and drama, as well as such crafts as leatherworking and pottery making; "Vocational," which encompassed a wide variety of offerings, including auto mechanics, radio, forestry, surveying, and accounting; and "Instruction on the Job," with a great diversity of courses, ranging from bridge and road building to landscaping.[59] Typical activities covered by CCC education courses at camps in North Carolina included making and repairing fishing nets, making fly hooks, radio (sending and receiving), conservation of forests, soil conservation and erosion control, beekeeping, mechanical drawing, surveying, the reading of blueprints, music, the raising of chickens and swine, gardening, making hooked rugs, and journalism.[60]

A national survey conducted in 1935 revealed that, within the total CCC educational program, 16,142 persons were teaching 172,962 enrollees. Of those

Robert Fechner, CCC director, had a keen interest in education for the enrollees and promoted the production of numerous teaching aids such as this one for a woodworking class. From the Great Smoky Mountains National Park Archives.

teachers, 1,346 were camp educational advisers; 1,266 were assistant educational advisers (overhead staff); 2,829 were army officers; 4,235 were from the work supervisory staffs, such as foremen; 4,121 were gifted enrollees; 1,048 came from the ranks of the WPA; approximately 292 were from the traditional teaching profession; and 1,005 were classified as "others."[61] The educational program established at Camp NC F-7, Company 407, at Hot Springs is indicative both of the types of teachers involved and the subjects taught at the camp:

It was while Captain Gravatt was in command, 1933-1934, that an educational program was launched. He was ably assisted by other Army officials and members of the Forestry staff, as well as by Miss Roberts and Miss Edwards, two young ladies from Dorland-Bell school, and by Mrs. George Corbett, who is associated with the State Adult Education Department. In March, 1934, Thomas J. Greenlee, Marion, N.C., was assigned as the Educational Adviser. Classes were organized in typewriting, shorthand, algebra, plane geometry, history, English, and first aid. Those members who could neither read nor write were required to attend classes three nights each week.[62]

A similar statement came from Camp NC SCS-16, Company 3416, at Monroe, which reported that within the span of one year the educational program had grown from enrollee/instructor to twelve teachers, consisting of one adviser, two army officers, four teachers from the National Youth Administration, one teacher from the WPA, two soil conservation foremen, and two enrollees. The camp also made provision for a Spanish-speaking enrollee to be tutored daily in the speaking and writing of the English language, for an enrollee with college training to pursue the study of law through a correspondence school, and for an enrollee with an extremely low I.Q. to receive individual tutoring.[63]

UNITED STATES DEPARTMENT OF THE INTERIOR SOIL EROSION SERVICE

Polkton, North Car.
Company 437
April 30, 1935

My dearest Cornelia,

I wrote you last night but didn't mail it until this afternoon in Wadesboro. I thought maybe I could mail it in Wadesboro this morning so I didn't put it in the camp mail. I went through there this morning but I didn't know I was going that far when I left camp and left the letter here.

Captain Byrley picked the black head in my ear this morning but it wasn't quite ready. It has been paining right much today. I wish you were here to squeeze it for me. I think it will be alright in a few days.

We have messed around and havn't make much headway in catching up with my work today. Price and I went down to Wadesboro to run off the forms on the Membograph mechine but we cut the stinsel for the form that was holding me up to wide for the roll. I guess I will have use carbon paper and type off enough to catch up with until I get a chance to go back to Wadesboro. Cox was working on a truck last night and kept me awake until about 12:30. I thought I would go to sleep to-day after diner in spite of all I could do.

I am still in love as much as I was yesterday and continue that something must be done. The more I date other girls the more I appreciate you. But that is a happening of the past now. I told Price today that I didn't intend to ever date another girl other than you. We finally got up a bet.

You know sweetheart it is going to be might hard to go two weeks with seeing someone that is so dear to me. But I guess I will have to go home and indorse that check for Bernece. Has she written you this week?

Hildreth, the blacksmith, is going to teach a saw sharping class over here tonight. I guess I will hang around and see him try to put forth the fundimental principles. He was bitten by a mad dog Sunday and had got to take the Rabbi treatment.

Lovingly yours always,
Chas.

The last paragraph of this letter mentions a saw-sharpening class to be offered at Camp NC SCS-2, Company 437, in Polkton. Charles Brooks to Cornelia Harris, April 30, 1935. Courtesy of Becky Brooks Wallace, Lillington, N.C.

LEFT: Most camps composed and published their own newspapers. Some were quite sophisticated, as was this one from Balsam Grove, while others were mimeographed reports. RIGHT: This cover for *The Ivy Squall* reveals the admiration enrollees had for President Franklin D. Roosevelt. Both images from the Mars Hill College Archives.

Camp newspapers became a very popular teaching aid for educational advisers. They provided hands-on instruction in English, journalism, typing, mimeographing, printing, and business management. North Carolina camps featured a variety of newspapers, ranging from quite sophisticated printed publications (such as the *Balsam Breeze*, issued by Camp NC F-14, Company 428, at Balsam Grove) to a simple two-page mimeographed handout. The newspaper's name often reflected a sense of humor and place: the *Little Tattler* of Camp NC SCS-15, Company 3415, at Newton; or the *Mountain View Times*, which incorporated the name of Camp NC SP-5, Company 3422, at Hanging Rock State Park; or the *Sand Spur*, which was most fitting for a camp stationed at Southport on the coast. The most aptly named camp newspaper in the state would have to be the one issued by the white veterans' camp at Lillington: *Scars and Gripes*.[64] A wide variety of subject matter was standard fare for camp papers: sports events and scores, outcomes of inspections, personnel changes, upcoming events, church services, recent camp improvements, and almost anything that the editors thought might please readers. Humor, too, played a leading role, as did the tall tale.

Still another aspect of camp life in which there was great variation was interaction between CCC enrollees and the local community. Some camps were established within towns and cities. Thus, the cultural and recreational resources available, including movie theaters, retail stores, skating rinks, barbershops, and bowling alleys, were readily available all week long. Other, more isolated, camps had to transport their enrollees into towns for weekend liberty outings, allowing the men a much briefer time to pursue recreational activities. Some cities were friendly and some quite hostile to sudden and frequent inundations of virile, adventure-seeking young men, whose personal conduct provoked a variety of responses. One newspaper reported that a local citizen had fired his pistol at a truckload of CCC boys. The shooter allegedly was intoxicated, and the boys, as they passed him on the road, directed some derogatory remarks at him. He thereupon pulled the pistol and blasted away at them, hitting the truck but missing the enrollees. The shooter was subsequently arrested.[65]

In one North Carolina mountain town, citizens complained that the boys from the local CCC camps were reckless drivers who endangered the lives of people in the community. But another resident championed their cause, saying: "We are all alike; men are just grown up boys—if you don't believe it, just watch their actions."[66] Another local resident likewise defended the CCC boys, blaming the resident riffraff, especially bootleggers, for some of the alleged enrollee misconduct: "We are sorry for the boys that must come into town for recreation and be beset by carrion like we have here. . . . To err is human; to yield to temptation is a trait that has been handed down from the time of Old Adam, and is especially hard for the young fellows who spend month after month in camp to turn a deaf ear to the serpents that crawl into the grass and beset the boys with their devilish wares in order to make a little money."[67]

Local boys, in particular, resented the influx of CCC enrollees, who were eager to catch the eye of any buxom lass anywhere. A former student at Mars Hill College when the CCC camp was stationed nearby recalled: "Huh, we gave them a rough time. We didn't want them dating either our college girls or the girls in the community."[68] But despite that attitude, which was more or less general throughout the state, a number of local girls did date CCC boys, and it was not at all unusual for an enrollee to marry and remain in the community after leaving camp.

Of course, the open-house activities that most camps frequently sponsored, coupled with the very popular company dances, provided an open door for Cupid to enter, as well as a means for community and camp to establish and promote congenial relations. The open house occasionally became a major event, as when, in 1940, to celebrate the seventh birthday of the CCC, the members of Camp Virginia Dare, at Manteo, hosted people from the community and enrollee families from at least twenty eastern North Carolina counties. Moreover bonding between enrollees and local citizens often resulted when the boys provided emergency relief for threatened communities, such as rescue from life-threatening floods or fires. It was also a rather common occurrence for enrollees to be called upon to aid in search-and-rescue missions to locate missing children, strayed senior citizens, lost hikers, or storm-stranded persons. One co-ed at Mars Hill College owed her life to the labors of a battalion of CCC enrollees, who hastily equipped one of their trucks with chains and then shoveled snow for five hours, enabling the student, very ill with acute appendicitis, to travel some twenty-five miles from Mars Hill over roads deemed impassable, to reach the nearest hospital, at Asheville, where she underwent emergency surgery.[69] In similar fashion, an enrollee in Pisgah National Forest came to the rescue of the operator of a motorized grader who had accidentally plunged deep into the Davidson River and become submerged and entangled in the wreckage. Almost half an hour of artificial respiration was necessary before the victim was revived; he survived because his rescuer had paid attention in a CCC first-aid class.[70]

Moreover, enrollees lent a hand to check the ravages of fire and flood. One newspaper told of 125 men from the CCC camp at Newton working side by side with the Hickory fire department to curb a raging forest fire near Lake Hickory that was threatening lives and property.[71] Then, in January and February 1936, when the Ohio and Mississippi rivers went on a devastating rampage, flooding and endangering a vast area, CCC camps from North Carolina provided aid by transporting supplies and materials to the needy and by assisting the Red Cross in its ministry to the victims.[72]

Another very significant aspect of camp life was the cultural exchange that took place when local civic clubs visited the camps or the officers and men from the camps provided programs for the clubs. More exciting exchanges resulted when rural and urban boys from North Carolina intermingled at CCC camps with youths from all over the South, as well as with boys from New York or New Jersey. Most remarkable of all, though, was the inpact that resulted when Tar Heel enrollees were sent to the Ninth Corps area of the far western United States. Many rode their first Pullman car, played the slot machines of Las Vegas, stuck a foot in the Pacific Ocean, snowballed in Yellowstone Park, encountered their first Mormon, or experienced the thrill offered by such national parks as Sequoia and the Grand Canyon.[73]

CCC enrollees helped control forest fires, as this promotional brochure indicates. From Record Group 95, National Archives.

Thus, from short-sheeting to open house; from talks on Central American customs to hosting civic clubs; from dubbing a colleague with a nickname to selecting the name for a camp; from the classroom to the mess hall; from Southport, North Carolina, to San Francisco, California—all provided new, meaningful experiences for thousands of young North Carolinians who, in reality, were moving from adolescence to manhood. Mrs. Annie L. O'Berry, director of emergency relief in North Carolina, perhaps best summarized the overall impact that camp life had on the lives of those young men:

All our administrators remarked upon the change in appearance and attitude of the boys upon their returning from a period in camp. They were in better health; they had come to have more regard for their personal appearance; and their attitude toward the world had generally changed. Many of them went from homes of poverty and discouragement where they had developed a feeling of bitterness and indifference towards things in general. They came back from camp with a new self-respect, with purpose and ambition[,] and for the first time they had some ray of hope for their future.[74]

5 "Fire in the Hole!": Work Accomplishments

*M*any locales in North Carolina, from the towering 6,000-plus-foot peaks of the Great Smoky Mountains, devastated by the ravages of the oriental chestnut blight and by wanton, mindless timbering, to the beaches of Cape Hatteras, viciously eroded by tide and wind, felt the healing hands of the Civilian Conservation Corps between 1933 and 1942. At the cry of "fire in the hole" and similar safety-related calls, those hands labored diligently to bring new life and a vibrant new beauty to the state's sadly depleted natural resources. So artfully did the corps accomplish its tasks that millions of residents and tourists presently enjoy that beauty, from the mountains to the sea, without giving a thought to the fact that a great deal of loving care by committed CCC workers made much of that enjoyment possible. Moreover the CCC survived for nine years without being seriously demeaned or categorized as a federal boondoggle or even a dole. Robert Fechner, director of the CCC, made sure the public understood that his agency was not created to perform "made work." He delighted in explaining that the "establishment of the CCC made available for the first time to federal, state, and local governments an adequate supply of manpower and funds with which to carry out urgently needed conservation programs."[1] To counter the "dole" label, Fechner often said: "We feel that one of the best things we do is to teach the boys, most of whom have had little occupational experience, the importance of hard work and of doing a job well."[2]

An observer, witnessing the activities of enrollees at the CCC camp at Globe, Caldwell County (Camp NC F-6, Company 412),

had this to say: "This is no recreation camp but a fine school in lifecraft wherein the curriculum is laborious effort, pride of achievement, adaptability to problems of life on the basis of common sense, [and] awakening of confidence . . . in human potentialities." He added:

> It is unfair and even criminal to entertain the idea or discuss as a fact that this governmental activity is a dignified "dole" or in terms less refined which carry the sting of ridicule. If labor is worthy of its hire, it cannot be tainted with the stigma of "dole." To apply "dole" to the work at these conservation camps, such as the one at Globe, is unjust, discouraging and untrue. . . . In the formative stage of this activity it may have been considered an experiment of questionable value, but these young men have removed it, by the spirit of cooperation and labor, from the experimental stage to one of real achievement. They are deserving of full recognition.[3]

The process of teaching CCC enrollees the importance of an honest day's labor often required the employment of numerous professionals from a variety of backgrounds, who found a whole new career in the CCC programs. Included in the supervisory staffs of the National Park Service, the U.S. Forest Service, and various state agencies were landscape architects, foresters, engineers, historians, archaeologists, geologists, biologists, and others. They earned, learned, and taught their skills to thousands of eager CCC boys, many of whom took up their mentor's trade.[4] Between October 1, 1935, and March 31, 1936, sixty-six CCC camps were located in North Carolina. Sponsoring agencies for the 66 camps were: the Soil Conservation Service, 22 camps; national forests, 18; private forests, 9; the National Park Service, 6; state parks, the Tennessee Valley Authority, and the U.S. Army, 3 each; and state forests and the biological survey, 1 each.[5] When it is considered that approximately 13,600 persons were employed at those camps and that every workday required the skills of such professionals, there was little chance that a dole philosophy would or could take root.[6]

The number of camps allotted to North Carolina, as well as those assigned to the individual technical or sponsoring agencies ("using services"), varied considerably. For example, when the CCC began in 1933 the national forests and the national park system had well-defined labor needs and thus quickly qualified for 14 forest-related camps and 4 park-related ones. At the peak of the program, 1935-1936, the number of forest-related camps increased to 18, and the number of park-related ones totaled 9. As the CCC program drew to a close in 1942, there was but a single forest camp and 2 park camps. When the program began, there were no soil conservation camps, but by 1935-1936 there were 22 such facilities in the state. That number dwindled to 2 by 1942.[7]

Generally speaking, CCC enrollees conducted more than 150 major types of work throughout the nation within nine major categories:

In addition to employment for needy young men, the CCC provided a wholly unexpected career opportunity for professional adults, including superintendents, foremen, engineers, and landscape architects. Shown here is the supervisory staff at Camp NC F-14, Pisgah National Forest. From the Mars Hill College Archives.

1. forest culture
2. forest protection
3. erosion control
4. flood control, irrigation, and drainage
5. transportation improvements
6. structural improvements
7. range development
8. wildlife
9. landscape and recreation

All of these except range development were diligently pursued in North Carolina (although Tar Heel enrollees dispatched to the western United States did engage in that practice).[8] The following discussion will review the accomplishments of the various sponsoring agencies in North Carolina.

THE GREAT SMOKY MOUNTAINS NATIONAL PARK, NATIONAL PARK SERVICE

The CCC camps established in the North Carolina portion of the Great Smoky Mountains National Park were responsible for the clean-up and improvement of more than 200,000 acres of parkland. A total of thirteen camps existed in the park between 1933 and 1942:

CAMP NUMBER	HOST COUNTY	POST OFFICE
NP-4	Swain	Smokemont
NP-5	Swain	Smokemont
NP-7	Haywood	Mount Sterling
NP-9	Swain	Bryson City
NP-14	Swain	Smokemont
NP-15	Swain	Smokemont
NP-16	Swain	Bryson City
NP-17	Haywood	Waynesville
NP-18	Swain	Ravensford
NP-19	Swain	Ravensford
NP-20	Haywood	Cove Creek
NP-22	Haywood	Cove Creek
NP-23	Swain	Proctor[9]

The vital need to develop the newly created Great Smoky Mountains National Park encompassed practically all of the major work categories, and nine years of CCC labor did much to create the striking beauty that characterizes the park at present. Unfortunately, however, by the time the CCC enrollees arrived there, the park's vast tracts of chestnut trees were already being devastated by a blight, filling its woodlands with dead or dying chestnuts, requiring workers at the Forney Creek camp to fell some six thousand dead trees.[10] In the spring of 1936 one area newspaper reported that more than two million cords of dead chestnut had been brought down, with about one-tenth being burned for CCC camp fuel and a small portion utilized to construct rustic bridges and cabins.[11] Later that year the national newspaper of the

CCC estimated that more than eighty thousand acres of dead but standing chestnut trees had been felled and flattened in the park to eliminate the hazard of forest fires and promote new growth.[12] In accord with standard conservation practices, the park administration quickly established nurseries and implemented a major reforestation program—the result of which is the "virgin forest" acclaimed by present visitors. During the period between November 1, 1934, and March 25, 1935, alone, a forty-man crew "dug, transported, and planted about 24,500 plants . . . ," including trees and shrubs.[13] (That quantity, of course, represents only a tiny sampling of the vast amount of planting done throughout the park in the course of nine years of labor.)

Another important park-improvement program was a "Motor Trail Cleanup." That activity, practiced by about fifty men at Camp NC NP-4, commenced at Smokemont and progressed up Bradley Fork for about five miles, resulting in the cutting and storing of a winter's supply of firewood and the removal or safe burning of "a tremendous amount of trash and debris."[14] Similarly, Camp NC NP-5 at Kephart Prong was charged with landscaping N.C. Highway 107, the roadway that ran through the park via Newfound Gap, connecting Cherokee, North Carolina, and Gatlinburg, Tennessee. The camp reported that between December 1, 1933, and April 15, 1934, it had planted more than eleven thousand trees and shrubs along the route and that, amazingly, only 405 of them had failed to survive.[15] Camp NC NP-5 accomplished many other projects, among them constructing twenty-two fish-rearing ponds capable of caring for one million fish annually; creating sixty-five miles of class A horse trails; constructing and beautifying areas sufficient to handle approximately six hundred automobiles; reducing fire hazards on about four thousand acres of parkland; maintaining fourteen miles of a mountain highway; and constructing a water system for a parking area at Newfound Gap.[16]

Meanwhile, a sister camp, NP-9 at Forney Creek, was likewise deeply involved in improving the section of the park assigned to it. The following table summarizes its accomplishments during the six-month period between December 1, 1934, and June 1, 1935:

TYPE OF WORK	TOTAL AMOUNT COMPLETED	TOTAL MAN-DAYS EXPENDED
Telephone lines	5 miles	136
Roadside clearing	5.5 miles	201
Trailside clearing	19.2 miles	44
Truck trails	6 miles	3,972
Minor road maintenance	6 miles	456
Highway maintenance	6 miles	152
Horse trails	5.3 miles	1,012
Vehicle bridges	15 bridges	2,124
Stream improvement	3 miles	340
Landscaping	10 acres	509[17]

Fish hatchery operations, such as this one at Kephart Prong, quickly enhanced the fish population of the park, to the delight of fishermen. From the Great Smoky Mountains National Park Archives.

The so-called "Wop Brigade," Company 1211 at Smokemont, well demonstrated that its city-bred enrollees had acquired some new muscles. For the six-month period from April 1 to September 30, 1935, it was credited with landscape work involving fine sloping and grading of more than 25,000 square yards of earth, or nearly 18,500 cubic yards removed; digging up, moving, and planting 5,000 trees; developing 15 acres of public picnic grounds; and seeding and sodding 6.6 acres of land.[18] Work of a different sort was credited to NP-20 at Cove Creek (even though it had only recently received a new

group of enrollees): "We started a dam at the gaging station on Cataloochee Creek, built 6 miles of telephone line, and worked on fire hazard reduction. The dam has been completed and the telephone line is about 75% complete. We have widened, sloped, and surfaced about ¾ of a mile of Highway #204. We have also opened about 15 miles of old trails for manways in case of fire."[19] A number of camps engaged in the collection of seeds. NP-14 at Smokemont, for example, in one six-month period collected approximately fifteen bushels of hardwood seeds, which were subsequently planted throughout the park to provide the eye-pleasing, varicolored forest of the present time.[20]

The section of the Appalachian Trail that bisects the Great Smoky Mountains National Park is a favorite of many hikers, probably few of whom realize how much hard labor CCC enrollees expended to make that pathway the delight it is today. A 1934 statement from Camp NC NP-7, then laboring at Big Creek, offers an insight into that extremely difficult undertaking:

This enrollee holds oak seedlings from Ravensford Nursery—seedlings that are today's major contributor to the park's renowned fall color. From the Great Smoky Mountains National Park Archives.

> White Rock Trail, which is a segment of the famous Appalachian Trail, does not show great mileage due to the fact that the construction was the most difficult yet encountered by this camp. At points it was necessary to blast the trail grade from solid rock and most of the remainder of the construction on this trail . . . entailed retaining wall construction, some of which reached unusual heights. However, every effort was used on this job to preserve natural effects and appearances, and the results obtained were satisfactory, considering the obstacles necessary to overcome.[21]

Another task peculiar to the Great Smoky Mountains National Park was the enormous amount of fire-hazard mitigation and clean-up made necessary by the haste with which timber companies abandoned their former landholdings. A project superintendent for NP-17, working at

Flat Creek, noting that his camp's efforts represented the "first opportunity for conservation work in an area that had been heavily logged," reported in 1934 that "the most important project was converting an old railroad grade into a motorway extending some 12 1/2 miles into the cut-over region. Ties were removed and disposal made by burning and hauling; the surface was graded and widened in places; ditch lines cleaned out; drainage structures installed, and the grade put into shape for travel. . . ."[22] Camp NC NP-15, at work on Mingus Creek, was likewise busy cleaning up after an abandoned lumber company. "At Ravensford, where the mill and other buildings stood, we have cleaned up 22 of an estimated 69 acres. . . . Approximately a thousand feet beyond Couches Creek, 40 acres have been cleared of dead timber as a fire hazard reduction."[23]

The multiplicity of tasks in the park provided a rare opportunity for college and university students to serve as interns. For example, three juniors at the University of North Carolina, seeking to become engineers, were put to work measuring and plotting trails, as well as conducting topographic surveys. Likewise, majors in landscape architecture at the University of Cincinnati and Ohio State University were apprenticed to the park's resident landscape architect. Two forestry students at North Carolina State College were provided with facilities and work opportunities, and a number of student naturalists were assigned quarters and facilities at various camps, enabling them to pursue a variety of tasks associated with the park's natural history.[24] The duties carried out by the naturalists evidently enhanced the quality of life for the wild

This undated photograph shows a typical logging train in the Great Smoky Mountains. CCC labor converted many such roads into hiking trails. From the Great Smoky Mountains National Park Archives.

creatures that lived there. Several project superintendents noted an apparent increase in the amount of wildlife in the park—turkeys, grouse, hawks, squirrels, foxes, wildcats, and bears. One superintendent declared that bears were quite in evidence and that they visited camp both day and night. Another said: "Forney Creek is literally running over with rainbow and mountain trout"— a result of stream improvement and stocking from the CCC-built fish hatcheries.[25]

CCC enrollees' labor and CCC funding made possible the park's visitor centers at Sugarlands (Tennessee) and Oconaluftee (North Carolina), shown here. From the Great Smoky Mountains National Park Archives.

Along with fire towers, trails (hiking and horse), motor roads, recreational facilities, reduction of fire-hazards, improvements to timber stands, and landscaping, the Great Smoky Mountains National Park also included preservation along with its conservation: it oversaw the renovation and rehabilitation of a number of historic buildings, including gristmills and other exemplary architectural structures, for cultural interpretation. The park also constructed the Oconaluftee Visitor Center, which remains the North Carolina gateway to the park, utilizing native stone, local chestnut timber, a Spanish-born master stonemason (Joe Troitino), and CCC labor.[26]

In reflecting upon how the CCC program most benefited the park, the superintendent during the CCC era enumerated "the removal of fire hazards, the building of motorways and trails, erection of fire lookouts, study of White Pine Blister Rust conditions, landscaping, telephone construction, and others."[27] He recalled that the park, before the advent of the CCC, had been greatly handicapped in promoting any significant development by the lack of personnel and funding, as well as by the inaccessible nature of the terrain. The arrival of the CCC greatly alleviated those adverse conditions. With the CCC came an abundant labor supply, funds, and equipment sufficient to reduce fire hazards, develop motor roads and trails, and rehabilitate forests ravaged by destructive timber practices and the chestnut blight.

THE BLUE RIDGE PARKWAY, NATIONAL PARK SERVICE

The Blue Ridge Parkway, like the CCC, was born of the Great Depression, a child of necessity, created to link two new national parks—the Shenandoah and the Great Smoky Mountains—and simultaneously to provide work for mountaineers suffering from oppressive unemployment. The nation's first rural national parkway was conceived in 1933, and construction began in September 1935; like the two new parks it connected, it offered potential employment opportunities to thousands of people. The official charged with the parkway's design and development, Stanley W. Abbott, the parkway's resident landscape architect, was a graduate of Cornell University who came directly from the pioneering Westchester County, New York, park system. His brilliant design concepts called for 469 miles of roadway with a vast support system of recreational parks, trails, lodges, and service facilities. President Roosevelt's New Deal programs, especially the Works Progress Administration (WPA) and the CCC, provided much of the funding and labor for fulfilling Abbott's vision.

Three sources of labor were marshaled for the construction and beautification of the proposed parkway: contract, WPA, and CCC. Once land was purchased and rights-of-way were conveyed, contract and WPA labor went into action quickly, but there was a five-year delay in obtaining CCC labor. Abbott, mindful of the vast additional amount of construction that could be accomplished by CCC enrollees, filed with the chief architect of the National Park Service in 1937 a request that nine CCC camps be established for parkway use. He proposed creation of four camps in Virginia: one each at Peaks of Otter and Pine Spur/Smart View and two in the vicinity of Rocky Knob. For North Carolina,

he sought five camps: one each at Tomkins Knob, Cumberland Knob, and Basin Creek, and two in the vicinity of Bluffs Park. Abbott even suggested the possibility of having CCC labor from both the Shenandoah National Park and a U.S. Forest Service camp at Sherando, Virginia, assigned to the parkway. Moreover, he recommended the establishment of some permanent CCC camps along the parkway in lieu of projected maintenance facilities. He estimated that just one aspect of needed labor—landscape improvement—could employ one camp of two hundred men continuously for a year. In addition, Abbott viewed the development of wayside recreation parks, the installation of guardrails, the sloping of banks, erosion control, planting, and similar essential endeavors so labor worthy that he declared: "I believe we can safely guarantee the use of nine camps over at least a ten-year period."[28]

For unknown reasons, the request for nine CCC camps received such little support that the parkway obtained only four. The Virginia section received three: NP-14, located in the Rock Castle Gorge of Rocky Knob Park; NP-15, situated at Kelso; and NP-29, erected on the parkway near Galax. The North Carolina section received but one—NP-21, established adjacent to milepost 240 near Laurel Springs in September 1938 and abandoned in July 1942.[29] With the addition of the four camps, Abbott's work reports took on new dimensions. In reporting on landscape development along one section of the parkway in North Carolina, Abbott noted that "Selective cutting by the CCC has been in progress. . . . As a result of the cutting several excelling bays of Catawbiense Rhododendron have been opened up, and an excellent view has been cleared into Devil's Garden. By proper cutting it was also possible to eliminate a

NP-21, Company 3420, named Camp Meadow Fork, was established in September 1938 and remained active until July 1942. The white structures in the foreground are maintenance buildings still in use. The area occupied by the camp is now a white-pine forest. From the Blue Ridge Parkway Archives.

few scrubby oaks and expose the alpine-like character of several pine trees growing on the rugged ridges which drop down into Devil's Garden."[30]

CCC enrollees in the North Carolina portion of the Blue Ridge Parkway labored from September 1938 to July 1942, and their handiwork was augmented by that of WPA laborers, adult family men who, unlike the CCC enrollees, lived at home and commuted to work daily. Virtually every report Stanley Abbott filed with the parkway's regional or Washington office included information on the specific accomplishments of the WPA and CCC work forces. An example follows:

Section 2-B: Planting of trees, shrubs and ground cover is complete on the first two and one-half miles except for the pond site. Work was done by WPA.

Selective Cutting: The first two cuts and about half the third cut are complete for the first six miles of the section. Work has been discontinued due to lack of sufficient men at NP-21 to carry on all the projects.

Seeding: This has been started by the CCC forces at the end of the planting, working back toward the beginning of the section. Topsoil has been spread for about ¼ mile, but seeding has started.

Section 2-D: Seeding of open area on the first mile of the section was done by WPA. Preliminary Improvement by CCC forces is complete on the first ten and one-half miles of the section.[31]

It was not at all unusual for WPA laborers and CCC enrollees to work as a team, one group doing one portion of a project and the other another. Here a WPA crew is constructing the entrance road to Camp NC NP-21 at Laurel Springs, Alleghany County. From the Blue Ridge Parkway Archives.

The projects described in the foregoing passage were, of course, just a few of the tasks performed by one CCC camp during forty-five months of labor on the North Carolina portion of the parkway; three others were laboring on the Virginia portion. Contrary to popular belief, however, the CCC did not actually construct the parkway. That task was accomplished by professional road builders on public contract. But it was the touch, care, and labor of the CCC that enabled the landscape architects and contractors to plan and create one of the world's most scenic national parkways. Those young men followed behind the rough gougings of the bulldozers and the blasters, performing fine-tooth, tender-loving-care landscaping. Their work involved slope reductions to prevent soil erosion; planting a wide variety of shrubbery and trees; spreading tons of fertilizer and grass seed; mitigating fire hazards; building rail fences; constructing facilities such as campgrounds, trail shelters, picnic grounds, rest-room accommodations, waterlines, and pumping stations; and producing the rustic, hand-routed signs that are so characteristic of the parkway. Not only was their labor responsible for creating maintenance and utility buildings at North Carolina points of interest such as Doughton Park, Gillespie Gap, and Cumberland Knob, but CCC funding also helped make such facilities possible. Moreover, Cumberland Knob became one of the nation's pioneer recreation demonstration projects, designed to illustrate that worn-out, submarginal land could be rehabilitated and that conservation of natural resources such as water, soil, forests, and wildlife could be integrated into attractive, viable public recreational facilities that included trails, trail shelters, spacious playing areas

CCC enrollees did not construct the Blue Ridge Parkway, but their efforts at slope reduction, landscaping, planting, fertilizing, and seeding did much to promote its beauty. From the Blue Ridge Parkway Archives.

with picnic grounds, and concession structures.[32]

But what is most remarkable about the work of both the CCC and the WPA is that the landscape designers performed their work so deftly that motorists moving along the parkway at present find it difficult to believe that all the beauty they encounter is not simply Mother Nature's gift. Rather, it is her bounty, richly fertilized and artfully planted—the crowning achievement of superb, purposeful design by master landscape architects, aided by the diligent labor of CCC and WPA hands. Stanley Abbott, reminiscing after the CCC had been dismantled, paid it and the WPA the highest tribute a landscape architect could possibly give to the practitioners of landscaping:

Much of the present beauty of the Parkway stems from the landscaping efforts of CCC enrollees such as these. From the Blue Ridge Parkway Archives.

Over the period of depression years in which the Parkway has been two-thirds built, four CCC and four WPA projects averaging 150 men each were assigned to the Parkway. These emergency agencies accomplished many worthwhile projects. Much of the work might otherwise never have been realized[,] for the jobs were of a nature hardly suited to contract forms, and funds . . . were not procurable. Major construction of the Parkway by contract has necessarily shown the marks of large scale road building in the modern manner. While better controlled than usual, the great earth moving machines have left a rough trail across the mountains, a wayside ravelled with many threads to be caught up. It has been in this re-knitting, in the healing over, and finishing that the emergency programs have made of a mountain highway a mountain parkway. Without such follow up much would be lost in the Parkway's beauty, and much that makes it practical as well. . . . No recapitulation of project accomplishments could estimate the real worth to the Blue Ridge Parkway of the emergency agencies.[33]

THE U.S. FOREST SERVICE

The national forests in North Carolina were relatively new in 1933, having been in existence less than two decades. Nevertheless, that newness, coupled with the need to manage the thousands of acres of land encompassed by federal holdings in the state, especially in the western section, provided an effective argument for establishing CCC camps for the specific purposes of improving the forests and promoting recreational development. Much of the land, like that in the neighboring Great Smoky Mountains National Park, had been adversely affected by the chestnut blight, ill-advised farm practices, and highly intensive timber cutting, largely by non-native lumber companies. Thus, federal forest officials were quite thrilled at the prospects the newly proposed CCC held for them. From the chief forester in

Washington, D.C., to the forest supervisor in Pisgah National Forest in North Carolina, the Forest Service ardently supported the new conservation program and quickly suggested projects in which it might become involved, lending both credibility and viability to President Roosevelt's ideas.[34]

When the CCC was implemented in 1933, there were two major national forests in North Carolina: the Nantahala, with approximately 1,349,000 acres of forest land in portions of Cherokee, Clay, Graham, Jackson, Macon, and Swain counties and headquarters in Franklin; and the Pisgah, with 1,178,000 acres of woodlands in portions of Avery, Buncombe, Burke, Caldwell, Haywood, Henderson, Madison, McDowell, Mitchell, Transylvania, and Yancey counties and headquarters in Asheville. Because they were southern Appalachian forests, they presented a magnificent variety of flora and fauna. The Forest Service pointed out that on a trip from Marion, North Carolina, to the top of Mount Mitchell, a distance of some thirty miles, a traveler would "encounter more species of trees than he would in crossing Europe from the British Isles to Turkey."[35] Moreover, within the two forests stood many rugged peaks a mile or more in elevation; and since the average annual rainfall was higher than the national average, those peaks were the headwaters of such rivers as the French Broad, the Catawba, the Tuckasegee, and the Davidson. Likewise, the relative health of those forests and their ability to serve as watersheds exerted a major influence on the well-being and prosperity of many communities that surrounded them or received water from them and made it essential that they be managed with great care.

Traditionally the most important aspect of forest management is protection against

A deadly chestnut blight, combined with the careless cut-out-and-get-out policies of the timber companies that originally owned thousands of acres of North Carolina's timberlands, left acres of ugly debris like this. From the Great Smoky Mountains National Park Archives.

fire, because unchecked blazes bring a host of dire consequences: scorched humus, ash-filled streams, death-dealing damage to young timber, a frightful toll on wildlife, years of delay in harvesting timber, and major loss of recreational value. But for the entire life of the national forests in North Carolina prior to 1933, there had never been sufficient funding to properly protect, manage, or professionally develop the federal holdings. Moreover, much of the land was practically inaccessible because of the rugged terrain and lack of roads. So a vast acreage with potential value for precious water resources, choice hunting and fishing, quality timber production, and an unparalleled recreational experience lay undeveloped and under-utilized for lack of funds and management. For the Forest Service, then, the CCC was a true godsend, bringing with it money and manpower sufficient to design, lay out, and construct much-needed roads, trails, fire towers, and telephone lines for protection and to augment the protective measures with some of the most remarkable recreational facilities in the entire nation.[36] As a result, nine years of diligent, admirably supervised CCC labor built the infrastructure of the modern national forests in North Carolina, advanced managerial achievements a full generation, and enhanced the region's economic and recreational opportunities.

To accomplish those goals, it was necessary to establish numerous CCC camps within the state's vast federal forest lands. The following table lists those camps, their locations, and the date each was occupied.

CAMP NUMBER	POST OFFICE	COUNTY WHERE LOCATED	DATE OCCUPIED
F-1	Pisgah Forest	Transylvania	May 19, 1933
F-2	Hendersonville	Henderson	May 19, 1933
F-3	Old Fort	McDowell	May 25, 1933
F-4	Marion	McDowell	May 25, 1933
F-5	Mortimer	Caldwell	May 20, 1933
F-6	Globe	Caldwell	May 20, 1933
F-7	Hot Springs	Madison	May 27, 1933
F-8	Barnardsville	Buncombe	May 30, 1933
F-9	Franklin	Macon	May 24, 1933
F-10	Aquone	Macon	May 28, 1933
F-11	Tellico Plains, Tenn.	Cherokee	June 26, 1933
F-12	Rainbow Springs	Clay	June 28, 1933
F-13	Topton	Cherokee	June 21, 1933
F-14	Balsam Grove	Transylvania	June 22, 1933
F-15	Maysville	Jones	Aug. 15, 1935
F-16	New Bern	Craven	Oct. 19, 1933
F-17	Troy	Montgomery	Nov. 20, 1934
F-18 [no record of]			
F-19	Highlands	Macon	Oct. 6, 1934
F-20	Franklin	Macon	July 2, 1935
F-21	Maysville	Jones	Sept. 3, 1935
F-22	Asheville	Buncombe	July 14, 1935
F-23	Otto	Macon	July 14, 1935
F-24	Robbinsville	Graham	Aug. 21, 1935
F-25	Canton	Haywood	July 6, 1935
F-26 [no record of]			
F-27	Marion	McDowell	Dec. 17, 1937
F-28	Brevard	Transylvania	May 22, 1938
F-29	Murphy	Cherokee	Sept. 26, 1939[37]

The following table lists the work projects assigned to Camp John Rock (NC F-28), Company 428, located in the Pisgah National Forest, Transylvania County, for a single six-month enrollment period:

PROJECT NUMBER	DESCRIPTION	NO. OF APPROVED MAN-DAYS
42-A	Truck Trail Construction	1,309
64	Boundary Survey	500
67	Telephone Line Construction	2,500
82	Telephone Line Construction	11,000
100	Truck Trail Maintenance	400
124	Foreman's Residence	125
125	Administrative Office	155
151	Truck Trail Maintenance	1,300
154	Warden's Residence	10
166	Truck Trail Construction	500
168	Lookout Tower	300
172	Privy	10
173	Well	5
175	Lookout Tower	350
179	Privy	10
180	Well	5
191	Telephone Line Construction	800
195	Recondition Area Ranger's House	120
197	Brushing, Telephone Lines	160
198	Firebreak Construction	555
219	Eye Bolt Construction	4
221	Forest Blasting	400
222	Timber Cruise	75
223	Recondition Area Forester's House	150
224	Fire Construction	2,100
225	Install Bath Toilet & Septic Tank	25
240	Fighting Forest Fires	500
245	Map Making	20
247	Fire Suppression	500[38]

A brief history of Camp NC F-22, Company 3402, of Asheville serves to illustrate how Forest Service camps were established and where their enrollees came from. On June 14, 1935, an advance cadre from Camp NC P-57, Company 433, stationed at Morganton, arrived to establish a new camp on the Rocky Cove Road in the Bent Creek Forest. On July 24 a full contingent of enrollees from North Carolina, Mississippi, Georgia, and Florida arrived. Its basic task was to assist the Appalachian Forest Experimental Station achieve its goal of establishing a more useful, efficient, and attractive experimental forest and accompanying field laboratories. The company's daily projects focused on the construction of roads and trails; clean-up and planting; and the establishment and maintenance of permanent sample plots on which studies of fire, insect and fungi damage, rodent control, stream flow, and similar forest-related concerns could be carried out.[39]

In August 1933 one newspaper reported that men from nearby Camp NC F-4, Company 401, had improved more than a thousand acres of forest lands and had completed, in less than three months, nearly half of a five-mile-long road it was constructing over Sugar Tree Cove.[40] Another declared that between 1933 and 1935 the CCC had expended more than ten million man-days of work in improving southern national forests, including the following specific tasks:

Public Camp Ground Clearings	526 acres
Public Camp Ground Buildings	58
Miscellaneous Camp Ground Improvement Projects	455
Reforestation	18,243 acres
Bridges	17,637
Recreational Dams	36
Telephone Lines	10,918 miles
Fire Breaks	26,864
Lookout Towers	347
Forest Stand Improvement	1,118,042 acres
Topography and Timber Surveys	6,220,676 acres
Check Dams	337,609
Trees Planted	11,282,382[41]

Still another paper announced in November 1938 that a large forest fire that had ravaged about 3,000 acres in Watauga and Caldwell counties for five days had been extinguished "after about 300 citizens and as many boys from nearby CCC camps battled the blaze day and night."[42] A similar story reported that 200,000 acres of land in Alleghany and Wilkes counties had been destroyed by forest fires before CCC and relief workers could be hurried to the scene to bring them under control.[43]

One CCC camp, F-8, Company 409, stationed at Barnardsville, Buncombe County, distinguished itself by making a number of improvements at Craggy Gardens, site of a spectacular array of rhododendrons and a popular destination

Pictured here is a stream-flow control project at the Coweeta Experimental Forest, Nantahala National Forest, Macon County. This 1937 photograph shows enrollees working to reduce soil erosion. From the Southern Highlands Research Center, UNC-Asheville.

Among the contributions made by the CCC were the many picnic shelters and sites still in service in the national forests of North Carolina. This unit was built at the famous "Pink Beds," Pisgah National Forest. Courtesy Nick Lanier.

of visitors to Asheville's annual Rhododendron Festival. Before the advent of the CCC, miles of foot trails provided the only access to Craggy Gardens. In 1937 the CCC enrollees at Camp NC F-8 constructed a road from Barnardsville to Craggy Gardens, created a parking space there, improved a trail connecting the parking lot to the gardens proper (at Craggy Dome), and beautified the nearby picnic and camp grounds. Moreover, the men placed rustic benches at convenient intervals along the trail and at its midpoint constructed a handsome, hewn-log picnic shelter (which is still in use).[44] The road they constructed made it possible for Asheville's annual Rhododendron Queen to be crowned in the midst of the namesake plants at Craggy Gardens.

One unique endeavor of the CCC in North Carolina was its activity in connection with the state's deer population. CCC enrollees designed and scattered throughout the Pisgah Game Preserve, a section of Pisgah National Forest, some 164 large wood-and-wire traps and left them there throughout the year so that the preserve's resident deer would become accustomed to them. During the late-spring trapping season the men set the traps, baited them with apples, visited them daily, retrieved any captured deer, placed them in large crates, and transported the animals to a holding pen. The deer were subsequently shipped to game-depleted state and federal forest areas and released. The program had the added benefit of helping to maintain the resident deer herd of the Pisgah National Forest at a manageable level. Moreover, CCC enrollees often participated in an annual Forest Service-sponsored "fawn hunt," usually in early June, by obtaining official permits to capture fawns and conveying them to a central holding area, at which they were fed a special diet and monitored until autumn, when they were mature enough to be sent to some other forest.[45]

Camp NC F-14 had one of the most unusual tasks of any camp in North Carolina: capturing young deer and shipping them to numerous national forests. From the Mars Hill College Archives.

Roads were a high priority for all national forests, providing quick access for fire control and timber stand improvement projects. From the Southern Highlands Research Center, UNC-Asheville.

An activity common throughout the forests of North Carolina was road building. CCC enrollees stationed in Caldwell County won praise for constructing a road to connect the Globe community and the town of Lenoir by a route "some five miles shorter than the existing route by way of Collettsville."[46] Camp NC F-25, Company 3455, stationed near Canton, declared that road construction was its principal work project, with its main efforts concentrated on building a road (present-day N.C. Highway 215) from the camp to the Blue Ridge Parkway. "At the present time," the camp reported in 1937, "approximately five and one-half miles of this road have been rapidly built, and it is progressing rapidly as steam shovel and trail builders, manned by enrollees, push forward. As it winds up the mountain, the road crosses the river several times on picturesque stone bridges built by the enrollees."[47] The superintendent of Camp F-24 ("Camp Santeelah"), Company 3447, stationed at Robbinsville, provided the following description of a forest road constructed by the men he supervised:

A road project has been under construction since Camp Santeelah was organized. The road is known as Number Thirteen Tatham Gap. We have completed four miles of this road. Camp NC F-13 completed nine of it. It leads from the town of Robbinsville to the town of Andrews, going through the forest all the way. It makes many places easy to get to and saves many miles of travel for the Ranger and other Forest Service officials when they want to come into the Graham County Forest. It also gives the public the most scenic trip in this county. It opens up wide spaces of forest lands that is a treat for the eye to behold. A lover of nature could not travel this road without worshipping the act of God in making the mountains and then decorating them with such a beautiful forest.[48]

Another superintendent, who served at a number of forest camps in western North Carolina, recalling his career with the CCC, reflected on the wide range of duties and opportunities for community service and self-improvement the corps brought into his life:

> My experience with the CCC was a very meaningful, character building, and constructive part of my life. There were new and varied experiences offered that many men do not have the opportunity to share in a lifetime. The challenge to excel was great and I was the Project Superintendent of my first camp after being with the CCC for about one year. I was only twenty-nine at the time and looked forward to the new experience offered us daily.
>
> We built roads, fought fires, built forest ranger stations, fore roads, observation towers, and constructed telephone lines. These jobs all required the cooperation of each and every man. It did not matter if he was a ditch digger or a leader, everyone had to pull together.
>
> We tried to add to the communities we were in and help the locals whenever possible. There was a lady that passed away at the north end of the camp. There was no way her family could get a vehicle up to the cemetery. The family asked us to help get her up to the burial site. The CCC boys went to the home, with a foreman, and carried the deceased to her place of rest. They had to carry her about three-quarters of a mile distance.[49]

The CCC's stewardship of North Carolina's national forests transformed the woebegone remnants of thousands of acres of overtimbered and neglected woodlands into productive, attractive, and desirable places of beauty and utility. The lands that came under their care were largely rejects, submarginal, and unsightly. Indeed, most of the acreage had been sold to the U.S. government by former owners more than happy to dispose of their unproductive holdings. Yet that same acreage is presently considered a treasure house of resources—scenic, timber, wildlife, mineral, wilderness, and recreational. That remarkable rehabilitation demands applause for two entities—the U.S. Forest Service and the CCC.

THE TENNESSEE VALLEY AUTHORITY

The Tennessee Valley Authority (TVA) and the CCC were two of the most innovative of the New Deal programs, born in the exhilarating first one hundred days after the inauguration of President Franklin D. Roosevelt. Each program stemmed from major reclamation problems, and each was a bold experiment in converting man-ravaged lands into productive acreage through wise husbandry. Indeed, the TVA was envisioned as the means by which a national disgrace, a vast rural slum area the size of Great Britain, could be restored to the condition it once enjoyed—"one of the fairest agricultural regions in the land."[50] Sorrowfully, the toll of more than two centuries of prodigal, mindless, unconscionable, unscientific farming had resulted in the loss of many millions of tons of fertile soil, accompanied by a dire loss of productivity. An official 1933 TVA report clearly established man's exceedingly poor stewardship of the valley: "At the time, erosion afflicted an estimated 85 percent of the Valley's 13 million acres of cultivated land, with 2 million of those acres so gullied that experts questioned whether the land could ever be revived."[51]

To reverse that devastation was the basic purpose for which the TVA was created. The agency's enlightened leadership proposed to accomplish that task by utilizing regional planning, modern engineering skills, and a gigantic conservation program, including flood control, soil erosion control, and reforestation. One of the principal mechanisms relied upon to fulfill that purpose was the CCC. All states encompassed by the TVA were allotted CCC camps, with the number per state determined by the needs of the various projects deemed necessary to rehabilitate the entire region. North Carolina's location astride the eastern continental divide assured its participation. The vast mountain ranges in the western part of the state, with such rivers as the French Broad and the Little Tennessee draining massive watersheds endowed with unusually high annual precipitation and subject to frequent and devastating flooding, were prime targets for the TVA conservation program. Moreover, the efforts expended by CCC enrollees in the Great Smoky Mountains National Park and the national forests in North Carolina dovetailed neatly into the conservation aims of the TVA; indeed, the TVA established three camps of its own in the state: TVA-1, Company 2432, stationed at Bakersville, Mitchell County, established July 25, 1935, and abandoned October 4, 1937; TVA-2, Company 3424, headquartered at Mars Hill, Madison County, established July 22, 1935, and abandoned March 10, 1942; and TVA-3, Company 413, located at Arden, Buncombe County, established July 22, 1935, and abandoned January 1, 1936.[52] The camps well suited the TVA's desire to reseed, reforest, and rehabilitate the vast acreage it had inherited.

The North Carolina TVA camps, in an unusual but effective bureaucratic arrangement, were placed under the jurisdiction of the U.S. Forest Service, which functioned as a contractor. The TVA retained absolute administrative charge of the camps and oversight of all their work projects. The Forest Service, in turn, was responsible for all of the major administrative details, such as the hiring of personnel, project supervision, purchasing, and all work accomplishments. The TVA inspected the projects as they were being done and upon completion to ensure that the work met its plans and specifications.[53]

A PEACE TIME ARMY:

The Tennessee Valley Authority - Civilian Conservation Corps, 1933-1942

Front page cover of TVA's CCC history publication. From the Mars Hill College Archives.

Individual projects had two basic aims: "(1) to save farm lands from the disastrous effects of erosion, and (2) to prevent the local farmer's land from washing downstream and clogging the newly built dams with silt."[54]

To counter years of unbridled waste and destruction, the TVA CCC enrollees launched their conservation offensive in the late summer of 1935 with five western North Carolina counties the focus of intensive, painstaking attention: Buncombe, Henderson, Madison, Mitchell, and Yancey. By the spring of 1938 varying numbers of enrollees, from two

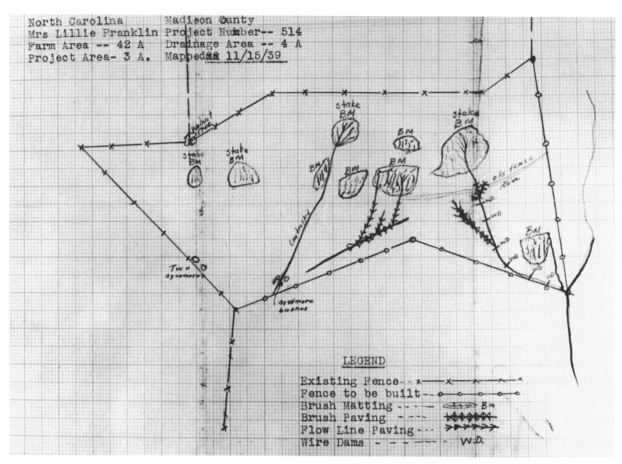

This TVA sketch shows work to be done on land in Madison County. From the Mars Hill College Archives.

hundred to six hundred at times, had carried out erosion work on four hundred farms within the five counties. Included in that work was the planting of nearly three million trees, among them thousands of locusts, pitch pines, yellow poplars, and supposedly blight-resistant chestnuts. The TVA was reported to be employing eight distinct methods of controlling soil erosion in the five-county area: strip cropping; mulching, or straw matting; brush paving; construction of diversion ditches and check dams; terracing and building terrace outlets; contour plowing; and planting trees or vegetation.[55]

As a means of affixing and retaining the local soil, the TVA placed considerable emphasis on the planting of trees. The CCC did double duty in that regard—they gathered seeds and planted young trees. In 1937 alone the Mars Hill camp was credited with gathering nine hundred bushels of pine seeds. Small seedlings from the agency's nurseries were planted at the rate of two thousand per acre. To ensure that the seedlings had a good chance of surviving, the farmer on whose land they were planted signed an agreement stipulating that for five years he would protect them from grazing livestock. Any farmer willing to cooperate was eligible to receive the CCC planting services. Two full-time TVA career employees—an erosion engineer and a forester—supervised the cooperative agreement for the five counties.[56] Some conservative farmers eyed the TVA's soil-erosion program with skepticism in its initial stages, but once

These young boys from Camp Joe (Camp TVA-2) in Mars Hill could easily have been poster enrollees for CCC publicity. Across the state many thousands of trees were planted to improve timber stands and prevent erosion. From the Mars Hill College Archives.

they saw the beneficial results on demonstration farms, most began seeking the service for their own holdings.[57]

The work of the TVA camps at Bakersville, Mars Hill, and Arden was augmented by other camps in the region. For example, in 1939 workers at Camp NC P-66, Company 3448, located at Brevard, initiated a TVA erosion-control and reforestation program in Transylvania County. Two crews of twenty men each combated gullies, mulched eroded lands, and planted pine and locust trees as a means of slowing erosion at the very

headwaters of the Tennessee Valley.[58] Moreover, Camp NC F-7, Company 407, stationed at Hot Springs, reported in 1940 that it had twenty enrollees engaged in planting TVA white pines and yellow poplars.[59] The first annual report (October 1935-June 1936) of Camp NC TVA-2, Company 3424, headquartered at Mars Hill, provides a glimpse of the specific types of work being done to check soil erosion:

TYPE OF PROJECT	AMOUNT	MAN-DAYS INVOLVED
Fence Building	3,278 rods	1,020
Bank Sloping	551,251 sq. rods	4,372
Check Dams, Permanent	5	36
Check Dams, Temporary	918	2,882
Seeding and Sodding	598,895 sq. rods	8,359
Tree Planting	203,011	875
Sheet Erosion Planting	183 acres	1,100
Seed Collecting	20 bushels	28
Forest Fires	—	34[60]

From July 1935 through March 1942, CCC camps sponsored or supported by the TVA labored on the farms and forest lands of western North Carolina. The total impact of the labor provided by those camps is beyond measure, but the TVA's praise of them is suggestive of their value: "As late as 1963," according to a TVA study of the agency's cooperative ventures with the CCC, "a land survey in the Tennessee Valley indicated that the acreage cared for by the CCC yielded $20 more per acre than similar land that did not have the assistance of the Corps. Although TVA has rightfully received credit for its soil conservation work, its success would not have been attained without the daily labor provided by CCC recruits."[61]

Private land throughout North Carolina benefited immensely from the enormous amount of labor expended by CCC enrollees, as the erosion-control measures carried out on this farm by Camp NC P-54 demonstrate. From the Mars Hill College Archives.

THE SOIL CONSERVATION SERVICE

This federal government agency began life as the "Soil Erosion Service" under the Department of the Interior but was renamed and put under the jurisdiction of the U.S. Department of Agriculture in 1934, with North Carolinian Hugh H. Bennett as its head. It was established to battle the enormous problem of soil erosion that plagued the nation. In 1934 it estimated that 50 million acres of farmland were "essentially ruined" by erosion, that another 50 million were "almost ruined," and that 100 million were "seriously eroded." Worse, the process of erosion accelerated in the 1930s as 3 billion tons of topsoil washed away annually.[62]

North Carolina counties were major contributors to this dismal record. In the Tar Heel State alone more than one-fourth of the topsoil from more than 5.5 million acres had been lost to erosion; more than 2 million acres had lost more than 75 percent of their topsoil; more than a million acres had been completely abandoned; and in the ten Piedmont counties most affected by erosion, one-fourth of the land had been abandoned as no longer suitable for cultivation.[63] A Burlington newspaper reported that 26,650 acres of the total of 314,880 acres that comprised Alamance County—or approximately 8 1/2 percent—had been abandoned because of severe erosion.[64] An extension specialist for erosion control declared that "rain washes as much plant food from Piedmont soils in one year as a farmer's crops take from out of the soil in 20 years."[65] In May 1940 the commissioners of Stokes County, seeking assignment of a CCC camp to alleviate their erosion problems, spelled out the problem in painful detail:

Of the total land area in Stokes County only 18 percent, or 55,296 acres, show no erosion. Fourteen percent, or 43,000 acres, have from one to twenty-five percent of the topsoil removed. Fifty to 75 percent of the topsoil has been removed by erosion from 30 percent of the land in the county, i.e., 92,160 acres, and more than 75 percent of the topsoil has been removed from 20 percent of the land, or 61,440 acres. There is no question but that the soil erosion situation is not only severe, but critical. It is Stokes county's biggest problem.[66]

Plainly, the needs were there, but the political powers had not yet met them. It will be recalled that North Carolina's first CCC camps were assigned to the national park and forest lands in the spring of 1933, largely because the latter's management teams had quickly grasped the enormous possibilities that President Roosevelt's civilian conservation program entailed for the land in their charge and had conceived extensive project proposals to utilize the potential new labor sources. Thus, the first camps in the state were heavily concentrated in the mountains. But widespread publicity about the evils of soil erosion in the state's Piedmont region finally caught the politicians' attention. In August 1935 North Carolina was awarded five of ninety-three soil-erosion projects to be established throughout the nation—the largest of any state besides Arizona and Texas. North Carolina's $1.5 million share of the total appropriation of $27 million was to create such projects in ten Piedmont counties of the state—Alamance, Anson, Davidson, Forsyth, Franklin, Guilford, Mecklenburg, Randolph, Rockingham, and Union.[67] Only a month earlier, newspapers in the state had reported that a total of twenty-three CCC camps were being constructed in twenty-two North Carolina counties and that those camps would be the centers for soil conservation work, with North Carolina headquarters to be maintained at High Point.[68]

The twenty-three camps were assigned as follows:

AGENCY NO.	COMPANY NUMBER	LOCATION	COUNTY
NC SES-1	434	High Point	Guilford
NC SES-2	437	Polkton	Anson
NC SES-3	404	High Point	Guilford
NC SCS-4	3405	Mount Airy	Surry
NC SCS-5	3406	Yanceyville	Caswell
NC SCS-6	3407	Winston-Salem	Forsyth
NC SCS-7	3408	Lexington	Davidson
NC SCS-8	3409	Salisbury	Rowan
NC SCS-10	3410	Huntersville	Mecklenburg
NC SCS-11	3411	Gastonia	Gaston
NC SCS-12	3412	Oxford	Granville
NC SCS-13	3413	Burlington	Alamance
NC SCS-14	3414	Durham	Durham
NC SCS-15	3415	Newton	Catawba
NC SCS-16	3416	Monroe	Union
NC SCS-17	3417	Madison	Rockingham
NC SCS-18	3418	Lillington	Harnett
NC SCS-19	3419	Franklinton	Franklin
NC SCS-20	3420	Ramseur	Randolph
NC SCS-21	3421	Statesville	Iredell
NC SCS-22	3422	Rockingham	Richmond
NC SCS-23	3423	Shelby	Cleveland
NC SCS-24	3424	Forest City	Rutherford[69]

As early as November 1934—six months before the announcement concerning the twenty-three new soil conservation camps planned for North Carolina, one newspaper reported that the CCC was scheduled to inaugurate tree-planting work in the Deep River and Brown Creek watersheds of Randolph County in December and continue the project until

April 1935. According to the paper, the CCC was to supply the labor of approximately two hundred men to plant 1.5 million commercial tree seedlings.[70] The newspaper story represents one of the earliest reports of soil conservation activity by the CCC in North Carolina.

Throughout the spring and summer of 1935 the newly announced CCC erosion-control camps opened in numerous locations throughout the North Carolina Piedmont. The typical such facility consisted of a "camp superintendent, who will be in charge of conducting the general field program; an agronomist or agreement man, who will be in charge of working out cooperative agreements and farm programs with the individual farmers; an agricultural engineer in charge of the construction of terraces and other mechanical methods of controlling erosion; three technical foremen (forestry, engineering, and agronomy or soils); four junior foremen in charge of work in the fields; a draftsman, a mechanic, and a camp clerk."[71]

In order to administer the erosion-control program efficiently, the Conservation Service divided North Carolina into soil conservation districts and established a state coordinator's head-quarters at Raleigh, a soil conservation nursery at Chapel Hill, and an erosion experiment station in Iredell County. Moreover, it established demonstration land-utilization projects at Elizabethtown (Bladen County) and Hoffman (Richmond County), as well as eight demonstration-project areas in such counties as Alamance, Guilford, Randolph, and Stanly.

This photograph of the Erosion Control Nursery, U.S. Department of Agriculture, Soil Conservation Service, near Chapel Hill was made on December 2, 1935. Here CCC men are clearing and plowing a corner of an oak nursery. From Photographs, Forest Resources, North Carolina Division of Forestry, State Archives.

The pioneering Brown Creek district was the first in the nation to be chartered—in August 1937. It encompassed Anson, Montgomery, Richmond, and Union counties, which together represented 12,000 cooperating farms and 1,396,000 acres of land. The Tar River district was the largest in North Carolina, involving 15,415 cooperating farms and 1,414,000 acres of land in Franklin, Granville, Nash, and Vance counties.[72]

Each of the districts originated in cooperative efforts among representatives of erosion-control agencies, county agents, county commissioners, and farmers eager to save their farms. The farmer customarily provided the acreage to be improved, paid the cost of the machinery necessary to terrace the land, and pledged to maintain prescribed practices in the future. The county, as a rule, provided the terracing machinery. The CCC camps made available the labor required to rehabilitate the land, generally by constructing diversion ditches, controlling gullies, and carrying out reforesting.[73] At the heart of that cooperative program was the formation in North Carolina of a series of county soil conservation associations to work together, share information, and conduct demonstration projects conducive to erosion-control practices; forty-two such associations existed throughout the state in 1938.[74]

Once erosion-control work actually commenced, positive results quickly followed. For example, in October 1935 Forsyth County agent R. W. Pou announced that work was beginning on an initial three thousand acres of farmland in his county. The program had been made possible when Forsyth's commissioners had expended county funds to acquire a tractor and a terracing machine. With that equipment, Pou said, the land of one hundred farmers who had signed cooperative agreements could be terraced. He further noted that at least two years of work by the CCC would be required to accomplish that task and that approximately ten years of such effort would be necessary to terrace all the eroded land in Forsyth County that needed attention.[75]

In the Forsyth County example just cited, the terracing work was followed by additional activity by CCC enrollees, who installed scientifically engineered drainage ditches, diversion dams, and gully-stopping dams; conducted reforestation; and made improvements to timber stands.

An important anti-erosion activity practiced by the CCC was the planting of seedlings. Related to that activity was the diligent gathering of seeds, which were then shipped to the state forestry nursery at Clayton or to the Soil Conservation Service nursery at Statesville for sprouting, nurturing, and ultimately distribution as seedlings ready for planting.[76] One newspaper reported on the "immense" quantities of nuts and seeds that had been gathered by "scores" of CCC camp workers in Cleveland County.[77] A sister camp in Franklin County was cited for having collected "enough seed to produce 30,000,000 trees."[78]

The duties of a typical CCC soil conservation camp in North Carolina are neatly summarized by the following statement of work accomplished in one year by Camp NC SCS-19, Company 3418, stationed at Franklinton:

CCC enrollees dig a ditch at the State Forest Nursery in Johnston County in 1939. From Photographs, Forest Resources, North Carolina Division of Forestry, State Archives.

60 acres of gullied areas have been treated.

Over 60 wired check dams have been built and over a hundred stake checks put in.

7,000 feet of diversion ditches with 8,000 square yards of bank sloping and grading.

10 miles of terracing.

75 square yards of sodding.

13,000 feet of channel excavation.

19,000 trees have been planted.[79]

A similar report for Camp NC SCS-17 at Madison, Rockingham County, reveals that the camp entered upon soil conservation work on September 17, 1935, and that in one year signed up for its cooperative program fifty-two farmers holding a total of 9,954 acres of farmland. During that same year, moreover, the camp's engineering division staked 159,209 feet for terracing, while its soils department conducted a detailed erosion survey of 6,386 acres in Rockingham and Stokes counties to determine the type of slope, the degree of erosion, and the culture of the soil as a preliminary step to controlling erosion. (The difficulty of planning is suggested by the fact that seventy-five different soil types were identified in those two counties.)[80]

With more than twenty CCC camps dedicated solely to soil-erosion control in North Carolina, each day's labor represented a building block in reconstructing the foundation for untold savings of natural resources that otherwise would have literally washed away. Each camp demonstrated every workday that soil conservation and a wiser land-use policy not only were possible but also were in fact the most practical and economical thing to do. One editor, praising the work and worth of CCC labor in behalf of soil conservation in Catawba County, perhaps spoke for other counties and camps affected by the program: "It is impossible to estimate in dollars and cents the value of Catawba county soil that has been saved from total loss by erosion since the establishment of Camp Little (NC SCS-15), Company 3415, at Newton, on July 17, 1935. Soil experts, however, are generally agreed that the soil erosion control accomplished through this camp is worth far more to the county, especially with reference to future agricultural wealth, than the maintenance of the camp has cost the government."[81] By the end of the program in 1942, a giant step had been taken toward realizing the dream of a Shelby editor who had admonished his readers to "save what lands we now have as a heritage for our people."[82]

Men of NC SCS-15, Company 3415, in Newton build a terrace outlet channel for planting kudzu. From undated Company 3415 annual, n.p. Courtesy of Mrs. W. L. Harper, wife of the camp superintendent. From the Mars Hill College Archives.

STATE PARKS

One of the most unusual by-products of the CCC program was the enormous boost it gave to development of state parks throughout the nation. As early as April 28, 1933, Secretary of the Interior Harold L. Ickes pointed out the importance of state parks—particularly how their development could make a major contribution to the conservation of natural resources, as well as to employment for the needy. The secretary was building on the earlier work of national park leaders Steve Mather and Horace Albright, who in 1921 established the National Conference on State Parks as a means of initiating a support program for enlarging existing state parks and creating new ones as adjunct recreational units to augment the opportunities provided by national parks.[83] President Roosevelt readily saw the wisdom in promoting the development of state parks and on April 29, 1933, approved the use of federal funds and manpower to aid the states in enlarging their park programs. The Department of the Interior, through its National Park Service, thereupon established on May 15, 1933, four district offices to facilitate a cooperative program with the states and their park officials.[84]

Each interested state official filed formal requests for the establishment of CCC camps to perform park work deemed desirable to promote conservation of natural resources and provide recreational opportunities for their citizens. Moreover, to encourage each state's participation, the federal government agreed to provide funding, technical assistance, and CCC manpower. That the states sensed they were getting a bargain is reflected by the fact that the number of state-park CCC camps nationwide jumped from 102 in the first six-month enrollment period (early 1933) to 263 in the second (October 1933).[85] That federal-state cooperative program worked very successfully. One of the reasons why it did was the caliber of leadership provided by the National Park Service's top-echelon officials—men such as Conrad L. Wirth, chief National Park Service coordinator of CCC state park activities. Wirth operated on the principle that the program was mutually advantageous. He explained succinctly how it worked:

While the army finance officer paid the bills, we asked the state authorities to act as our procurement agents. The CCC camps were turned over to them, and although the camp superintendents and the technical men who supervised the work were paid out of federal funds, they reported directly to the state park authorities. . . . The state park offices prepared project plans and took care of employment and procurement. . . . At the request of various states, the National Park Service counseled them on drafting legislation to provide the necessary legal authority to plan, develop, and maintain state park systems.[86]

Mount Mitchell State Park

Unlike many other states, North Carolina already had an ongoing state park system, having established Mount Mitchell as a state park in 1915-1916 through the efforts of a handful of ardent conservationists who challenged Gov. Locke Craig to halt the environmental calamity being inflicted upon the highest peak in the eastern United States by intensive timbering and accompanying forest fires. Craig's leadership resulted in the creation of the first state park in North Carolina, as well as one of the first in the South.[87] Nevertheless, between 1916 and 1933, for a variety of reasons, little was done to develop the park. In April 1933, seeking to reinvigorate the development both of Mount Mitchell and Fort Macon, a stone fortification erected at the entrance to Beaufort harbor in 1826, the North Carolina General Assembly approved resolutions requesting federal funds.

The entrance to Mount Mitchell State Park, ca. 1930. It actually reads "Mt. Mitchell State Game Refuge." This photograph is from the State Archives.

In May 1935 J. S. Holmes, North Carolina state forester, announced that the high peak "is scheduled soon to have a program of development that should increase materially its accessibility and popularity for additional thousands of tourists. . . ." Holmes added that an advance cadre was already on the mountain, preparing a campsite for full occupancy. Moreover, said Holmes, the State Highway and Public Works Commission had given assurances that a toll road would be provided to the top of the mountain.[88] As part of the federal-state cooperative program, a federal landscape architect from the CCC camp at Fort Macon was supervising clearing operations on the mountain.

Thus it was that on May 13, 1935, a small detachment of CCC enrollees set up camp on Mount Mitchell, worked there until August 2, and then departed. On May 26, 1936, the CCC reappeared on the mountain with but thirty-five men, but on June 8 an additional fifteen arrived. A full contingent was scheduled to arrive in July and remain until October 1.

Thomas W. Morse, the state assistant in charge of parks, reported to the chief forester that "One of the most important projects being carried on at Mount Mitchell State Park is fire hazard reduction. This work involves removal of dead standing and fallen timber, brush, stumps, and other material which constitutes a fire risk."[89] Improving the overall appearance of the area was another important rationale for the CCC work. Among additional projects slated for these CCC workers were installation of permanent waterlines, pumping systems, and pump houses; installation of toilets for males and females near the top of the mountain; improvement of existing trails and construction of additional trails as a means of improving both hiking and fire control; and construction of facilitating buildings to house necessary tools and equipment.[90]

But an unfortunate turn of events delayed the CCC work atop Mount Mitchell: a lingering disagreement between the former owners of the mountain and the state over disposition of a toll road kept the road from being put in good condition. The army and the National Park Service in turn refused to establish a full camp, or even an advance detachment, on the mountain until the road was improved and arrangements made for unrestricted passage of their vehicles over the road at all times. The disagreement persisted throughout 1936, and it was not until May of the following year that Camp NC SP-2, Company 2410, a group of white veterans transferred from Troy, North Carolina, arrived to renew work on Mount Mitchell.[91] With an average of 121 enrollees turning out for work call daily, considerable progress was made on the site for the concession building, but by September 30, 1937, all work ceased, and the camp was abandoned.[92]

Meanwhile, officials of the National Park Service briefly considered the possibility that the state park land at Mount Mitchell might be acquired by the federal government and turned over to the NPS for development as a tourist destination in connection with the newly created Blue Ridge Parkway. What manifested that possibility was a report that a detachment from one of the CCC camps in the Great Smoky Mountains National Park would be sent to Mount Mitchell for the purpose of erecting overnight cabins, a hotel, and other tourist accommodations, as well as administrative facilities. Although the NPS officials feared that if Mount Mitchell remained under state control it might be adversely exploited by private interests, they ultimately decided that such facilities could be better provided at points elsewhere so as not to disrupt the primitive character they sought to see preserved on the highest peak in eastern North America.[93]

Two years later another disagreement threatened to curtail CCC activities on the high peak when the private owner of the toll road near the mountain's summit reneged on his earlier agreement not to charge tolls for use of the roadway and also brought suit against the state, seeking compensation for portions of the road located on state-owned land.[94] Finally, the state settled the suit brought by the toll-road operator and established an improved, toll-free road leading almost to the summit of the mountain. Thereupon, on July 10, 1940, Camp NC SP-2, Company 5487, reoccupied the site abandoned by the veterans three years earlier and continued the work of its predecessors until October 1941.[95]

With the removal of the obstacles that had delayed much-needed labor by the CCC, Company 5487 made its mark on Mount Mitchell State Park. "The CCC

CCC workers helped preserve the natural beauty and "primitive character" of Mount Mitchell. This 1934 photograph is from the Albert Barden Collection, State Archives.

camp," a historian has written, "was no small operation, consisting of thirty-six buildings located one mile south of Mount Mitchell's summit. Perhaps the major accomplishment of the one hundred to two hundred workers was the construction of a facility still in use at the present time: a large wooden refreshment stand and rest room complex located just below the summit. The CCC also constructed a plumbing reservoir . . . and laid a pipeline from there to the summit area. In addition, it accomplished considerable trail work and fire hazard reduction."[96]

Thus, despite the loss of many man-hours of what could have been most meaningful work, CCC funding and labor did help prepare North Carolina's first state park to receive and reasonably accommodate a vastly expanded visitation brought about by construction of the nearby Blue Ridge Parkway. But a lodge and tourist cabins were not constructed at Mount Mitchell. On the other hand, visitors to Mount Mitchell State Park now drive upon a well-paved, gently sloping highway to an attractive reception area that facilitates a brief walk to the summit, all of it toll free, a legacy of the CCC.

A view of Fort Macon State Park and the CCC camp there in October 1934. From Photographs, Forest Resources, North Carolina Division of Forestry, State Archives.

Fort Macon State Park

Fort Macon, easily one of the most unique parks in the entire state system, the guardian of Beaufort Inlet and gateway to Morehead City and Beaufort, was constructed in 1826. But it was the Civil War that dramatically changed its course of history. Confederate forces seized the federal fortification in 1861 but lost it in April 1862. Thereafter it served as a coaling station and a federal prison until 1876. Although it was phased out of use in April 1877, it briefly returned to active service in the Spanish-American War and then was once more retired. The passage of time gave the fort the promise of a new life when it became the property of the state in 1924. But, tragically, little was done to make it a vital link in the state park system until the Great Depression brought new preservation concerns—and a most dynamic new conservation force in the form of the CCC. In a classic example of mutually beneficial cooperation between state and federal agencies, the North Carolina Department of Conservation and Development and the National Park Service joined hands and in 1934 established at Fort Macon the first state park CCC camp in North Carolina.[97] So it was that in April 1934 CCC Camp NC SP-1, Company 432, was established at Morehead City in Carteret County to rehabilitate Fort Macon and convert it to a first-class state park.[98]

When the CCC first occupied the area, the only approach to the fort was either by boat or by automobile up the beach. To improve access, the corps built a road from Atlantic Beach, about seven miles to the west, to Fort Macon. The construction and hard-surfacing of that road greatly facilitated rehabilitation of the fort.[99] One year after the CCC had entered upon its duties at the fort, a newspaper reported that:

Completion of the restoration and development of Fort Macon . . . is expected early this summer. State Forester J. S. Holmes announces a CCC camp has been engaged in the work for several months and will finish in a few months. The road leading from the causeway . . . to the fort has been completed and is being landscaped but will not be open until the work at the fort is finished.

The force is now engaged in repairs and improvements to the fort proper. The huge doors and barred windows have been restored and arches and masonry work inside and out are being done over.

The old cabin used by campers is being remodeled and a residence for a caretaker, construction of a dock for visiting craft, and provisions for public picnickers will be provided.[100]

L. A. Sharp, regional inspector of state parks for the National Park Service, had supervised the restoration work in cooperation with state officials. He was so pleased with the results that he ventured the opinion that Fort Macon, newly refurbished with CCC funds and labor, would easily become one of the major tourist attractions in the region.[101] Just as pleased were North Carolina's state park officials, one of whom reported: "Fort Macon State Park was officially opened to the public on May 1, 1936, with appropriate exercises. This is the first state park completed in North Carolina and in the Third Region of the National Park Service[,] and considerable interest has been shown by officials of the Park Service in its operation. They seem to feel that its operation and maintenance are being carried on along sound lines." The official also revealed that from May 2 through June 30, 1936, an admission charge of ten cents was levied to help defray expenses of operating and maintaining the park. "In this way," he noted, "$288.10 has been collected without, so far as is known, a single complaint from the public." He added that the picnic area at the fort was receiving so much use that an additional caretaker was needed. His concluding remark was a poignant testimonial to the work of the CCC: "The area is in such excellent condition that many compliments have been received on it."[102]

Morrow Mountain State Park

This park, located in Stanly County between Albemarle and Badin, astride an ancient mountain range bearing the Indian name "Uwharrie," is a resounding testimony to what a handful of dedicated citizens, a few philanthropists, a small army of politicians, and a large force of WPA and CCC workers could achieve. James McKnight Morrow, for whom the mountain is named, was a prominent citizen of Albemarle who is generally credited with being the first to envision that the area held the potential for becoming a fine public recreational space. During the 1920s Morrow and a small group of citizens, including A. C. Honeycutt, publisher of the *Stanly News and Press* (Albemarle), labored assiduously to secure local and state support for establishing a park there. But the arrival of the Great Depression halted the movement, which then lay dormant for years until the creation of the CCC and the accompanying cooperative program between the National Park Service and state governments to develop state parks brought it out of its slumber. Indeed, a park at Morrow Mountain was just the sort of project visualized when the cooperative program was conceived.

A key step in the process was taken when Morrow and others secured a visit to the area by L. A. Sharp, regional inspector of state parks for the National Park Service, on February 8, 1935. Impressed by the sincerity of the local boosters and by the recreational potential of the site, Sharp declared that if the proper cooperation of local citizens could be secured, there was strong justification for creating a park. In a follow-up meeting, Morrow pledged to donate from seven hundred to one thousand acres of land, and others agreed to contribute considerable acreage. Thereupon, Sharp said that he would officially recommend creation of the park, provided enough land could actually be secured. He estimated that the proposed facility would cost between $200,000 and $300,000.[103] Then, in late February 1935, Sharp approved the project, more land was

The classic beauty of Morrow Mountain State Park in Stanly County is a fitting testimony to the labor of many CCC enrollees, including veterans of foreign wars. From the North Carolina Division of State Parks.

acquired, and the North Carolina General Assembly authorized Stanly County to issue $20,000 in bonds to purchase additional land for the park.

In April 1935 Stanly County authorities delivered to J. S. Holmes, state forester, deeds to 2,500 acres, and all necessary applications were filed, whereupon the federal government approved the park program. On May 14, 1935, President Roosevelt gave his approval for a CCC camp to be assigned to Stanly County for state park work. (Behind the scenes, U.S. Rep. Robert L. Doughton had been pressing unceasingly for establishment of the camp; his efforts were rewarded not only by assignment of the camp but also by having the unit named "Camp Doughton" in his honor.)[104] So it was that CCC Camp NC SP-3, Company 3421, came to Morrow Mountain State Park, beginning with the arrival on July 8, 1935, of an advance cadre of twenty-five men previously assigned to Camp NC SCS-2, Company 437, Polkton, and the subsequent arrival on August 20, 1935, of 175 new enrollees from Florida. With the two hundred enrollees at the site, the real work on Morrow Mountain began:

> Roads were constructed and repaired. Fire hazards were reduced by clearing the mountain of brush, dead trees and logs. Literally acres of mountainside were cleared of dead mountain laurel, and as the work advanced one could see and appreciate the change that was taking place. Dry brush, dead trees, and decaying logs were giving place to clean ground and a fresh green undergrowth of mountain laurel. Rock was quarried for use in the development of the park— thousands of cubic yards of rock, quarried and transported to places where rock will be needed.[105]

In June 1940, a local newspaper summarized the accomplishments of the CCC camp assigned to the park:

1. Five miles of graded rock road, running through the area to the summit.

2. Landscaping and erecting stone retaining walls throughout the park.

3. Building a semi-enclosed picnic pavilion with open fireplace and grill.

4. Constructing native stone comfort stations.

5. Laying 9,000 feet of water mains.

6. Building fifteen miles of woodland trails.

7. Construction of a 1,500,000 gallon water reservoir.[106]

Nearly forty years later, a comprehensive plan for the park reviewed the early contributions made by the CCC enrollees:

> During 1939 and 1940 these workers completed two entire water systems (one for the swimming pool, another for the other park buildings and use area), the family picnicking areas (including the picnic shelter, toilet buildings, septic systems, and picnic tables), a 100 car parking area at the lodge, and the concession buildings at the swimming pool. By 1942, before the CCC camp disbanded, two ranger residences, a part of the maintenance service area (a garage, tool house, and shop), a barn, a barracks for summer employees, and enlargement of the parking area on top of Morrow Mountain had been completed.[107]

To accomplish those tasks, three CCC companies, including one composed of war veterans, are credited with serving at Morrow Mountain at one time or another from July 1935 to April 1942. In commemorating their work and that of others, a reporter described in 1940 what visitors to the park would see as a result of their labors: "lovely mountain vistas, overlooking lakes and rivers, a democratic spot, designed for spending leisure time joyfully."[108]

Cape Hatteras State Park

Along North Carolina's easternmost shores, a necklace of sand that forms present-day Cape Hatteras National Seashore Recreational Area originated as Cape Hatteras State Park. Like Morrow Mountain State Park, it owes much to the CCC and its accompanying state park cooperative program between the federal government and individual states. The area, historically important for its famed Cape Hatteras Lighthouse and for its reputation as the "Graveyard of the Atlantic," readily qualified for CCC rehabilitation work, especially as a means of checking widespread, debilitating beach erosion.

LEFT: A sand fence of dead hardwood at Cape Hatteras State Park, 1935. RIGHT: Sand-control work completed by the CCC under J. E. Byruss near Cape Hatteras State Park in 1936. Both images from Photographs, Forest Resources, North Carolina Division of Forestry, State Archives.

On August 12, 1935, an advance detachment of CCC enrollees crossed Pamlico Sound to Hatteras and began at Buxton the process of establishing CCC Camp NC SP-6, Company 3423, which was charged with reestablishing sand dunes by countering beach erosion. On August 23, 1935, an additional 173 enrollees arrived. Reaching their isolated campsite, virtually surrounded by water and inaccessible by land, was an achievement in itself: the men were ferried across the sound a few at a time whenever it was possible to obtain a boat.[109] A report published a year later described their activities: "At Cape Hatteras State Park . . . the major work being done is sand fixation and the control of wind erosion. So far about twelve miles of sand fences have been built, some of which have been practically filled with sand. It will be necessary to build additional fences on top of those already built until dunes of the desired size are produced. About forty acres of grass and about twenty thousand plants have been planted on this area."[110]

The work was challenging: erosion from tides and high winds, the movement of salt water into freshwater lakes, and the migration of windward sand ridges were among the aggravating factors that militated against the proper erection of sand fences.[111] Nevertheless, one state park official reported with pride on July 9, 1935,

that "bad storms during the past year have failed to tear down the man-made dunes which have been built to heights as great as 25 feet."[112] In addition to the work of sand fixation, the camp was assigned the task of constructing roads, a sanitary sewer system, concession, maintenance, and administrative buildings, and a museum. Separated from the mainland by forty miles of water, the camp employed a barge to transport enrollees and supplies to and from the mainland. During storms, which sometimes raged for days, crossing Pamlico Sound was impossible. On one occasion the camp received no mail for eight days, and sometimes the men experienced anxiety about being separated from their supplies of food.[113]

Conrad L. Wirth had eagerly followed the progress being made at Cape Hatteras. Through his influence, a national recreational demonstration-area program, designed to reinforce the idea that broad conservation measures could convert submarginal, eroded lands into attractive recreation areas, was developed. Soon the state park was redesignated a recreational demonstration area, then, finally, at Wirth's urging, it was incorporated into Cape Hatteras National Seashore, the first such designation in the national park system.[114]

These swimming facilities at Hanging Rock State Park, Stokes County, built by enrollees from Camp NC SP-5, are classic examples of project accomplishments achieved via state park and National Park Service cooperation. From the Mars Hill College Archives. Courtesy Nick Lanier.

Hanging Rock State Park

Hanging Rock State Park, located near Danbury in Stokes County, featuring spectacular remnants of the ancient Sauratown Mountain range, is a unique jewel in the North Carolina state park system. Its peaks jut upward more than 2,400 feet, dominating the Piedmont lowlands that surround it.[115] A newsman who visited the mountains in August 1935 was enthralled by the dramatic contrast between the lowlands and the Sauratown peaks. He wrote: "Visitors . . . are immediately impressed by the variety and character of natural growth, unique in this section. Here the silent majesty of the northern woods meets the mystery of the southern savannas as hemlock and cypress, holly and rhododendron mingle on the slopes . . . in a riot of year-round color. Rare plants and fungi, products of this

blending of northern and southern flora, flourish along the streams, to the delight and astonishment of flower lovers."[116]

Although the beauty of the mountain range had long been recognized and efforts to capitalize on it had been advanced periodically, a variety of obstacles, including the gigantic scope of the undertaking, as well as the huge cost of acquiring land, proved too daunting, and the range remained virtually untouched. As early as September 1933, a prominent citizen of Stokes County appealed to Gov. J. C. B. Ehringhaus for a CCC camp, citing both the beauty of the region and the economic misfortunes that four years of drought and countywide bank failures had imposed. He pointed out to the governor that even though the Sauratown range was situated in the populous

Piedmont, fifty miles east of any other major mountains in the state, it nevertheless remained "inaccessible in so far as motor travel is concerned."[117] As in many other instances throughout North Carolina, when regional planners learned of the impressive achievements possible through the National Park Service's cooperative agreement program with the states to promote their parks, boosters in Stokes County immediately took advantage of it.

What made the park possible was a pooled effort involving the Stokes County commissioners, the North Carolina Department of Conservation and Development, and the National Park Service. Local supporters secured the acquisition of a crucial three thousand acres of land, including the proposed park's namesake peak. Then they invited to Stokes County the ubiquitous L. A. Sharp, regional inspector of state parks for the National Park Service, whose immediate reaction to the visit was a booster's dream: "No park in the East, in my opinion, surpasses this one in scenic beauty and potential usefulness to those seeking out-of-doors recreation, under the finest conditions." Shortly thereafter came the announcement that Hanging Rock Mountain and its immediate environs in the Sauratown Mountain range of Stokes County would be developed as a state park, using CCC labor.[118]

On July 2, 1935, as was customary in the wake of such an announcement, an advance cadre of enrollees was dispatched—in this case, from Camp NC P-55, Company 438, at Purlear in Wilkes County—to establish the new camp at Hanging Rock, which was designated as NC SP-5, Company 3422. On August 25 of that year a full complement of enrollees arrived from Florida to become the creative hands that would make the new park more accessible, recreationally more enjoyable, and, in the words of a

Winston-Salem booster of the facility, "a great boon to the rank and file of our people. . . ."[119]

The range of work accomplished by the CCC enrollees at Hanging Rock is perhaps best summarized by the following report, issued approximately one year after the men arrived in the summer of 1935:

> At Hanging Rock State Park . . . an average of about 110 men have been available for work projects. . . . Work is well underway on a portion of the Park Road. Stone is being crushed and stock-piled for the surfacing of this road. . . . Topographic surveys have been made of the lake site and of the drainage area. . . . The plans for the earth dam have been completed and the plans for the masonry dam should be completed within the next three or four weeks. . . . Plans are being completed for the construction of a bath house on the lake shore and tentative studies have also been made for the combination recreation and administrative building. As at other State parks, the tremendous amount of work necessary to provide roads, trails, cabins, camping and picnic areas will take considerable time. . . . In addition to the actual work program a great deal of surveying has been done and is still necessary in order to establish the boundary lines and property lines of the Park area.[120]

The CCC workers practiced their arts at Hanging Rock from 1935 to 1942. Their accomplishments, which transformed an isolated, inaccessible area into a welcoming and highly popular state park, included neatly landscaped, paved access roads; two dams and a twelve-acre lake; an intricate, enjoyable trail system of more than two hundred miles; an imposing stone bathhouse adjoining a clean, attractive swimming area; picnic shelters; water and sewer systems; and reforestation of the entire surrounding area.[121]

Those achievements were proudly commemorated on October 26, 1991, when many of the CCC alumni returned to the park to reminisce about their youth and their labors and to witness the unveiling of a plaque commemorating the addition of their handsome stone bathhouse to the National Register of Historic Places, the first CCC structure in North Carolina to receive that honor. At the gathering, pride was as prominent as gray hair. "I forged all that ornamental ironwork," or "I laid that portion of this bathhouse wall," or "We quarried the stone, every bit of it," and so on, as each participant recalled the days of their hard times and happy days.[122]

William B. Umstead State Park

This park, originally established in 1937 as Crabtree Park in Wake County, is situated within a brief drive of metropolitan Raleigh, Durham, Cary, and nearby Piedmont population centers and is another classic example of how New Deal relief programs facilitated the improvement of state parks in North Carolina. It is also a vibrant testimony to the fact that long-abused and poorly managed land can be converted into appealing recreational resources. Indeed, land that now forms the very heart of Umstead was acquired in 1934 by the federal Resettlement Administration as a means of reclaiming a wasteland that

CCC structures located in the Crabtree section of William B. Umstead State Park. From the State Archives.

had resulted after farmers had made futile attempts to grow cotton in already worn-out soil adjacent to Crabtree Creek. Then, as at Cape Hatteras, Fort Macon, Morrow Mountain, and Hanging Rock, the North Carolina Department of Conservation and Development collaborated closely with the National Park Service to provide and improve public pleasuring grounds in what became known as the Crabtree Creek Recreation Demonstration Area.[123] Accordingly, on August 1, 1940, CCC Camp NC NP-24, Company 446, was established to provide funding and continuing labor for that purpose. The camp worked in cooperation with an ongoing program developed by the Works Progress Administration.

To provide easier and more available funding and to mitigate the possible threat of political interference, a trainload of CCC enrollees from Brunswick, Georgia, arrived on August 2, 1940, to take over the work previously performed by WPA labor. At the Wake County camp, the CCC was instrumental in implementing the standard state park facilities: roads, trails, picnic grounds, a lake, erosion control, and reforestation.[124] The coming of World War II terminated both the CCC and federal funding for the park's development, but sufficient reclamation had been accomplished to allow Crabtree Creek State Park to open—through a transfer of title from the federal government to North Carolina and by official proclamation by the state. In 1955 the name of the park was changed to honor the memory of William Bradley Umstead of Durham, who had been elected governor of North Carolina in 1952 but died unexpectedly in office in 1954.[125] Modern-day visitors to the 5,439-acre park are basically unaware of its history but are keenly conscious that it is a delightful place for recreation.

These workers are strawing seed beds at Hoffman in Richmond County, 1935. From Photographs, Forest Resources, North Carolina Division of Forestry, State Archives.

South Mountains State Park

This facility, located in the South Mountains of southwestern Burke County, is a relatively new one, established in 1975. Because of this, CCC enrollees never actually labored within a "South Mountains State Park," but it was their work on the land the park now occupies that made it accessible and the resulting park possible. The park was a by-product of the diligence of CCC Camp NC P-57, Company 433, established at Enola, Burke County, on July 20, 1935, to improve the watersheds for the city of Morganton and for Broughton Hospital, located there. That small army of workmen brought roads to the remote areas of the South Mountains, developed trails, erected fire towers, and accomplished a multitude of similar tasks to improve the natural resources of the region.

STATE FORESTS

North Carolina's state forester, J. S. Holmes, was charged with general supervision of CCC work done on private lands and in state forests. The great bulk of that labor was engaged in projects directly related to the control of forest fires, fighting soil erosion, and reforestation. During the period 1935 to 1942, at least three camps were designated state forest camps: NC SF-65, Company 5424, at Maysville, Jones County; NC SF-68, Company 4482, at Elizabethtown, Bladen County; and NC SF-76, Company 3448, at Hoffman, Richmond County.[126] The North Carolina Department of Conservation and Development annual reports for these camps are replete with their accomplishments, including road-building for fire-control access, erection of fire towers, establishment of nurseries, improvement of timber stands, the running of extensive telephone lines, construction of facilitating buildings, wide-scale timber mapping, erosion control, well drilling and construction of related water systems, game-management programs, fire suppression, and seed collecting.[127]

The School of Forestry at North Carolina State College allowed freshmen to spend two months of their summer enrolled in a CCC forestry camp, thus acquiring a measure of hands-on experience. A newspaper reported in 1936 that "The boys get a taste of camp life, sleeping in dormitories, eating at the 'mess,' even having a truck take them to a movie in the next town at night, and back to 'lights out' by 10. Another night they had the experience of responding to a call from the next county for fire-fighters and went with the boys from the CCC camp. . . ."[128] Appropriately enough, both the work site and the CCC camp were named in honor of Dr. Julius V. Hofmann (1882-1965), who established the forestry program at State College—thus "Hofmann Forest" and "Camp Hofmann." CCC funding and labor greatly enhanced the development of the forest. A considerably expanded experimental program there included studies of loblolly and slash pines to determine whether or not they were suitable tree varieties for North Carolina to invest in and promote. CCC labor greatly pleased Hofmann because it made possible the construction throughout the forest of much-needed access roads, which were in turn utilized for logging, timber cruising, fire fighting, study tours, special studies, and access for fishermen and hunters.[129]

BIOLOGICAL SURVEY (FEDERAL MIGRATORY BIRD REFUGE)

North Carolina's location and coastal topography made the state an ideal place in which to establish a type of CCC activity that few other states enjoyed: biological survey camps dedicated to establishing and promoting federal migratory bird refuges. On June 30, 1933, CCC Camp NC BF-1, Company 424, was created to perform work at the Swan Quarter Bird Refuge in Hyde County. Then, in the latter part of 1934, CCC Camp NC P-63, Company 436, at Manteo, Dare County, was converted into CCC Camp NC BF-2, Company 436, to work, from the same site, on the Pea Island Migratory Waterfowl Refuge. Still later, in November 1937, the camp at Swan Quarter was moved to the Mattamuskeet Migratory Waterfowl Refuge at New Holland, Hyde County, retaining the same company number but changing the project designation from BF-1 to BF-3.[130]

Much of the work of Camp NC BF-2 at Manteo centered on anchoring, or attempting to anchor, constantly shifting sand. The goal was to retard, insofar as possible, the subtle but relentless movement of the shoreline inland as a result of pounding ocean waves and currents and to prevent wind-driven sand from covering highways, buildings, or other unprotected objects.[131] The problem was quite severe. "Before the camp started operating," one article pointed out, "the sand blown from the sound beaches had been piled up almost to the tops of trees near the shore and had drifted in huge waves[,] threatening to cover the paved highway in the vicinity."[132] Many of the enrollees assigned to checking the migrating sand came from inland counties and had never before seen the ocean. Nevertheless, they earnestly labored at building a series of brush fences along the oceanfront to halt the wayward sand. When the sand reached the top of the fence, another was erected on top of it, and that process continued until the desired height and width of the barrier was achieved. Then grass and shrubs, as well as trees, were planted to hold the sand. A 1936 report credited the camp with

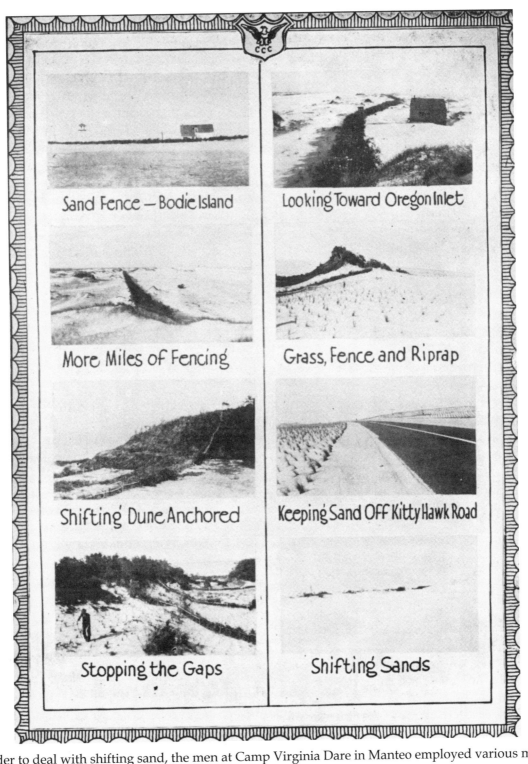

In order to deal with shifting sand, the men at Camp Virginia Dare in Manteo employed various methods of containment. From *High Tide,* page 11.

constructing more than twenty-one miles of sand fences and planting 1,713 acres of grass, and with plans to begin planting at least 70,000 tree seedlings as a first step toward reforestation.[133] Such work laid the foundation that enabled the rehabilitated historic land to be designated, a short time later, as Fort Raleigh National Monument, under the guardianship of the National Park Service.

In the meantime, enrollees at CCC Camp NC BF-1, Company 424, worked from 1933 until 1942, developing at Swan Quarter and New Holland land and water resources that quickly became a vital component of the national wildlife refuge program. One important aspect of that program was a gigantic reclamation project being carried out at Lake Mattamuskeet in Hyde County. Long before the advent of the CCC, the huge lake had been drained and its lands converted into farms as an investment venture. A protracted series of misfortunes, among them the devastation visited upon the market for farm products by the Great Depression, brought failure to the massive drainage project. In 1936 the federal government acquired the drained former lake site and assigned the CCC the daunting task of returning the entire tract to its pre-drainage condition in order to restore it as a vital link in the nation's migratory waterfowl refuge program.[134]

One of the most unusual of the CCC's achievements was the conversion of the former pumping station at the lake into a lodge to accommodate visitors. (CCC workers even handmade the lodge's furniture.) Even more striking was the conversion by the corps of the gigantic smokestack of the former pumping station into an observation tower for superb viewing of migrating waterfowl. Enrollees even participated in the counting of

waterfowl. One of them recalled: "They'd peck the living daylights out of you if you weren't careful." "It was the most unique thing I've ever done in the wild-life field."[135] Robert Fechner, director of the CCC, visited the camps at Swan Quarter and New Holland in 1936. When he paid a return visit there two years later, he was astonished at what had transpired at the camps during his absence—"more geese and swan on the lake than anybody had believed would ever be seen anywhere. Yesterday, they were counted . . . and there were 55,000 of them. There were also 12,000 swan. . . . The sky was black with them."[136]

The lodge is now vacant, awaiting some inspiration to give it still another adaptive life. But the adjacent fields are routinely planted in grain—not to feed man or beast but for the pleasure of the migratory waterfowl that annually appear by the thousands. The formerly drained and plowed areas are now a patchwork of water, grass, shrubs, wetland, and forest—home to a variety of wildlife, including deer, raccoons, swans, and geese. A dream of conservationists undid the nightmare wrought by developers and returned Lake Mattamuskeet to a much more productive life as a national wildlife refuge, a transformation made possible by some remarkable planning and a great deal of diligent labor by CCC enrollees.[137]

* * *

When the total accomplishments of the CCC workers in the Great Smoky Mountains National Park, on the Blue Ridge Parkway, in the national forests of North Carolina, in the Soil Conservation Service, in the Tennessee Valley Authority, in the biological survey, in North Carolina's

One of the most remarkable feats by any Tar Heel CCC camp was the conversion of an old water-pumping station into a hunting lodge, with the former chimney serving as an observatory. This was accomplished by Camp NC BF-3, Company 424, New Holland. From the Mars Hill College Archives.

state parks, and on private lands are added up, they equate into a most magnificent contribution to the well-being of North Carolina's natural resources, to the remarkable expansion of recreational facilities throughout the state, and to the economic and cultural benefits that accrued to the citizens who reside there.

6 "Not in My Backyard" v. "The Best Years of My Life" Tar Heel African Americans and the CCC

"The CCC was the best life I ever lived. It was beautiful," exclaimed an African American senior citizen in Cleveland County when the fiftieth anniversary of the corps was being commemorated in 1983.[1] This remark apparently held true for many others who enrolled in the Civilian Conservation Corps, for studies have revealed that in North Carolina, and in all other southern states, the average length of service for African American enrollees exceeded that for white enrollees.[2] According to *Happy Days*, the national newspaper of the CCC, more than 350,000 African Americans served at one time or another during the nine years of corps activity. Moreover, the African American camps were sponsored and supervised by basically the same agencies as those of whites, among them the army, the U.S. Forest Service, the Soil Conservation Service, and the North Carolina Forest Service. Indeed, at least forty companies served in approximately twenty-five North Carolina counties, with most companies stationed at more than one place during their lifetime. For example, Company 3404 began its existence as part of Company NC P-69 in Butters (Bladen County) on June 18, 1935. It was quickly moved to Ramseur (Randolph County) as NC SCS-20 on August 9 of that year. After laboring at that location for almost four years, it was moved again—to Raleigh as NC SCS-29 on September 27, 1939. Finally, the coming of World War II mandated still another move—this time to Jacksonville to serve the New River Marine Base as NC NP (D)-11, on May 1, 1942.[3]

But despite the provisions of the enabling act that created the CCC program, African American enrollees, almost without exception, served in racially segregated camps. At the insistence of the sole African American serving in Congress at that time, Oscar de Priest, Republican of Illinois, the enabling act plainly stipulated that "in employing citizens for the purpose of this Act no discrimination shall be made on account of race, color, or creed."[4] Nevertheless, despite the unambiguous wording of the enabling legislation and the objections of the National Association for the Advancement of Colored People (NAACP), segregation in the CCC was, from the outset, based upon race and was most definitely practiced. Furthermore, Robert Fechner, director of the CCC, decreed that no more than 10 percent of CCC enrollment could be made up of African Americans, because that group then represented 10 percent of the national population.[5]

Then, in 1934, the War Department's adjutant general made it very plain that racial segregation was an acceptable practice when he issued the following statement: "Colored personnel will be employed to the greatest extent practical in colored units within their own states of origin. In the future[,] segregation of colored men by company, while not mandatory, will be the general rule and earnest effort will be made to reduce the total number of colored men in white units."[6] On July 5, 1935, the War Department's policy concerning formation and location of "Colored Civilian Conservation Corps units" became even more restrictive: "Complete segregation of

African American Camp Nathanael Greene, NC F-12 (C), Company 425, (Rainbow Springs), 1934. Note that the supervisors (*second row, left*) were white. Shown here is the right-hand side of a photograph from a CCC annual. From the Mars Hill College Archives.

white and colored enrollees is directed. Only in those states where the colored strength is too low to form a company will the mixing of colored men in white units be permitted." The same authority also decreed that "Colored companies will be employed in their own states, except where located on a military post and then within their own corps."[7]

As a result of those rulings, North Carolina's CCC camps were racially segregated. Moreover, a number of African American enrollees spent their entire enrollment in camps located on military bases, such as Fort Bragg. Regardless of where the camp was situated, the military personnel and the supervisory work staff were, almost without exception, white. Nonetheless, such matters as rates of pay, regulations, housing, food, medical care, uniforms, discipline, and work assignments were basically the same for both races. By 1940, when North Carolina's total authorized quota of young non-veterans was 7,000, approximately 21 percent of those accepted were African American, whereas,

according to the 1930 census, 29 percent of North Carolinians were of that race.[8]

Moreover, as was the case with white enrollees, those accepted for African American camps were divided into two groupings: one of young men ("juniors") and one of veterans, with the word "Colored," or its abbreviation, "C," always specifying a company of African American men. For example, "NC F-12 (C), Company 424" indicated a camp composed of "Colored Juniors," whereas "NC P-60 (CV), Company 2411" identified a camp of "Colored Veterans." (Incidentally, North Carolina established two camps for African American veterans—one at Hollister in Halifax County and the other at Rockingham in Richmond County.)[9]

As might have been expected from a demographic standpoint, most of North Carolina's African American CCC camps were located in the Piedmont, with fewer in the Coastal Plain and fewer still in the mountains. A number of them were situated at Fort Bragg in Cumberland,

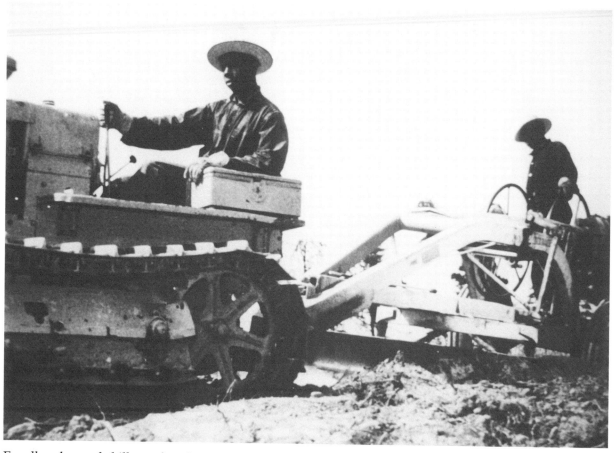

Enrollees learned skills, such as heavy-equipment operation, that proved to be valuable credentials for securing a good-paying civilian job. From Record Group 35, National Archives.

Hoke, and Moore counties. The U.S. Forest Service sponsored camps in such counties as Clay, Jones, and Macon. Camps were established on private lands in various counties, among them Bladen, Caswell, Columbus, Halifax, Jones, and Pender. The Soil Conservation Service had a large number of camps scattered across the Piedmont in such counties as Alamance, Cabarrus, Caswell, Cleveland, Durham, Guilford, Montgomery, Orange, Person, Randolph, Richmond, Rutherford, Union, and Wake.[10]

The historian for CCC Camp NC Army-4(C), Company 410, provided a brief summary of the origins of his unit and the various duty stations to which it was assigned at Fort Bragg: "Company 410 was among the first junior colored companies organized in the Fourth Corps Area. Company 410 was organized at Fort Bragg, N.C. in June, 1933, and has been stationed continuously on the reservation since then, having occupied four different camp sites and two side camps. It is now stationed in the southwest corner of the reservation, ten miles from Aberdeen, N.C., and thirteen miles from Raeford, N.C."[11] Prior to July 1935 the company's work efforts were directed primarily toward landscaping, grading, and planting in connection with an overall modernization of Fort Bragg from a World War I-era army post to a more modern facility. After that date, Company 410 built roads to facilitate access to the artillery firing range and to expedite approaches for CCC crews assigned to fire-fighting duties. It also installed a telephone system to allow for more efficient reporting of forest fires, cut many miles of firebreaks, and erected a number of arched steel bridges to accommodate heavy artillery traffic.[12] Little did the enrollees realize how beneficial their work would prove within a short time, when the exigencies of World War II made Fort Bragg a most essential military training center.

The work accomplishments of Camp NC Army-3 (C), Company 1497, stationed at Raeford, were quite similar to those of Company 410: "the cutting of firebreaks, saw milling, road building, and the constant erection and upkeep of telephone lines."[13] Camp NC P-3 (C), Company 429, organized at Fort Bragg in June 1933, established camp at nearby Manchester and immediately encountered obstacles: "Difficulties were experienced in many respects. The using service was without tools and could not get started on the work project. The road into camp was a trail with water standing at a depth of several feet in places. There were no electric lights, and water had to be carried in tank wagons." Nevertheless, the traditional CCC "Can Do" philosophy ultimately prevailed, and the situation quickly changed: "The camp developed little by little. Electric lights were made available and run to all tents. A small platform was constructed and covered with a tent fly, which provided a space for the piano and tap dancing. This hit the spot. Who can forget the shrill sounds of 'Stormy Weather' resounding about camp from one extreme to the other, with everyone making an attempt to join in, even if not in harmony."[14]

The Soil Conservation Service widely utilized the services of African American CCC enrollees. A reporter for NC SCS-20 (C), Company 3404, which was established at Ramseur in January 1936, wrote of that unit's arrival:

> The white citizens in this vicinity say that they had never before seen such a lively group of lively, husky enrollees from the descendant of Ham. And it took only a short while to prove to the citizens that the two hundred and eighteen colored enrollees had been trained by Uncle Sam in his usual thorough and superior fashion. The work of Company 3404 on this area, and in the field, has won friends and admirers of both races. This can be proved by the fact that when it was rumored that the camp was to be disbanded, letters poured into headquarters from many important individuals and organizations, all of them commendatory.[15]

North Carolina's African American CCC camps emphasized hands-on training that would provide skills useful to those seeking civilian jobs or self-employment. An example of such a camp was NC SCS-5 (C), stationed at Yanceyville. Enrollees there were engaged in such diverse skilled tasks as operating a Caterpillar tractor, using a surveyor's transit to map a field, and beekeeping.[16] Camp NC P-53 (C), Company 429, at Fort Bragg, was likewise diligent in making available educational opportunities to any ambitious enrollee. Class offerings included house wiring, plumbing, elementary science, cooking, reading, writing, arithmetic, letter writing, and arts and crafts.[17] Similar offerings were found throughout the North Carolina camps. Invariably there was a frontal assault on illiteracy; an emphasis on highly employable skills such as carpentry, plumbing, and auto mechanics; and such elementary or high school subjects as the camp educational adviser deemed useful.[18]

Meanwhile, at Shelby, Camp NC SCS-23 (C), Company 5425, was busy helping farmers in their battle against soil erosion: "Over 15,000 acres of farm land is being improved, 36 miles of terraces have been laid out, one mile of diversion ditches,

On-the-job training, such as that received by this apprentice surveyor stationed at a soil conservation camp at Yanceyville, prepared numerous enrollees for attractive civilian employment. From Record Group 35, National Archives.

7,000 square yards of gully banks sloped and seeded; 40,000 trees, shrubs, and vines have been set out, and more than 110,000 collected to set out. Over 100 terrace outlets have been constructed and many more designed."[19] Camp NC F-15 (C), Company 5420, stationed at New Bern, was dedicated to the well-being of the Croatan Forest. Its tasks included "building of roads, fire breaks, fire towers, and protecting this vast domain from forest fires. A constant vigilance is maintained day and night to protect the Government's 307,000 acres of forest land in this section. . . . During the past six months the Company has responded to 80 alarms, 30 of them false, and four the work of incendiaries."[20]

The African American enrollees generally proved to be good students and adept at learning specific skills. One 1936 report declared: "The vast majority of them knew nothing whatsoever of skilled work such as they have learned in the forestry service, in drainage control, in road building, and similar activities. Boys who had never had anything but a hoe in their hands have become experts in handling tractors, trucks, and road machinery. Boys who never knew what order was have learned that first lesson in civilization—A PLACE FOR EVERYTHING AND EVERYTHING IN ITS PLACE."[21] For many of them, however, one of the most meaningful—and valuable—experiences was learning to read and write:

Then there is the shy pride among these boys who have learned to write their names. Of course it took a little strategy to overcome the reluctance to admit they were illiterate, but when faced with the announcement that no pay would be given any boy who could not write his name, stiff fingers that had seldom grasped a piece of wood smaller than a plow handle began to adjust themselves to the delicate lines of a lead pencil and make marks that the writers themselves couldn't read, but it passed muster on the payrolls and admitted the practitioner to a new world.[22]

Happy Days, the national newspaper of the CCC, waxed almost poetic in crediting the corps with altering the basic attitudes of its African American enrollees:

Not only are these enrollees (from a Soil Conservation Camp at Yanceyville) receiving a new lease on life, but the very soil on which they stand is also getting a new opportunity to resume a productive life. From Record Group 35, National Archives.

They have a new attitude toward life, a new sense of responsibility, a new sense of capability, and more than all, perhaps, a new sense of *belonging*. This latter thing is almost revolutionary. From long years of experience with indifference and neglect many Negroes in America feel that somehow they don't *belong*. But the CCC camps have changed that for the Negro youth who have felt its uplift and inspiration. Here they find someone interested in them; here are camp commanders urging them to improve themselves, their clothes, their surroundings, their health. Here are leaders urging them to make something of themselves, to strive for advancement, to learn the *how* and *why* and *what* of the things they are doing. Here they find that they have similar jobs, the same equipment, the same opportunities that other boys receive. From that time on[,] the colored boy has a new incentive to live for: *he is walking up a street, not up a blind alley.*[23]

In working closely with white officers and work supervisors, African American enrollees sometimes experienced, for the first time in their lives, the realization that whites were capable of feeling goodwill toward them. As one commentator phrased it, "If the CCC camps did nothing more than reveal the latent capacities of black boys in the south and the latent good will in southern white men toward these same black boys, it would be worth every dollar that has been spent on them."[24] Time and again, year in and year out, local CCC administrators earnestly sought approval for enrolling in the corps more of their minority population. From the CCC administrator at Rocky Mount, for example, came this plea to the Raleigh office: "I am writing to ask, if possible, to give us a liberal quota of negro boys. Negro families are our problem. Boys from these families are anxious to go and always make good. I would like three-fourths or even more of our quota to be negroes for this next enrollment."[25] In similar manner, from Concord to the Raleigh office came a telegram on the subject of quotas: "CAN HANDLE QUOTA OF TWENTY-FIVE CCC RECRUITS BUT PREFER ONE HALF COLORED." From Hoke County came this telegraphed inquiry: "HOKE COUNTY'S CASE LOAD MORE THAN HALF COLORED. PLEASE ADVISE IF POSSIBLE TO CHANGE PART OF THE WHITE QUOTA TO COLORED." From Orange County: "If there is anything you can do toward allowing for a considerable number of negroes instead of white men it would certainly help out our local relief situation." And from Forsyth County: "We would, in fact be glad to have a larger quota for negroes. If any counties are unable to fill their negro quota, we would be glad to have an additional allotment granted us."[26]

Invariably, however, the state CCC administrator summarily rejected such requests, reminding his correspondents that national CCC policy allowed for no flexibility in the realm of quotas. For example, in 1934 he wrote to the relief administrator for the city of Winston-Salem:

We have just wired you that we are unable to increase the quota of Negro applicants for enrollment in the CCC. The entire quota allotted to the state is only 217. We have distributed this number as equitably as we know how to give the city Negroes this opportunity rather than those from the rural counties. Undoubtedly, we could recruit 2,000 or more Negroes without difficulty. Unfortunately, however, work camps have been established and no change will be made in the character of these camps. We, therefore, can only fill vacancies as they occur and we have no discretion as to the number of Negroes to be selected.[27]

Moreover, quotas allotted the various counties were based not only on population, but also upon such pertinent factors as the availability of employment, the number of applicants in a county, overall relief needs, the personal qualifications of applicants, the amount of federal and state funding being expended in a county, the basic economic health of a county, and such critical factors as prolonged drought or crop failures. For April 1935, for example, total CCC enrollment in North Carolina was set at 2,010, of which 201 were to be African Americans; and that 201 were to be supplied from a handful of counties, in the following numbers: Mecklenburg, 43; Forsyth, 34; Guilford, 30; New Hanover, 30; Wake, 30; Cumberland, 12; Durham, 12; and Wilson, 10. Only whites were to be enrolled from all other counties.[28]

The tragic reality was that in any community, rural or urban, it was much more difficult to locate and establish an African American work camp than a white one. A policy statement issued by the adjutant general made the point with little subtlety: "The assignment of a colored unit will be made by the Corps Area Commander to a locality offering no protest to its employment. If this be impractical or objection is raised to such an assignment because of local hostility, the Governor of the State will be formally asked in writing to indicate at what particular project in this state he desires such a unit to be located."[29] In pursuance of that policy, Maj. Gen. George Van Horn Moseley, commander of the CCC's Fourth Corps Area, wrote Gov. J. C. B. Ehringhaus in August 1935:

We are meeting with objections to the assignment of colored companies in several locations in North Carolina, particularly to the following projects:

> NC SCS-21, Statesville, N.C.
> NC P-67, Washington, N.C.
> NC P-69, Butters, N.C.
> NC SCS-22, Rockingham, N.C.
> NC P-68, Elizabethtown, N.C.

We also anticipate objections to the following assignments of six new colored companies due to the last increase:

> NC NP-14, Smokemont, N.C.
> NC NP-15, Smokemont, N.C.
> NC NP-16, Bryson City, N.C.
> NC NP-20, Cove Creek, N.C.
> NC P-64, Laurinburg, N.C.
> NC F-15, New Bern, N.C.

As if to assure Governor Ehringhaus of the wisdom of approving those camps, the general added:

We have uniformly found that when a community became familiar with the administration of the colored companies all their objections were withdrawn. . . . The colored companies are commanded by white officers, inspected by white inspectors who maintain close liaison with the adjacent communities, and keep a close check on the administration of the companies. Their work is supervised by white superintendents and foremen. There have been no untoward results to arise in connection with the assignment of colored companies anywhere else in the Corps Area.[30]

The governor responded to General Moseley: "I shall be glad to cooperate with you and your Department in every way possible in the selection of locations for colored companies of CCC workers."

But, as Ehringhaus was soon to discover, the "not-in-my-backyard" standard-bearers were already on the march, clearly and vociferously affirming that they did not want, indeed, were strongly and fervently opposed to, having an African American CCC camp pitched in their midst. For example, the general manager of the Butters Lumber Company in the tiny Bladen County community of Butters sent the governor both a letter and a telegram of protest. The telegram read: "PLEASE USE EVERY EFFORT POSSIBLE TO HAVE CCC CAMP AT BUTTERS OCCUPIED BY WHITE MEN LETTER FOLLOWS." That letter said: "We will greatly appreciate your using your efforts to have the CCC camp here occupied by White boys. We allowed the War Department to pick out this site in the edge of our little saw mill village adjacent to the White section and we had not the slightest idea that it would be occupied by Negro laborers. While they have a few Negroes here at this camp already we would greatly appreciate it if you can have the change made."[31]

A number of North Carolina's representatives in Congress, among them Sen. Josiah W. Bailey, received similar letters. When the senator filed an inquiry with Robert Fechner, director of the CCC, asking about the assignment of the Butters camp, Fechner replied, somewhat defensively: "I want to state emphatically that no one in authority made any statement to the Butters Lumber Company or to anyone else regarding the personnel that would occupy this camp. No one except the War Department has any knowledge of what company will occupy any given CCC camp. It may be a junior company or a war veteran company. It may be white or black." Fechner continued: "Responsibility for the assignment of companies to camp locations rests solely with the Corps Area Commander," and added: "In the case of negro companies the Corps Area Commander is directed to consult with the Governor of the State before assigning a negro company to a camp location in the state." He assured the senator that "Every negro company in North Carolina is composed of North

Carolina negroes. No negro company is sent to any state from another state." Fechner concluded by telling Senator Bailey that he knew of no fairer method of handling the matter than to consult with the governor as to where specifically to assign Negro CCC enrollees: "I can only suggest that interested parties should confer with the Corps Area Commander and with the Governor."[32]

When Governor Ehringhaus learned of Fechner's statement to Senator Bailey, he promptly responded by quoting to the senator portions of Fechner's letter, then vigorously rebutting one of Fechner's main contentions:

> This language seems to infer [*sic*] that this office was consulted before location at Butters, an impression which I desire of course to correct, as we have no record in this office concerning the location of this camp. I am sure that Mr. Fechner did not intend to convey this impression, but I am writing this letter so that it may be corrected. Our first advice concerning location of this camp came from a telegram from the Butters Company, making objections, which telegram was promptly transmitted to our Conservation Department.[33]

When Fechner was informed of Ehringhaus's rebuttal, he quickly wrote the governor a letter of apology, saying about his earlier letter to Senator Bailey: "I keenly regret that my letter may have conveyed a wrong impression. . . . I thank you for correcting the impression that my letter to the Senator may have caused." Fechner then used the occasion to offer this assurance to the governor: "Definite instructions have been given to the War Department not to send a negro company to a Civilian Conservation Corps camp if the people in the locality of camp definitely object to having the camp occupied by a negro company." The director added this brief caveat: "This may result in the work project being cancelled if there is no white

company available to send to that particular camp."[34]

Coincidentally, almost at the very moment Fechner was composing this communication, the general manager of the Butters Lumber Company was sending General Moseley the following most remarkable communiqué in which they were withdrawing their protest against the "negro company."[35]

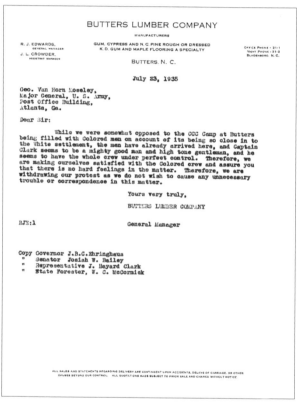

This letter is one of only a few filed in the Governor's Papers that reported satisfaction with a "Colored crew" instead of protesting its presence "so close to the White settlement." From CCC Camps (colored), 1935, J. C. B. Ehringhaus, Governor's Papers, Box 50, State Archives.

But that was by no means the end of the "not-in-my-backyard" activities. On July 9, 1935, Governor Ehringhaus received the following telegram from North Carolina congressman Lindsay C. Warren:

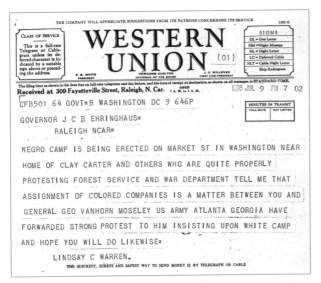

This telegram is from Federal Relief Program, 1933-1937, J. C. B. Ehringhaus, Governor's Papers, Box 50, State Archives.

Two days later the governor replied in a telegram to Congressman Warren that he had wired General Moseley as follows:

> AM ADVISED BY CONGRESSMAN WARREN . . . THAT PRESENCE OF NEGRO CC [SIC] CAMP AT WASHINGTON NORTH CAROLINA IS JEOPARDIZING FRIENDLY RACIAL RELATIONSHIP AND UNSATISFACTORY TO LOCAL CITIZENSHIP . . . I SUGGEST YOUR CHANGING THE ASSIGNMENT TO SOME LOCATION WHERE NO IRRITATION WILL EXIST.

On that same day Congressman Warren dispatched this very brief but significant telegram to Governor Ehringhaus: "THANKS FOR THE WIRE SUCCEEDED YESTERDAY IN GETTING GENERAL MOSELEY TO LOCATE WHITE CAMP IN BEAUFORT COUNTY."[36]

The historian for the camp that was ultimately assigned to Washington, North Carolina (Camp NC P-67), provided this account of the affair:

> On or about July 1, 1935, Captain T. M. Evans, commanding an advance detachment consisting of colored CCC enrollees from Company 410, Fort Bragg, N.C., arrived at the local camp site, which was located on 15th Street at the end of North Market Street in Washington, N.C.
>
> The inhabitants of Washington were dissatisfied at the thought of having a colored CCC camp in the very outskirts of their town, so a formal complaint was made, resulting in having the colored enrollees removed and replaced by an Advance Detachment from Camp NC BF-1, Company 424, Swanquarter, composed of twenty five white enrollees. . . . This replacement was made on Friday, July 12, 1935.[37]

A very similar series of events transpired when an African American camp prepared to occupy a site about a mile northeast of Statesville. A cadre of African American enrollees left Fort Bragg for Statesville and began construction of a standard CCC camp. But as they were in the midst of erecting the camp, something totally unexpected happened. On August 23, 1935, an advance cadre of *white* enrollees from the Maysville camp relieved them, and the camp to be established at Statesville, NC SCS-21, Company 3420, was soon afterward staffed by white enrollees from Alabama and Georgia.[38] Similarly, a story that ran in the Raleigh *News and Observer* in January 1938 detailed the "bitter" opposition engendered by the possibility that a white CCC camp at Southport might be replaced by colored enrollees. The proposed change was portrayed as a political stratagem reflecting a power struggle between Forest Service officials and politicians. And once again the final decision favored the "not-in-my-backyard" element. The resolution of the matter was succinctly framed in one sentence: "Captain D. G. Wilson of District A, CCC, at Fort Bragg . . . learning of the pronounced hostility . . . stated that the Negroes would not be sent."[39]

Meanwhile, as the CCC administrators at Fort Bragg sought to replace other white camps with colored companies, they were barraged with protests. For example, the mayor of Mount Airy cited the "great cooperation" that then existed between his community and the nearby white CCC camp. He also praised "the most delightful comradeship between community people and the officers and the boys." Then his upbeat mood changed, as he sought to document why sending African Americans to staff the existing white camp would be an unwise move:

> Few colored people in the county.
> No colored high school.
> No substantial number of colored people to associate with.
> No recreational provisions for colored people.
> County able to furnish means of extraordinary instruction to white boys and to provide recreation for them—none to colored people.
> Opinions of our people that camp not so situated as to allow the change.

Furthermore, the Mount Airy Merchants' Association, its chamber of commerce and Kiwanis Club, the town's chief of police, the president of its ministerial association, and the superintendent of its schools all went on record against the proposal.[40]

Similarly, at Danbury the citizens were happy with their white CCC camp and wished to retain it, declaring: "Stokes has no paid police protection. Negro population too small. Thirty-five miles to nearest recreation and even there Negro population a bad element and venereal disease prevalent." From Burlington representatives, including the mayor, the Rotary Club, and the Exchange Club, came a familiar refrain: "Highly pleased with the present White camp." The city commissioners frankly stated that even

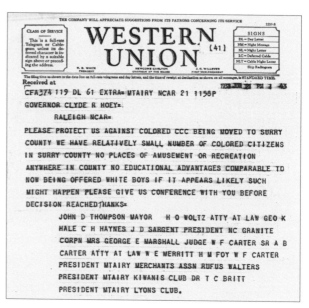

Telegram from CCC, Clyde R. Hoey, Governor's Papers, Box 64, State Archives.

though they did not expect any opposition toward an African American camp, retaining the existing white facility would be preferable for the following reasons: "(1) Now cordial relations; (2) No recreational and other facilities for Negroes; (3) Many white enrollees are residents of this region and change would send them further away." Likewise, when a CCC inspector surveyed the citizens of Gastonia on the question of a possible exchange of African Americans for white enrollees, the local residents quickly declared that the installation of African Americans and the removal of whites would result in "strenuous protests from the citizens of Gastonia." They also expressed the opinion that the campsite originally had been given to the government with the stipulation that only whites would occupy it, and they added that the presence of African American enrollees would adversely affect real estate prices, inasmuch as the camp was situated in the heart of the city's residential district and was surrounded by substantial residences.[41]

In Albemarle the CCC inspector found a similar response, with interviewees filling his ears with such negative comments as:

> A very dangerous Negro settlement adjoins the camp.
> There are cuttings and fights every night and to add more Negroes to the community would mean increasing the police force and would result in murders.
> Camp located on main road in city and Negroes would have to travel Main Street to town
> People owning the houses adjacent to camp would move and property would be depreciated.
> Camp near High School.
> Negroes would not work on project because WPA White workers are on the same project.
> County has spent $20,000 and city $30,000 for parks and swimming pools and they do not want Negroes in the town to spoil their project.
> City has too great Negro population and does not want more.
> There are no colored stores, colored movies, or colored eating places.
>
> Our citizens are very much exercised over the proposed change in the personnel of our local CCC camp. With the camp located as it is, well within the town with homes of the white people on three sides, with only a street between the camp and these homes, you can readily understand why we feel colored boys would be undesirable.[42]

From Salisbury came the very same lament: "Too many Negroes in Salisbury and more will add to feeling against them." Said the mayor: "Do not want Negroes, rather lose the camp. Bad Negro situation already and more will add to it." The president of the Salisbury Chamber of Commerce was of the same mind. From Dobson in Surry County came a June 1938 telegram from the superintendent of schools in the small town to Gov. Clyde R. Hoey:

PLEASE PROTECT US AGAINST THE TRANSFER OF A NEGRO CAMP TO CAMP HANCOCK, NEGRO POPULATION THIS COUNTY SMALL. POOR EDUCATION AND SOCIAL ACTIVITIES FOR CARING FOR THE NEGROES. UNANIMOUS SENTIMENT OF THE COUNTY AS A WHOLE.

In response, the governor wired back: "I WILL OPPOSE LOCATION OF A NEGRO CAMP IN YOUR COMMUNITY. YOU MAY SO ADVISE THE OTHER SIGNERS OF THE MESSAGE."[43]

At about the same time, the Raleigh *News and Observer* reported in a headline story that Durham and Alamance counties had joined hands to oppose the replacement of their local white CCC camps with Negro enrollees from Fort Bragg and had sought the aid of Congressman William B. Umstead, inasmuch as army officials had notified authorities in both counties that they would have to accept the Negro companies or see their camps abandoned. A number of mitigating circumstances attended this particular case. The county spokesmen were particularly upset because the white enrollees had been carrying on an effective soil conservation program, whereas the African Americans under consideration were assigned to forestry units. It was that change in program that was most irksome: "Farmers have highly commended the work done in halting soil erosion and consider it of greater importance than forestry work." And, too, there were claims that the army had targeted the camps in Congressman Umstead's district because he was "slipping out of the picture as a member of the nation's law-making body."[44]

Whether they were simply racist in origin or grounded in genuine concerns that well-received soil conservation projects might be negatively affected, the protests in Durham and Alamance counties were in vain. In that one instance, at least, the "not-in-my-backyard" element lost the battle: Camp NC SCS-14 (C), Company 410, took up residence in Durham County; and NC SCS-13 (C), Company 1497, entered upon its labors in Alamance County. Of course, these two African American units were soil conservation camps and not forestry camps, as the local farmers had feared.[45]

On Monday, May 29, 1939, the headline in the *Monroe Enquirer* screamed: "NEAR RIOT HERE SUNDAY BY THE CCC"; a secondary headline added: "NEARLY 100 NEGRO ENROLLEES STAGE RAMPAGE TO NORTH MONROE." The accompanying story said that the "First signs of trouble were seen about 9:30 o'clock [P.M.] when several groups of the camp members came noisily into the uptown section pushing over garbage cans, forcing towns people from the sidewalks, and causing considerable disturbance."[46] Two town policemen and a state highway patrolman hurried to the scene, and the commanding officer of the facility to which the unruly African Americans were assigned, SCS-26, Company 5425, was summoned from his residence to aid the police in quelling the disturbance. But before being persuaded to return to camp, the African Americans allegedly ran up and down the streets of North Monroe, breaking windshields in automobiles and attempting to turn over at least one car. As they retreated toward camp, there were reports of "missiles" being thrown at several automobiles, as well as rumors of white citizens being shoved off the sidewalks.[47] As word of the incident spread, a number of local whites began to gather in the uptown area. Meanwhile, the enrollees at the camp were hastily assembled in the facility's recreational hall for a roll call. Simultaneously, according to a news report, a large number of automobiles packed with whites began circling the camp, heightening the tension. Reportedly a gun was fired from one of the circling vehicles, but no one was injured. By 11:30 P.M. the incident quieted down, with no deaths or disabling injuries reported.

The next morning the commanding officer of the camp publicly apologized, saying that he and his staff deeply regretted the occurrence and that an investigation had been launched. Meanwhile, the Monroe Board of Aldermen was summoned into session to discuss the incident and to determine what course of action, if any, to take. Simultaneously, a battery of regular army soldiers was dispatched from Fort Bragg to the camp, ostensibly on "maneuvers."[48] The next issue of the *Monroe Enquirer* announced that the local CCC camp was to be moved to Fort Bragg within the week.[49] The removal order came on the heels of an investigation into the North Monroe incident conducted by a Fort Bragg CCC official, Maj. W. A. Metts Jr. Metts interviewed city officials, local police officers, and numerous local citizens, seeking facts as to what had motivated the incident. He was told that the camp enrollees, when visiting an African American section of Monroe known as Newton, had to pass through white North Monroe, and as they passed were regularly "rocked" by a group of white boys. Furthermore, he learned that efforts by local police and CCC officers to identify and arrest the white offenders had failed to halt the harassment. He was advised that the precipitating factor that brought the matter to open confrontation was the action of the white boys in so severely beating one of the enrollees that he lost consciousness. It was at that point, so a number of witnesses reported, that seventy-five or more of the camp members decided to take matters into their own hands, whereupon the rampage began.[50]

In the meantime, the Monroe Board of Aldermen appealed to Gov. Clyde R. Hoey to have the camp removed and requested further that it be immediately quarantined. The board likewise expressed concern for the safety of Monroe's citizens and property and made this charge:

> Last night the whole personnel of the camp, exclusive of officers, practically took over the town, committed several assaults, destroyed some property, and generally disturbed the peace by cursing and threats of violence. For the past few weeks the enlisted men, or large groups of them, have generally disturbed the peace by traveling around in large groups, forcing the white citizens, both male and female, to yield the sidewalks to them and generally acting in a rude and boisterous manner. Last night's occurrence created a good deal of resentment in this community, much of which had been smoldering for a long time. The example set by the enlisted men at the camp has created a new problem in the handling and discipline of certain elements of the local native negro population.

Mincing no words, the aldermen closed their appeal: "In the light of the above stated facts and in consideration of many other things which are too numerous to tabulate, we respectfully request Your Excellency take immediate steps to have this camp put under control and removed from our community." Then, to cover all bases, they asked the governor: "If your Excellency does not have the power to effect the relief asked for, will you kindly advise us, by wire, what steps to take."[51] The appeal by the aldermen, coupled with the investigative report by Major Metts, brought an immediate order from the Fourth Corps Area commanding general to vacate the camp and remove its enrollees to Fort Bragg.

The editor of the *Enquirer*, apparently unsatisfied with the outcome of the matter, fulminated against what he perceived as the army's lack of authority to control the actions of CCC enrollees. "The army," he wrote, "has supervision over the camps but control over the enrollees is limited to quarantining a violator for a week or discharging him from the Corps. Little wonder that the negroes did not hesitate before rampaging down Monroe's streets! They simply did not fear the consequences because they know their officers had no authority to deal severely with them."[52] The editor then offered his assessment of what he perceived the problem to be and offered a solution:

> The point is that the United States Government has placed these groups of young men, many of them absolutely irresponsible, in communities and has not provided for their control. The Monroe incident is a most emphatic illustration of why all Civilian Conservation Corps camps should be put under military control and all the enrollees subject to military discipline. Much as Union county needs the work being done by the Soil Conservation [Service] and the CCC, citizens here do not feel that their work is worth risking a recurrence of the Sunday night incident.[53]

The farmers in the nearby Union County town of Marshville apparently did not feel the same way. Pointing out that the Piedmont section of North Carolina was one of the worst-eroded areas of the nation and that for several years the CCC had been aiding greatly in remedying the situation there, they requested a CCC camp for their vicinity. Nonetheless, the War Department, through U.S. Representative W. O. Burgin of North Carolina's Eighth Congressional District, not only rebuffed their request but also declared that it would refuse to sanction a camp anywhere in Union County.[54] The War Department's action reinvigorated the editor of the *Monroe Enquirer*, who wrote: "Congressman Burgin has written citizens at Marshville that CCC officials will not approve placement of a camp there until they are assured that the negroes 'will not be molested.' Viewing the action of the enrollees here recently, Marshville citizens should demand that they be assured that they will not be 'molested' by the negroes. Evidently, CCC officialdom is attempting to place the entire blame for the incident here on the townspeople." To make clear his opinion of who was responsible for the incident, the editor quoted a fellow editor: "The Monroe camp was filled with young bucks who simply ran wild under stress of mass urge." "So now we know!"[55]

Ultimately it was the farmers who resided in the vicinity of Mount Gilead, Montgomery County, who benefited from the incident at Monroe. Through the efforts of Congressman Burgin, the town was assigned the camp that previously had served Monroe—even though a number of other communities had sought the facility. Soon afterward the enrollees previously stationed in Monroe were moved from Fort Bragg to Mount Gilead to engage in soil conservation projects similar to those carried out in Union County. And thereupon the "Monroe incident" faded from the news.[56]

From time to time in North Carolina, similar CCC-related community disruptions occurred as a result of strained race relations. A typical example involved NC SCS-23 (C), stationed in the Cleveland County seat of Shelby. Like most of its Piedmont neighbors, Cleveland County was plagued with major economic hardships attributable to severe soil erosion, and, also like its neighbors, was eager to obtain relief through the services offered by the CCC. When it became apparent that the county would soon receive a CCC camp, rumors began to circulate that the enrollees of the incoming camp would be African American youths. The editor of the Shelby *Cleveland Star* characterized the rumor as "Well founded" and expressed the opinion that the "idea is a bit startling at first thought but second thought reveals little objection." He elaborated:

In the first place, the work to be done here is precisely the kind of work that negroes do better than white men. It will be ditch digging, terracing, and drainage work, with picks, and hoes, and shovels. A gang of negroes . . . can do that kind of work better and happier than any other crew. In the second place, the colored boys are more tractable. The presence of some 200 young white men on the edge of town has its attractive points, but from what we can gather from cities that have nearby CCC camps, these youngsters are generally full of enterprises and ambitions that make too often problems in society and the police courts. The negroes, on the other hand, are more impressed with the uniforms of their army officer commandants, and think they are really in the army.

Such a statement was, of course, a gross overgeneralization, but to his eternal credit the editor closed his remarks with a gesture of welcome: "However, whichever they may be, white or black boys, they'll be pretty welcome to Cleveland."[57]

When it became public knowledge that the camp would indeed be staffed with more than two hundred African American enrollees, the *Star* acknowledged that the report "came as somewhat of a shock to Shelby residents" but also confirmed that "most fears have already been allayed." Perhaps the atmosphere of equanimity could be attributed to the army officer in charge of the enrollees, who announced to local citizens that the "Army guarantees to handle these men. As a matter of fact, they have a record of behaving much better than [enrollees at] the white camps. You see, we can send them out of camp immediately if they don't behave." Further, the army construction engineer in charge of erecting the camp was even more specific in his reassurances: "Why, we have been controlling negroes in the south for more than 400 years. As a matter of fact, most of the progress of the Southland has been built on the broad shoulders of black boys just like these. They'll be no problem to the city at all, whereas white boys often are."[58]

Despite these remarkable assurances, however, the specter of actually establishing the camp raised an immediate outcry. The citizens of the Belvedere community of Shelby, where the prospective camp was to be situated, were fearful the construction of a graveled access road through their previously sheltered property to the proposed campsite would generate a great deal of traffic and a large accompanying amount of dust. White owners of land surrounding the proposed site banded together and refused to grant easements through their property for roads, water, or electric lines. The commanding officer of the prospective CCC unit attempted to overcome the objections of the property holders by assuring them that:

> These negroes are under the direct control of the United States Army. We can restrict the men from any district we wish, and we can send them home for any serious misconduct. Anybody who has a complaint about the men can make it to the commanding officer and be assured that it will receive prompt attention. At the same time, the boys are subject to civil laws when they are in town—which won't be often. The cops can lock them up at any time, with no objection by the Army. What we are trying to get across is that the Army is here to cooperate in every way. We are a service unit sent here to please the people of Cleveland.[59]

In the meantime, the editor of the *Cleveland Star* voiced what was likely the majority opinion: "We do not feel that the objection is racial but is based on the annoyance and discomfort the residents would undergo because the road entrance to the camp is unpaved and runs directly through the residential section. The dust from the traffic of campers and visitors would be annoying, but we do not believe that the proximity of a colored camp would be any more objectionable than one for white boys, if there is any objection at all." Then he touched the key issue:

> What we are mainly concerned about, however, is the retention of the camp. If General McCloskey [commanding general of District A, Fourth Corps Area, at Fort Bragg] gets the idea that we are opposed to the camp because it is for colored youths, he would immediately move it away. He would not relish any racial clash. The negro boys are sent here to do manual labor on Cleveland county farms. Soil erosion and forestry work are needed and all of us would benefit—farmers, merchants, and professional men. We hope, therefore, that a new entrance to the camp, satisfactory to all parties concerned, or a new site is selected, so that the camp will be retained in the county.[60]

Meanwhile, General McCloskey was reported to have said: "If the people of Belvedere in Cleveland County don't want a Negro CCC camp in that vicinity to engage in soil erosion control, they need not fear that it will be kept there." He added: "We try to please the people of the affected community before we establish a camp. If they don't want it we can put it in another section or county." McCloskey's frank statement apparently produced a sudden change of heart among Cleveland County farmers, who stood to lose a great potential boon if the camp was moved elsewhere. Some five hundred of them assembled at the Cleveland County Courthouse in Shelby, formed a soil erosion control association, and dispatched to General McCloskey at Fort Bragg a letter that emphasized their desire to cooperate with the CCC program and urging that the proposed camp not be removed from Cleveland County under any circumstance.[61]

In the interim, the commanding officer of the prospective camp had been relieved

CLASS OF SERVICE DESIRED	
DOMESTIC	FOREIGN
TELEGRAM	FULL RATE CABLE
DAY LETTER	DEFERRED CABLE
NIGHT MESSAGE	NIGHT CABLE LETTER
NIGHT LETTER	WEEK-END CABLE LETTER
SHIP RADIOGRAM	RADIOGRAM

Patrons should check class of service desired, otherwise message will be transmitted as a full-rate communication.

Postal Telegraph
THE INTERNATIONAL SYSTEM

Commercial Cables   All America Cables

Mackay   Radio

RECEIVER'S NUMBER

CHECK

TIME FILED

STANDARD TIME

Send the following message, subject to the terms on back hereof, which are hereby agreed to   Form 2

Hon. Robert Fechner, Director,   October 4, 1937.
Civilian Conservation Corps,
Washington, D. C.

I am advised that you contemplate removing the colored CCC camp at Shelby, N.C.
to some other point in North Carolina.   I have been in conference with the War
Department representative and we are experiencing some difficulty in finding a suitable
location for this camp.   I have looked into conditions at Shelby, N.C., and find
that the citizens and farmers are especially anxious for this camp to be retained
there and the project is unfinished.   The farmers have made arrangements and are
cooperating fully with the camp and it is doing a good work at Shelby, and I would be
greatly pleased if you can find it possible to let the camp continue there and
complete the work which it has begun.   If possible to do this please advise the
War Department.

                                   CLYDE R. HOEY,
                                   Governor of North Carolina.

CHG/ EX. Dept.
DAY LETTER.

Here is a later example of efforts to retain the colored camp at Shelby. "Day letter" from CCC, Clyde R. Hoey, Governor's Papers, Box 64, State Archives.

of duty, and General McCloskey had sent one of his military representatives to Shelby with orders to remove the facility: "If they don't want the camp, move it right out."[62] Suddenly, there came an abrupt reversal of opinion, as, with but "a few minutes to spare," a group of Cleveland County's civic and business leaders "saved the soil erosion project for the county by finding a new camp location on the A. W. McMurry farm. . . ."[63] With that action, the air of indignation from the "not-in-my-backyard" faction evaporated to insignificance. The camp was soon established as NC SCS-23 (C), Company 5425, and was put to work immediately to help farmers reclaim their eroded lands. The following year, the camp's historian reported that "Many

commendations for the good behavior of the members were received in the first month or two of the camp's life."[64]

When African American enrollees were moved into the small town of Maysville (Jones County) as Camp NC SF-65 (C), Company 5424, to work on some 83,000 acres of land owned by the University of North Carolina, Burton M. Graham, CCC regional liaison officer, questioned whether the African American enrollees possessed sufficient skills to accomplish such tasks as type-mapping. The engineer in charge answered that he was quite optimistic about the abilities of the enrollees, especially since he had in his company several men who were high school graduates and even a few who had attended college. He mentioned that he had been checking the work of the white enrollees who had preceded the African Americans in the company, especially their type-mapping skills, and had found so many glaring errors that he was convinced that the African Americans could do no worse.

On the other hand, the state forester appealed to the regional CCC liaison officer to have a group of enrollees then assigned to a side camp at the state nursery at Clayton (Johnston County) switched from African American to white for several reasons: because the cultivation and care of the nursery's some two million seedlings required much close attention, and that it would require much more supervision to obtain the desired results from African Americans than whites. Moreover, the forester believed that the nursery work experience would be of substantial benefit to the participants long after they were discharged from the CCC and that the white enrollees would take far more interest in the nursery assignments than would the African Americans.[65]

Another question concerning the relative skills of whites and African Americans occurred in regard to the operation of the Clayton side camp's automotive repair shop. The appeal in favor of replacing African American enrollees with whites made this argument: "The work done in this repair shop consists in most cases of entire rebuilding or complete overhaul of all [CCC] equipment assigned to the state. A Negro enrollee does not have the ability of a white boy to do this type of work." Also included in the appeal was the argument that a change in enrollees from African American to white would provide a better quality of work, both in the nursery and in the repair shop, as well as being much less expensive: " . . . the figures show

that this repair shop is approximately 30% less efficient than those operated by white enrollees. This same efficiency would, of course, apply in the case of the operation of this nursery." However valid or invalid these statements may have been, they secured the petitioner's desired results: the African American-staffed side camp at Clayton was eliminated. A new location was selected for a substitute camp, and as soon as new buildings were erected, a white side camp took over the nursery and automotive repair work previously done by African American enrollees.[66]

In retrospect, when the various aspects of the CCC program for North Carolina are examined and evaluated, allowing for the usual bureaucratic nuances, it becomes statistically clear that the percentage of African Americans enrolled in Tar Heel CCC camps was relatively close to the percentage they represented in the state's total population. It is also clear that once an African American cleared the hurdle of enrollment, he was much more likely than his white counterpart to remain for several enlistment terms. What is not clear to the general public is the remarkable number of African American camps and the admirable accomplishments of those camps—on military reservations, with soil conservation projects, working on state and private lands, or improving the national forest lands in the state. Nor is the average citizen aware of what serving in the CCC did for the average African American enrollee. For the great majority of them, it provided a new sense of self-respect, a greater capability to cope with life's problems, and especially a new awareness that life was perhaps not a dead end but, with the inspiration and practical skills provided by the CCC, a newly opened avenue of hope.

For many African American enrollees, their time spent in a CCC camp represented "the best years" of their lives. This unidentified photograph could have been a scene from any of the African American camps. From Record Group 35, National Archives.

One former CCC worker at the soil conservation camp in Cleveland County alluded to above, reminiscing about those bygone days, spoke for many of his co-workers, as well as himself, when he said: "The CCC did keep a lot of kids off the streets. For me, it was the best years of my life."[67]

"I Want a Job and I Don't Mean Maybe!": The Eastern Band of Cherokee Indians and the CCC

"We didn't know there was a Depression. Hard times were a normal way of life for us. Unemployment, lack of ample food and clothing, and hand-to-mouth existence were everyday routine for most Cherokee Indians," said one of their historians in a recent seminar.[1] Sadly, that statement all too accurately portrays the social and economic conditions that characterized the great majority of the nation's Native Americans in the 1930s, regardless of their geographic location. Moreover, because most of the Indian reservations were sparsely populated, the standard state quotas for CCC enrollment would not accommodate a significant number of Native Americans. To cope with that problem, President Roosevelt and his advisers developed a fitting solution for enrolling Indians and ensuring that both they and their reservations actively participated in and benefited from CCC funding: the entire Native American CCC operation was delegated to the Office of Indian Affairs, Department of the Interior. That agency thereupon assumed total responsibility for administration, enrollment, work planning, and work supervision, as well as day-to-day operations for the Indian CCC projects. That meant that the Native Americans had their own separate quota and operations, utilizing qualified Indians to plan and supervise CCC operations on the respective reservations.[2]

Another unique aspect of the CCC program for Native Americans was that the War Department had no role to play in their work camps. Indeed, there were few actual "camps," because most of the enrollees were married adults, resided at home, and commuted to the work projects to which they were assigned. In addition, each reservation's tribal council served the program as both administrative and using service, thereby eliminating the need for army regulations and day-to-day oversight by either the U.S. Forest Service or the National Park Service. Nonetheless, such contentious matters as rate of pay

The Cherokee Indian CCC program differed from the standard in that it was administered by the Bureau of Indian Affairs and the enrollees had no common camp, simply commuting from home to the work projects. From the Mars Hill College Archives.

(e.g., thirty dollars per month per enrollee) applied to Native Americans as well as to others.[3]

As a bona fide, federally recognized Native American tribe, the Eastern Band of Cherokee Indians, with its Cherokee Indian Agency headquartered in Cherokee, North Carolina, was eminently eligible for participation in the new CCC program. Its reservation encompassed 57,079 acres, much of which was so mountainous and steep that it was totally unsuited for productive agricultural endeavors. Indeed, one contemporary report indicated that less than one acre out of ten was suitable for agrarian use. Moreover, the ravages of the chestnut blight had not only devastated what had been promising timber products but had also glutted the market, inasmuch as the owners of woodlands attempted to cut and market their chestnut timber before the blight rendered them unmarketable. For a people who had depended upon the forest for their livelihood, this oversupply was as economically blighting as the chestnut virus was to the forest. With their woodland treasure depleted, with agriculture offering at best a sub-marginal existence, and with no industrial plants to provide jobs, the 3,622 Cherokee on the tribal roll desperately needed an economic boost. But because they were Native Americans, however, they were not permitted to participate in any of the federally sponsored relief projects such as the Works Progress Administration (WPA) in the two counties that abutted the Cherokee Reservation—Jackson and Swain.[4] The introduction of the CCC program for the Cherokee was, then, not only timely but also critical for their very economic survival. In its nine years of activity, the Cherokee CCC program provided work to at least 520 members of the tribe and expended some $594,000. Enrollees were selected upon the basis of need, with the stipulation that they be male and at least eighteen years old.[5]

Included among the 520 enrollees were men whose family names ranged from Adams and Arkansas to Wolfe and Youngdeer. Among the most commonly found enrollee surnames were: Bradley, Bushyhead, Chekelelee, Cornsilk, Crowe, Cucumber, Driver, Feather, George, Hardin, Hornbuckle, Jackson, Jumper, Lambert, Littlejohn, Locust, Lossy, McCoy, Maney, Owl, Panther, Partridge, Pheasant, Rattler, Rose, Saunook, Sequoyah, Smith, Squirrel, Standingdeer, Swimmer, Tahquette, Teesatesky, Toineeta, Wachacha, Wahyahnetah, Walkingstick, Welch, Wildcat, Wilnoty, and Youngbird.[6]

Relying upon the already established administrative infrastructure of the Cherokee Indian Agency, the Cherokee CCC program functioned through the superintendent of the agency, the tribal council, a small administrative staff, and some twenty Native Americans who occupied supervisory, facilitating, or skilled positions, such as group foreman, sub-foreman, tractor operator, trail locator, stonemason, and clerk-steno-grapher.[7] A 1937 report enumerated the following projects completed at the Cherokee Reservation during the 1935-1936 fiscal year:

One steel fire tower erected.

12½ miles of telephone lines built.

38 miles of fire lanes constructed.

29 man days fighting forest fires.

39 miles of truck trails built and 30 miles maintained.

2 equipment sheds, 24' x 90' built.

28 miles of horse trail constructed.

120 miles of Indian Boundary re-surveyed under the supervision of the General Land Office.

50 miles of the boundary line clearly marked with paint.

150 acres of land reforested.

250 acres of forest land improved by thinning and removal of nonmerchantable species.

7 vehicle bridges built.

500 acres of land benefitted by check dams in gullies, and five miles along the Oconaluftee River cleaned from debris.[8]

CCC enrollees gathered seeds by the bushels, planted them in numerous Park nurseries, such as this one at Ravensford, and then tranplanted seedlings by the thousands to enhance the Park's beauty. Cherokee Indian enrollees labored in this nursery in return for seedlings for their forests. From the Great Smoky Mountains National Park Archives.

These projects are indicative of the types of undertakings the Indian leadership deemed desirable to improve the reservation. A more detailed listing would include construction of bridges, garages, lookout cabins and towers, latrines and toilets, utility buildings, trail shelters, fences, guardrails, levees, dikes, jetties, telephone lines, truck trails, check dams, foot and horse trails; erosion-control activities; field planting and seeding; improvement of forest stands; nursery operations; combating forest fires; reducing fire hazards; development of public picnic grounds; forest education; establishing boundaries; preservation of trees; and an enrollee program aimed at upgrading the educational and recreational opportunities for all the Cherokee.[9]

The projects listed above were accomplished through the work of 150 men per month, but the men were allowed only two weeks' work per month, thus restricting their earnings to considerably less than the standard CCC wage of $30 per month. Indeed, funding of the Cherokee Indian CCC program was woefully inadequate to pay for work for the eligible needy. The going rate of pay for a Native American enrollee was $1 per day plus 50 cents per day for "board and quarters"; but in order to provide some income for as many needy enrollees as possible, the men were worked in two shifts of one-half month per shift. That policy equated into $10 for wages and $5 for board and quarters—a total of only $15 for two weeks' worth, an amount required to last an enrollee and his family an entire month, an obvious hardship. To offset the shortfall, the Cherokee CCC administrators encouraged each enrollee to plant a garden and diligently nourish it. Even so, by 1937 things got even worse, with the work month being divided into three shifts of ten calendar days each.[10]

Moreover, in 1938 the administrators, faced with minimal funding and the ever present needy, reviewed the list of enrollees and reduced it by twenty-five men, leaving only those who were supporting one or more dependents. The agency superintendent lamented the necessity of dropping the twenty-five men but noted that unless the current allotment was increased, the payroll would have to be cut by one-third, or even suspended entirely. He appealed to the Bureau of Indian Affairs for an additional allotment of $10,000, reminding the commissioner of that agency of the woeful economic conditions that prevailed, particularly in the local timber industry, and made this prediction: "If we are forced to lay off more men from the CCC work, there will be nothing for them to do."[11]

The Eastern Band of Cherokee Indians operated their own CCC program under the auspices of the Bureau of Indian Affairs. Their projects were diverse, including sawmilling and road building. From the Mars Hill College Archives. Courtesy Ray Kinsland.

A few months later the same superintendent informed the commissioner that the only way the Cherokee Agency could stay within budget for its CCC operations was to drop the entire supervisory staff and retain only enrolled labor on the payroll. He thereupon requested that his CCC supervisory staff be placed on immediate administrative furlough, April 15 through June 30, 1938, adding a personal commendation on the staff's spirit of cooperation. "They are a fine, loyal group of workers and the action taken herein seems a poor reward for their service," the superintendent declared. Two years later the superintendent voiced a similar plea:

It is my opinion that the Cherokee Indians have for the past several years received a relatively small CCC-ID appropriation in proportion to their needs. . . . Heretofore, the Indians have depended to a considerable extent upon the cutting of timber for their livelihood. Now, our chestnut is gone. A considerable inroad has been made into the other timber on the Reservation. It is now necessary to greatly restrict the amount of timber that may be cut, and the revenue to the Indian people from this source will be more than cut in half next year; for this reason, it is absolutely necessary that some source of income be provided for them in order to keep them from facing actual want.[12]

Along with the endless concern for adequate funding came a sincere effort, throughout the length of the CCC program on the Cherokee Indian Reservation, to promote educational opportunities. Work schedules were arranged in conjunction with school officials so that enrollees could attend school and work a scheduled slot with the CCC projects. As of 1939, for example, six enrollees were listed as "School Boys on the C.C.C." To facilitate the relationship between work and education, CCC administrators cooperated closely with school officials to ensure that enrollees actually attended school.

While the vast majority of Native American enrollees in the Cherokee CCC program were paid, at best, approximately half the amount of wages available to similar enrollees at traditional CCC camps, the relatively few Native American foremen and skilled workers who managed to retain their jobs on the Cherokee Indian Reservation were relatively well compensated. The paucity of work and the vital importance of even a little income made the CCC jobs on the reservation most attractive, and even a number of people who were not members of the Eastern Band of Cherokee Indians—one from as far away as Nevada—applied for employment there. One needy Native American applied for employment in a handwritten letter that stated his desperate need succinctly: "I want you to let me on this job down there on E.C.W. [CCC] in Snowbird. And I hear that they were able to use a couple more and I am asking you to let me have a job and I don't mean maybe. And I want you to let me know as soon as impossible [*sic*]. I got to do something to keep my family up."[13]

The Cherokee Indian Agency was required once a year to describe in detail the specific projects it desired to implement on the reservation, with man-hours and costs delineated for each one. For example, the following projects were enumerated for the 1941 fiscal year:

PROJECT NO.	NAME OF PROJECT	ESTIMATED COST
40-3	Soco Gap Truck Trail	$3,750.00
40-17	Jenkins Creek Truck Trail	1,500.00
40-17 A	Jenkins Creek Truck Trail, lower end	7,500.00
40-18	Lower Jenkins Creek Bridge	500.00
40-19	Upper Jenkins Creek Bridge	750.00
41-1	Fire Suppression, employment of enrollees	2,000.00
41-2	Truck Trail Maintenance	8,000.00
41-3	Telephone Line Operation and Maintenance	2,000.00
41-4	Fire Lane Maintenance	750.00
41-5	Foot Trail Maintenance	750.00
41-6	Williams Cove Truck Trail	12,000.00
41-7	Road Bank Stabilization	5,000.00
41-8	Enrollee Program	2,000.00
41-9	Cherokee Recreational Area	1,500.00
41-10	Snowbird Levee	1,000.00
———	Equipment	6,000.00
	TOTAL:	$55,000.00[14]

An urgent need for improved recreational resources prompted Chief Jarrett B. Blythe to seek funding for a community building at Big Cove on the Cherokee Reservation through the CCC program. Chief Blythe justified the project by pointing out that "the CCC program provides specifically for the conservation of natural resources and since our young Indian people constitute our greatest natural resource, I feel that it especially desirable to provide some means to furnish them decent recreational facilities." The chief also noted that a community building constructed at Cherokee in 1939 had been of little value to the Indians residing at Big Cove because it was too far away. "Most of them," he remarked, "have no means of transportation and[,] lacking recreational facilities at home, far too many of them are walking the roads at night, getting drunk, and causing trouble. It is believed that with a suitable building where they can gather for games, box suppers, and dances, they will have less desire for the periodic carousals which now constitute too great a part of their leisure time activities."[15]

Chief Blythe demonstrated a sensitivity to the needs of the Cherokee by proposing construction of a parking overlook at a gap in the main dividing ridge across the reservation, near Little Bald on the Soco Gap Truck Trail: "probably one of the greatest sources of wealth the Cherokee Indians possess is scenery. Because of the heavy increase in tourist travel in this region, . . . we should develop our reservation in every way possible to attract this tourist trade."[16] John W. Libby, project supervisor for the Cherokee CCC program, likewise supported a landscaping project, specifically planting portions of the Cherokee Reservation with "native species of flowering shrubs, plants, and trees, as well as plants used by the Indians for medicinal purposes, for making dyes, and for making their various native crafts."

Libby's proposal included the employment of a well-qualified instructor who would assist in the selection of plants and would conduct extensive educational activities with the CCC enrollees and other interested Indians, teaching them the identification, history, and uses of each plant. Libby felt that the landscape project would serve as a demonstration to the students and employees of the five schools on the Cherokee Reservation, as well as to the CCC enrollees, and would be of significant value to the Cherokee:

> The Cherokee Indian Reservation borders on the Great Smoky Mountains National Park which is rapidly becoming one of the chief summer tourist resorts of Eastern America. The Cherokee Indians themselves are one of the major tourist attractions of the area and nearly every Park visitor is also a Reservation visitor. It is believed, therefore, that it is to the best interests of the Indians to properly appreciate the unexcelled beauty of their own Reservation in order that they may properly present it to the visiting public, and it is necessary that they may be made to realize the necessity of conserving this beauty, if not for itself, for the monetary value to themselves which can be secured by capitalizing on the tourist trade.[17]

By the middle of 1942 the Cherokee Indian CCC program, like the national enterprise, was terminated. During its nine-year period of activity—March 1933 through July 1942—it expended a total of $594,000.00 on conservation measures, an amount equal to about $164.00 per tribal member, or approximately $10.40 invested in conservation improvements for each acre of tribal land.[18] But statistics alone lack the ability to state in human terms what the CCC activities did for the Cherokee Indians and their reservation. For the reservation itself, nine years of well-planned and ably executed conservation measures enhanced the quality of the tribal forest, as well as its ability to produce and regenerate forest products. The present beauty of that forest land and the timber products presently being marketed from it stem directly from the plantings, timber-stand improvements, and fire-protection programs put into effect by the Indian CCC. In similar manner, the majority of the roads and trails that characterize the reservation had their origins in CCC funding and labor. And so did a number of community and general utility buildings, which continued to serve various tribal needs long after the CCC was gone. The corps' landscaping and erosion-control efforts likewise contributed to the reservation's present-day attractiveness and livability, which in turn enhanced the reservation's appeal to tourists—just as CCC planners had envisioned.

Enrollees of the CCC division, Eastern Band of Cherokee Indians, are shown laboring to construct one of many fire breaks designed to protect their treasured forest, which composed much of the reservation. From the Mars Hill College Archives. Courtesy Ray Kinsland.

But, as Chief Jarrett B. Blythe well knew, it was the reservation's human resources that benefited most from CCC funding and activities. The Cherokee administration's emphasis upon conservation and care of the reservation's resources, particularly its abundant native plant life; its efforts to promote awareness among tribal members of the natural beauty of the area in which the reservation was situated and the economic and cultural value of that natural beauty; its day-to-day concern for the economic well-being of the entire tribal community; its interest in education; its desire to take advantage of a growing tourist industry; its awareness of the need for additional recreational opportunities—all were legacies, to a greater or lesser extent, of the Cherokee Indian CCC program, one of the great but relatively unknown and unsung milestones in the cultural evolution of the Eastern Band of Cherokee Indians.

8 "Boys Don't Need CCC Jobs Today": Liquidation of the CCC, 1942

The nine years that encompassed the life of the CCC, 1933-1942, witnessed a most remarkable evolution in America, socially and politically. In 1933 all eyes and attention were focused on the frightful Depression, which was totally engrossing the nation; whereas in 1942 an awesome and dangerous world war usurped all the energy, resources, and creativity of American democracy. The public image of the CCC reflected that evolution. When the agency was formed in 1933, President Roosevelt and his advisers determinedly emphasized the fact that the program was absolutely nonmilitaristic, indeed was purely and simply a corps of young men organized to promote conservation of the nation's natural resources. Press releases constantly stressed that theme. For example, in the early months of the CCC a western North Carolina newspaper reminded its readers that "*enlisting* for the six months work in the forest does not entail *joining the army* but rather a signing up with the federal government to stay on the job for the six months period."[1]

The basic handbook for public information about the CCC, *Emergency Conservation Work Bulletin Number 3*, took painstaking care to ensure that the American public *knew* that the CCC was not a military project:

It should be emphasized that the fact that the man goes to a United States Army recruiting station for enrollment does NOT mean that he joins the Army. The machinery of the Army recruiting stations is used because it is the most convenient and most effective way of handling the enrollment of 250,000 men scattered over the United States. However, the man does NOT enlist or become a soldier. He does NOT become liable to military law. He remains a civilian from the beginning to the end. Emergency Conservation Work [the CCC] has nothing whatever to do with the enlistment in the military forces of the United States or with any military draft.[2]

Moreover, army regulations succinctly spelled out the nonmilitary status of CCC enrollees: "No military training will be undertaken."[3] As late as 1939, CCC director Robert Fechner addressed a convention of the Sons of Spanish War Veterans that "It is not possible under present laws for the Civilian Conservation Corps to be inducted into the United States Army as a body. A CCC boy is a civilian and remains so. In war time his status is that of any other civilian. Enrollment in the CCC is not enlistment in a military organization of any kind."[4]

Despite these pronouncements, an examination of camp assignments and tasks in 1933 and 1942 will reveal a major shift in emphasis. Of thirty-one camps assigned to North Carolina in 1933, only one was actually situated on a military reservation; but by 1942 thirteen out of twenty-eight such camps were designated "defense operations" and located on army or marine bases.[5] The outbreak of war in Europe and the Far East, followed by the attack on Pearl Harbor, was, of course, the major precipitating factor. Thus, as early as 1939 came a much stronger emphasis on patriotism within the CCC. Robert Fechner, director of the corps, made the following remarks during a radio interview in Birmingham, Alabama, on September 19, 1939: "In my opinion this CCC is a splendid school for democracy which teaches our young men practical and workable lessons in the American way of living. In view of the world political developments during the past few years I know that an organization like the CCC, which demonstrates the usefulness and advantages of our democratic processes, is an extremely valuable institution for this country to operate."[6]

In 1941 Ovid M. Butler, secretary of the American Forestry Association and a strong advocate of the notion that CCC labor should be confined solely to strict conservation activities, wrote about the CCC in a monograph on American conservation for which he served as editor. Butler reported as follows on the "national defense training" aspect of the CCC program:

Military training has not been a part of the Corps. Nevertheless one of its contributions to national welfare now beginning to be appreciated is its fitting of young men better to defend their country during the present emergency. Work experience in the camps has equipped millions of youth to be truck and tractor operators, telephone linemen, fire fighters, bridge builders, powder men, radio operators, cooks and other more or less specialized workers in industrial and military fields. Of the 135 different types of work experience given by the CCC, it is estimated that seventy percent is now proving of direct value in the national defense field.[7]

Similarly, a 1941 publicity release by the CCC administration featured a number of pictures of CCC enrollees at work and indicated how those labors could readily be applied to national defense. For example, the caption accompanying a picture showing enrollees erecting telephone lines said: "Signal Corps? No, but the skills gained by CCC men building telephone lines . . . will be of value if Uncle Sam needs to defend his land." And, accompanying a picture of enrollees blasting for a mountain trail, the cut line read: "The experience will be handy if any

The skills learned driving a truck and delivering supplies could easily be applied to national defense. Note the distinctive license plate. Pictured is Wayne Roberts of Camp NC NP-21, Company 3420. From the Blue Ridge Parkway Archives. Courtesy of Bert G. Richardson.

of them should become engineer troops." With enrollees constructing a forest road: "CCC road builders . . . can build roads in quick order, whether for peacetime travel or the transportation of troops and supplies." And, with an illustration of enrollees loading a recently serviced tractor onto a truck, a most prophetic line: "Tanks and tractors are much alike."[8]

In the meantime, President Roosevelt in June 1939 moved to make the CCC camps truly "civilian" by issuing orders to discontinue the use of military reserve officers as camp administrators. Instead, beginning July 1, 1939, civilians bearing such titles as "company commander" or "subaltern" were to replace the military officials, who, in turn, would take up active duty in the army, navy, Marine Corps, or Coast Guard.[9] The switch from military officers to civilian administrators for the CCC camps made available well-deserved promotions to CCC administrators and enrollees whose work had been exemplary. For example, Willis F. Cox, company clerk for Camp NC F-14 at Balsam Grove, was sent to a camp near Clemson University in South Carolina so that he could attend that school and enter upon an upgraded career as a CCC subaltern. Similarly, Alonzo M. Deitz, who had served as project superintendent for a number of CCC camps, was promoted, because of his outstanding administrative accomplishments, to the position of commander of Camp Coweeta (NC F-23), Company 3446, located at Otto in Macon County.[10]

As dark forebodings of war emerged in Europe and the Far East, President Roosevelt removed military officers from CCC camps and replaced them with civilians called "subalterns." These men were from Camp NC NP-21. From the Blue Ridge Parkway Archives. Courtesy of Bert G. Richardson.

On December 7, 1940, James J. McEntee, who had been named director of the CCC upon the death of former director Robert Fechner, delivered a nationwide radio address in which he pointed out the role the CCC was playing in the national effort to rearm America and safeguard its national institutions. McEntee ended his address with these words: "This nation has seen the creation of a mighty asset in natural resources through the labors of the Civilian Conservation Corps. But probably more important has been its creation of a mighty asset of trained, disciplined, courageous youth upon which the nation must ultimately stand or fall. I do not doubt the ability of Young America to carry on in defending its country against any aggression, be it drought or foreign armies."[11] On April 23, 1941, McEntee, addressing graduating cadets at Clemson University, further defined the growing relationship between the CCC and national defense: "The United States today faces a great national task. It is the task of greatly expanding our defense to insure that this Democracy shall survive in a world gone mad with weapons of destruction, and our entire educational system will not have performed its full duty until the youngster growing up learns to honor our nation's history, revere its traditions, and keep firm his faith in Democracy's course. That, in part, is one of the principal goals of the CCC."[12] And on May 17, 1942—a day designated by presidential proclamation to be commemorated as "I Am an American Day," McEntee read a specially composed message to all CCC enrollees; the message included these lines:

You have come of age at a time when your government has the most urgent need for your loyalty and the best that is in you. As members of the Civilian Conservation Corps, I know that you are making a real contribution to the winning of the war. You are fitting yourselves for bigger contributions in the stern days that lie ahead of all of us. In the camps you have learned discipline. You have acquired physical stamina and you have learned how to work. Above all, you have developed a greater appreciation of your country and the democratic principles which this nation is fighting to preserve.[13]

Men like these enrollees from Camp Jim Staton at Old Fort were part of "that magnificent Army of Youth and Peace." They developed strong bonds of friendship and a greater appreciation of their country. From the Mars Hill College Archives. Courtesy of James Shuford.

Typical of the not-so-subtle shift in emphasis on the part of the CCC was the case of a company of some 140 enrollees at Camp Hatteras, a CCC facility in Dare County, which early in 1941 was transferred to Fort Bragg. Among its other duties, the camp had spent the previous six years attempting to stabilize Cape Hatteras Lighthouse against wave erosion. The Raleigh *News and Observer* pointed out that the Hatteras CCC contingent was but the first of a half-dozen camps in North Carolina that were being transferred to Fort Bragg to help with "the massive labor of making Fort Bragg ready for the seventy-odd thousands of soldiers who will be training here before the beginning of summer." Once the CCC enrollees reached Fort Bragg, one of their specific duties was to construct rifle and pistol ranges and similar facilities necessary to train soldiers at the installation.[14] By August 1941 the War Department issued a new order stipulating that CCC enrollees head-quartered at military bases be trained for military drills. The order read: "In order to improve the carriage and posture of enrollees and to attain more orderly movement of large groups of enrollees within the camps, it is desired that instructions in marching and simple formation be given to all junior enrollees. . . ."[15] Shortly thereafter, the entire administrative aspect of CCC activities in North Carolina was transferred from Fort Bragg (District "A") to Charleston, South Carolina (District "I"). In reporting the change, a newspaper remarked that "there is beginning to be less and less room for anything that is not military" at the fort.[16] Within a month came the not unexpected news that at least six of North Carolina's CCC camps were to be closed by November 1, 1941, because of "the clamor for reduction of non-defense expenditures."[17]

With the attack on Pearl Harbor and the declaration of war that quickly followed, the nation and its political leaders became intensely defense conscious. As a result, the Joint Appropriations Committee of Congress became a vigilant watchdog of all appropriations, insisting that each be relevant to the national defense program. One of the major non-defense funding programs the committee hastily targeted for liquidation was the CCC, recommending on December 24, 1941, that it be terminated and phased out by no later than July 1, 1942. President Roosevelt, ever the champion of the CCC, quickly came to its defense, contending that enrollees were truly performing essential defense work by constructing military training facilities (as they were indeed doing at Fort Bragg).[18] CCC director James J. McEntee, shrewdly observing the disagreement between Congress and the president, ordered that all camps be closed unless they actively engaged in military defense activities or were vital for the protection of war-related natural resources.[19]

Ensuing debates by congressional committees both praised and damned the CCC. One longtime opponent of President Roosevelt and the CCC, Republican congressman Albert J. Engel of Michigan, kept a sharp focus on the "useless expenditures" represented by CCC operations. On June 5, 1942, in one of his "no more funding for the CCC" speeches, Engel repeated a biting comment he had made in 1940:

The Civilian Conservation Corps has been a sacred cow. While the people have worshipped the cow the politicians have milked her. Thirty-two thousand four hundred and six civilian employees, most of whom are political employees, will receive . . . in 1940, $58,234,000 in salaries, while 270,000 Civilian Conservation Corps employees and their families will receive $101,000,000 in pay. I am not opposing the Civilian Conservation Corps. I am just trying to stop the politicians from milking the sacred cow.[20]

Speaking in support of Congressman Engel were others, such as Republican John Taber of New York, who accused the CCC of practicing "the most wasteful and the most destructive management . . . of almost any organization in the Government." "Is it not time," Taber asked, "we got through soliciting the public to go to the relief rolls or on the relief employment? Is it not time we got rid of these demoralizing agencies . . . ? Is it not time we got to the point where we begin to build up America instead of tearing it down?"[21] Tennessee's Senator Kenneth McKellar, once a supporter of the corps, added his voice to the chorus of criticism:

Mr. President, in its time the CCC was a proper activity. I voted for every appropriation ever made for it, from the beginning until this year. I have never failed to vote for appropriations to maintain it, because I thought it was needed. But now, when it is no longer needed for the boys, when it is no longer needed for the Army, when we are in a war that staggers the imagination in its ramifications throughout the world, why should we continue a wholly unnecessary, a wholly extravagant, a wholly wasteful activity such as this?[22]

Opposing the arguments of Engel, Taber, and McKellar were legislators such as Representative Malcolm Tarver, Democrat of Georgia, and a number of westerners such as Sen. Elbert D. Thomas, Democrat of Utah, and Sen. Harry M. Schwartz, Democrat of Wyoming, who fervently sought to retain the services of CCC enrollees, contending that their labor was absolutely essential to the defense effort, especially as a means of protecting American forces from Japanese arson. Congressman James F. O'Connor, Democrat of Montana, declared:

The camps assigned to forest protection are a part of our war effort. There is no doubt but that our forests will be attacked by our enemies if they can break through the coast protective zones. I do not have to tell this House of the disaster that would befall if a single plane was permitted to unload its incendiary bombs on a part of our forests which was unprotected. A huge fire in our western forests would disrupt war production, interfere with Army training, and screen the activities of our enemies.[23]

When the question of liquidating the CCC was offered for a roll-call vote in the Senate on June 26, 1942, the result was a tie, with each side receiving thirty-two votes. The Senate's presiding officer, Vice President Henry A. Wallace, broke the tie, supporting continuation of the corps.[24] But the House of Representatives voted 158 to 121 not to appropriate the $9,101,000 President Roosevelt had requested to maintain 150 CCC camps for the ensuing fiscal year and instead made available $500,000 to defray the cost of terminating the corps.[25] Soon afterward, *Happy Days*, the national newspaper of the CCC, reported that a joint House and Senate conference committee had declined to approve the appropriation requested by President Roosevelt for continuation of the CCC for another fiscal year but had provided eight million dollars for liquidating the program, a process to be completed "as quickly as possible, but in any event not later than June 30, 1943."[26]

The arguments against continuing the CCC that ultimately prevailed focused on contentions that the program was wooing away from the nation's farmers labor that they urgently needed to produce food, that the vast number of available defense jobs rendered useless an unemployment-relief program, that work on military bases was not "conservation" and was thus outside the legal scope of the CCC, and that further funding of the corps would siphon off funds better spent on true national defense activities.[27] In truth, the CCC program had never progressed beyond the "emergency relief" stage. There was never a sense of permanency. Its life expectancy had always been short, its activities calendared in six-month periods of enroll-ment and projects. Its image as a relief agency persisted even after welfare-based prerequisites for enrollment were eliminated. Thus, its enemies, by 1942, with America embroiled in a challenging world war, could readily attack it for being wholly unnecessary, extravagant, and wasteful.

In a lengthy and emotional farewell editorial, *Happy Days* hinted that a long-running vendetta waged by political opponents of any and all New Deal

programs, and not just the question of economy, lay behind the liquidation:

> The Civilian Conservation Corps was dealt out of the government by a Congress which for nine years had supported appropriations for the Corps, sometimes in amounts greater than that asked by the President.
>
> Most of the argument against the CCC was on the grounds of "economy" and "boys don't need CCC jobs today." The voice of some who voted against retention of the Corps during this wartime emergency sounded sincere but the voices of others seemed to offer only lip service to economy while shouting repressed defiance to salve wounded prides or give vent to prejudices.
>
> These latter sought every excuse to uphold their vote to kill this agency which they thought was close to the heart of the President.
>
> It will close up shop knowing it has performed a great service to the nation and to millions of its young men. . . . In dollars and cents, the CCC will return to the country many times its cost, in improved and reclaimed natural resources. In intangible assets it bequeaths the nation the future lives of more than three million young men who will be healthier, happier, and have more patriotic lives because of their training in a CCC camp.[28]

Among a host of additional nationwide tributes to the accomplishments of the CCC was the following:

> Who can say the Civilian Conservation Corps has not been the beacon which first lighted the way out of the wilderness of waste and destruction? The thousands of miles of truck trails, the acres of forest cultural improvement, the vast areas which have been saved from forest fires, the bridges, dams, campgrounds, the revegetation and soil conservation and tree planting accomplishments, all these and a multitude of other improvements have built a monument to the CCC which will live as long as the Republic exists.[29]

They've made the good earth better.

Creative Work

CCC

DAILY NEWS
NEW YORK, N.Y.
JULY 16, 1939

The CCC was remarkably free from public media ridicule. This *Daily News* cartoon dynamically reflects the high esteem of the general press. From Record Group 35, National Archives.

And in North Carolina, a high-ranking CCC administrator added: "There seems to have been no phase of the work done in the Federal Administration's social program more universally popular than the Conservation Corps. This feeling is found among the enrollees themselves, their parents, and the community as a whole."[30]

In a final report to the Federal Security Agency, which had assumed oversight of CCC activities following the vote in Congress to liquidate the corps, the state of North Carolina filed a brief summary of the agency's accomplishments in that state between 1933 and 1942. Introducing the report was a declaration that the corps had provided employment and training to more than 75,000 young men and war veterans in the state and had advanced erosion control and forest-management programs by twenty to thirty years. The report revealed that an average of forty-five camps had operated in North Carolina during each year of the program and that at one time a total of 81 camps with an enrollment of 16,000 was operating in the state. Insofar as money was concerned, the report estimated that the CCC had expended at least $82,385,406 in North Carolina and that Tar Heel enrollees had distributed $16,431,098 to dependents.[31]

But a mere quantitative listing of accomplishments, such as number of trees planted or gullies retarded, fails to reveal fully the remarkable human legacy that accompanied and characterized the work of the CCC in North Carolina. From the towering peaks of Mount Mitchell and the Great Smoky Mountains to the glistening beaches at Cape Hatteras, millions of people annually enjoy, frequently without the vaguest awareness as to the source, the benefits derived from the labors of the enrollees in the corps: the beauty of the Great Smoky Mountains National Park and the Blue Ridge Parkway, the bountiful diversity of natural resources in North Carolina's national forests, the unique and appealing attractions of the state parks, the extensive hiking trail system (including the renowned multistate Appalachian Trail), the gully-free productive farmlands in the Piedmont, the wildlife that abounds throughout the state, the multitude of scenic byways, and countless other blessings of nature.

Even beyond the vast numbers of physical improvements to North Carolina's natural setting, the CCC offered an uplifting spirit of hope and optimism to the people of the state during some of its darkest days. The following case study, conducted in Guilford County in 1935, is indicative of that contribution:

M and W, with their six children, live in an old garage that they have attached to the back of a broken-down house situated at the edge of the city. They have the use of several acres of ground. M had been working at odd jobs, cleaning basements, but was hardly able to eke out a living.

In June, 1933, their son, Murry, was sent to C.C.C. camp and remained until July, 1934. During that time his parents received $25 a month and with that money they bought a cow, horse, two pigs, some farming implements, seed, feed, and groceries. With these they have made a living as M puts it; he for the first time in years is practically an independent individual. . . .

Before the cow was bought W was in very ill health and unable to do her work efficiently. Since she was unable to get a large amount of milk to drink daily, she has gained 20 pounds and says that she has never felt better in her life. The health of the children also has improved.

Murry himself was delighted with his experience at camp. Before he went to camp he had been troubled with indigestion and was unable to work very much. Since his return he has been getting along splendidly. He was willing and anxious to get a job when he came back, and at the end of four months after his return he managed to get a job as a plumber's helper, making $2 a day. He learned the plumbing trade at the C.C.C. camp.[32]

CIVILIAN CONSERVATION CORPS

ROBERT FECHNER, DIRECTOR

A BRIEF SUMMARY OF CERTAIN PHASES OF THE PROGRAM IN __NORTH CAROLINA__
PERIOD__APRIL 1933 – JUNE 30, 1938__

MEN

AGGREGATE NUMBER OF NORTH CAROLINA MEN GIVEN EMPLOYMENT...... 49,858

This figure includes:
Enrollees.. 44,733
(Juniors, veterans, Indians)
Non-enrolled personnel....................... 5,125
(Reserve officers, work supervisors, etc.)
North Carolina enrollees in CCC on October 20, 1938..... 7,645
Number of CCC enrollees working in North Carolina
camps on October 20, 1938............................... 7,800

CAMPS

CCC CAMPS OPERATING IN NORTH CAROLINA AS OF OCTOBER 20, 1938....... 39
National Forest........... 8   National Park....... 5
Private Forest........... 5   State Park.......... 3
Soil Conservation.........15   Bur. Biol. Survey... 2
Tennessee Valley Authority....... 1

WORK
ACCOMPLISHMENTS

PROTECTION OF FORESTS FROM FIRE and their development for greater public
use and the extension of soil erosion control measures through agricultural areas have been outstanding work activities of the CCC since 1933.
Rounding out a varied conservation program, CCC boys have worked on
migratory bird refuges, on camps within the TVA area, on national park
lands and in the development of a fine system of state parks. Among
work accomplishments have been the following:
Truck trails and minor roads, miles.................... 2,430
Forest stand improvement, acres......................... 165,749
Forest fire fighting and prevention, man-days.......... 141,024
Erosion control check dams built, number................ 71,865
Seeding, sodding, tree planting, gully control, sq.yds.18,143,988
Lookout houses and towers, number...................... 113

EDUCATION

IN THE HEALTHFUL atmosphere of outdoor CCC camps, enrollees are taught
how to work and how to make a living. Millions of acres of forests and
parks and farm lands furnish the laboratory in which young men and war
veterans gain practical experience and training. All camp facilities
are utilized to instill in each youth sound habits of work, pride in
accomplishment and the importance of regular habits, orderliness, neat-
ness and clean living. About 87% of all enrollees attend camp education
and training programs.

MONEY

TOTAL OBLIGATIONS IN NORTH CAROLINA (ESTIMATED)............$50,467,000

Estimated allotments to dependents by enrollees...........$10,548,000
(Enrollees allot $22 to $25 of their $30
monthly cash allowance to dependents)

This report reflects a summary of CCC activity in North Carolina. From CCC, Clyde R. Hoey, Governor's
Papers, Box 64, State Archives.

In a similar vein, one enrollee, who had spent thirteen months at a CCC camp in Polkton, composed an essay titled, "What the CCC Has Done for Me," in which he credited the corps with the following specific improvements to his life:

> It has taught me the necessity of discipline and to take orders from those in command.
>
> It has taught me the value of cleanliness and helped me to form good habits.
>
> I have learned the value of making friends and to appreciate the fundamental virtues of a person instead of the superficial characteristics. My whole life has been broadened.
>
> I have learned the value of the conservation of our natural resources, and to protect that which God has given me.
>
> The CCC has taught me the value of thrift and how to spend money to get the greatest benefit from it. I think that the money which I earn by the sweat of my brow is more appreciated and gives more pleasure than any other money, and that I am more apt to spend it wisely.[33]

A case study conducted in Wilson County told of a boy who was considered the only normal member of a family of four children. (One brother and one sister were deaf and dumb. Another brother was evaluated as "not so apt in his studies.") The boy dropped out of school while in the eleventh grade, but not before completing a two-year course in typing and bookkeeping. When he entered the CCC in 1934 he was sent to a camp at Belle Island, where he eventually became secretary to the camp's commanding officer. His work was so outstanding and efficient that he was granted an honorable discharge from the corps in order to accept a civilian position as "Biological Clerk" for technical services at Camp NC P-68, Company 434, Belle Island. In commenting upon his CCC experience, he declared that the months spent at camp had meant more to him than anything else in his life ever could, and that

it gave him confidence in himself. The caseworker said of the boy: "He has the self respect and a new determination to rise to the top. He faces the future with confidence, and there is something deeply personal in his attitude toward his work."[34] Likewise, from Person County came a similar report from a caseworker:

> When Johnny left us [to enter the CCC] he carried his clothes in a clean, white flour sack and wore patched blue overalls. His hair had been cut at home and his shoes mended by his father. The last we saw of him he was gazing anxiously at the fast disappearing town with his few possessions clutched wildly in his arms. Five months later he stepped from the bus with his suitcase in his hand. There was a new light in his eyes, a new assurance in his carriage, and his step was easy and carefree. He had come home from camp a new man to accept employment near home. During the time that he was [at camp] he learned to read and write to some extent.

The caseworker added that his charge had "discovered that there was a world beyond his own small horizon and was keenly enjoying its advantages and privileges. He had learned how to live with other people, how to play, and how to work cooperatively with others for a common purpose."[35] Similar stories could be gathered in abundance from every county in North Carolina.

Ben Dixon MacNeill, former feature writer for the Raleigh *News and Observer*, succinctly portrayed the essence of the CCC's influence upon its generation of needy young men. In a 1938 article titled, "Beggars' Thumbs to Workers' Hands—for Thousands of Boys CCC Shows the Way," MacNeill related how the CCC experience changed thousands from "sometimes menacing thumbs of hitchhikers to the purposeful and tool-trained hands" of enrollees. With keen insight, the columnist

Some enrollees parleyed skills acquired in the CCC into very successful business careers. Petro "Pete" Kulynych (*center*) helped build the Blue Ridge Parkway while working along the Virginia/North Carolina border. In his words he "was trained to work hard." As a result, he went on to become a top executive with Lowe's. From the Blue Ridge Parkway Archives.

credited a responsive government with "balancing the chances in favor of young men who were short-weighted in opportunity."[36] But to a North Carolina alumnus of the CCC, now deceased, goes credit for capturing the spirit of the corps in the fewest, but perhaps most vivid, words: "Our tracks are all over the place."[37]

Appendixes

Listing, by Sponsoring Agencies ("Using Services"), of All Civilian Conservation Corps Camps Established in North Carolina, 1933–1942

Alphabetical indicators appearing within parentheses at the end of company numbers denote the following:

"JR": young enrollees
"V": veterans
"W": white
"C": colored

The life-span of camps depended upon the availability of work projects in their respective locales. Some lasted only a few months, while others survived until the CCC program was discontinued in 1942. In instances where one company replaced another, the original camp number was generally retained, but the company number changed to that of the incoming unit.

NATIONAL PARK SERVICE CAMPS

A. Great Smoky Mountains National Park

CAMP NUMBER	COMPANY NUMBER	CAMP NAME	CAMP LOCATION (POST OFFICE/COUNTY)
NC NP-4	414 (JR/W)	Not recorded	Smokemont/Swain
NC NP-5	411 (JR/W)	Kephart Prong	Smokemont/Haywood
NC NP-7	415 (JR/W)	Zeb Weaver	Mount Sterling/Haywood
NC NP-9	413 (JR/W)	Forney Creek	Bryson City/Swain
NC NP-14*	3453 (JR/W)	William H. Thomas	Smokemont/Swain
NC NP-14*	1211 (JR/W)	Straight Fork	Smokemont/Swain (*twin camps)
NC NP-15	1215 (JR/W)	Mingus Creek	Smokemont/Swain
NC NP-16	1216 (JR/W)	Deep Creek	Bryson City/Swain
NC NP-17	414 (JR/W)	Black Camp Gap	Waynesville/Haywood
NC NP-18	1259 (JR/W)	Not recorded	Ravensford/Swain
NC NP-19	426 (JR/W)	Round Bottom	Ravensford/Swain
NC NP-20	1259 (JR/W)	Cataloochee	Cove Creek/Haywood
NC NP-22	415 (JR/W)	Not recorded	Cove Creek/Haywood
NC NP-23	3453 (JR/W)	Not recorded	Proctor/Swain

B. Blue Ridge Parkway

CAMP NUMBER	COMPANY NUMBER	CAMP NAME	CAMP LOCATION (POST OFFICE/COUNTY)
NC NP-21	3420 (JR/W)	Meadow Fork	Laurel Springs/Alleghany

C. Crabtree Creek Recreation Demonstration Area

CAMP NUMBER	COMPANY NUMBER	CAMP NAME	CAMP LOCATION (POST OFFICE/COUNTY)
NC NP-24	446 (JR/W)	Walter Hines Page	Raleigh/Wake

D. Cape Hatteras State Park

CAMP NUMBER	COMPANY NUMBER	CAMP NAME	CAMP LOCATION (POST OFFICE/COUNTY)
NC NP-1	3423 (JR/W)	Diamond Shoals	Buxton/Dare

U.S. FOREST SERVICE CAMPS

CAMP NUMBER	COMPANY NUMBER	CAMP NAME	CAMP LOCATION (POST OFFICE/COUNTY)
NC F-1	402 (JR/W)	John Rock	Pisgah Forest/Transylvania
NC F-2	404 (JR/W)	Mills River	Hendersonville/Henderson
NC F-3	406 (JR/W)	Jim Staton	Marion/McDowell
NC F-3	413 (JR/W)	Twin Oaks	Old Fort/McDowell
NC F-4	401 (JR/W)	McCloskey	Marion/McDowell
NC F-5	403 (JR/W)	Grandfather Mountain	Mortimer/Caldwell
NC F-6	412 (JR/W)	Big Globe	Globe/Caldwell
NC F-7	407 (JR/W)	Alex Jones	Hot Springs/Madison
NC F-8	409 (JR/W)	Big Ivy	Barnardsville/Buncombe
NC F-9	405 (JR/W)	Nawakada	Franklin/Macon
NC F-10	408 (JR/C)	Winfield Scott	Aquone/Macon
NC F-11	426 (JR/W)	Not recorded	Tellico Plains, Tenn./Cherokee
NC F-12	425 (JR/C)	Nathanael Greene	Rainbow Springs/Clay
NC F-12	3444 (JR/C)	Buck Creek	Franklin/Macon
NC F-13	406 (JR/W)	Not recorded	Old Fort/McDowell
NC F-13	435 (JR/W)	Bob Reynolds	Topton/Cherokee
NC F-14	428 (JR/W)	Balsam Grove	Balsam Grove/Transylvania
NC F-15	5420 (JR/C)	Patterson	New Bern/Craven
NC F-15	5420 (JR/C)	Not recorded	Maysville/Jones
NC F-16	294	Not recorded	New Bern/Craven
NC F-17	2410 (V/W)	Albert R. Ives	Troy/Montgomery
NC F-18	206 (JR/W)	Patterson	New Bern/Craven
NC F-19	455 (JR/W)	Horse Cove	Highlands/Macon
NC F-20	3445 (JR/W)	Cowee	Franklin/Macon
NC F-21	5424 (JR/C)	Gillett	Maysville/Jones
NC F-22	3402 (JR/W)	Zeb Vance	Asheville/Buncombe
NC F-23	3446 (JR/W)	Coweeta	Otto/Macon
NC F-24	3447 (JR/W)	Santeelah	Robbinsville/Graham
NC F-25	3455 (JR/W)	Haywood	Canton/Haywood
NC F-26	428 (JR/W)	Pisgah Forest	Brevard/Transylvania
NC F-27	401 (JR/W)	Joseph McDowell	Marion/McDowell
NC F-28	428 (JR/W)	John Rock	Brevard/Transylvania
NC F-29	2450 (V/W)	Not recorded	Murphy/Cherokee

TENNESSEE VALLEY AUTHORITY CAMPS

CAMP NUMBER	COMPANY NUMBER	CAMP NAME	CAMP LOCATION (POST OFFICE/COUNTY)
NC TVA-1	2432 (V/W)	Floyd Ramsey	Bakersville/Mitchell
NC TVA-2	3424 (JR/W)	Joe	Mars Hill/ Madison
NC TVA-3	413 (JR/W)	Not recorded	Arden/Buncombe

SOIL EROSION SERVICE AND SOIL CONSERVATION SERVICE CAMPS

CAMP NUMBER	COMPANY NUMBER	CAMP NAME	CAMP LOCATION (POST OFFICE/COUNTY)
NC SES-1	3443 (JR/W)	Hugh Bennett	High Point/Guilford
NC SES-2	437 (JR/W)	Recovery	Polkton/Anson
NC SES-3	404 (JR/W)	Not recorded	High Point/Guilford
NC SCS-1	434 (JR/W)	Hugh Bennett	High Point/Guilford
NC SCS-2	437 (JR/W)	Recovery	Polkton/Anson
NC SCS-3	404 (JR/W)	Not recorded	High Point/Guilford
NC SCS-4	3405 (JR/W)	Hancock	Mount Airy/Surry
NC SCS-5	3406 (JR/C)	Oak Grove	Yanceyville/Caswell
NC SCS-6	3407 (JR/W)	Nissen	Winston-Salem/Forsyth
NC SCS-7	3408 (JR/W)	Jerrico	Lexington/Davidson
NC SCS-8	3409 (JR/W)	Everest	Salisbury/Rowan
NC SCS-9	3420 (JR/W)	Not recorded	New Bern/Craven
NC SCS-10	3410 (JR/W)	Roosevelt	Huntersville/Mecklenburg
NC SCS-11	3411 (JR/W)	Gaston	Gastonia/Gaston
NC SCS-12	3412 (JR/W)	Granville	Oxford/Granville
NC SCS-13	3413 (JR/C)	Alamance	Burlington/Alamance
NC SCS-14	3414 (JR/C)	Carr	Durham/Durham
NC SCS-15	3415 (JR/W)	Little	Newton/Catawba
NC SCS-16	3416 (JR/W)	Old Hickory	Monroe/Union
NC SCS-17	3417 (JR/W)	Victor	Madison/Rockingham
NC SCS-18	2431 (V/W)	Avery	Lillington/Harnett
NC SCS-19	3418 (JR/W)	Vann	Franklinton/Franklin
NC SCS-20	3419 (JR/W)	Globetrotter	Ramseur/Randolph
NC SCS-21	3420 (JR/W)	Anderson	Statesville/Iredell
NC SCS-22	2430 (V/C)	Joe Robinson	Rockingham/Richmond
NC SCS-23	5425 (JR/C)	McMurry	Shelby/Cleveland
NC SCS-24	5423 (JR/C)	Post-Rogers	Forest City/Rutherford
NC SCS-25	3431 (V/W)	Anderson	Littleton/Halifax
NC SCS-26	5425 (JR/C)	Charles Young	Mount Gilead/Montgomery
NC SCS-27	3405 (JR/W)	Hoey	Elkin/Surry
NC SCS-28	2430 (V/C)	Crispus Attucks	Concord/Cabarrus
NC SCS-29	3404 (JR/W)	Geo. Washington Carver	Raleigh/Wake
NC SCS-30	3418 (JR/W)	Cooley	Nashville/Nash
NC SCS-31	3409 (JR/W)	Robinson	Peachland/Anson
NC SCS-32	3408 (JR/W)	Daniel Boone	Mocksville/Davie
NC SCS-33	1497 (JR/C)	Boone	Gibsonville/Guilford
NC SCS-34	410 (JR/C)	Edwin S. Lanier	Chapel Hill/Orange
NC SCS-35	3415 (JR/W)	Hickory	Hickory/Catawba
NC SCS-36	3411 (JR/W)	Houser	Cherryville/Gaston
NC SCS-37	3417 (JR/W)	Boone Trail	Sanford/Lee
NC SCS-38	429 (JR/C)	Not recorded	Roxboro/Person

STATE-PARK CAMPS

CAMP NUMBER	COMPANY NUMBER	CAMP NAME	CAMP LOCATION (POST OFFICE/COUNTY)
NC SP-1	432 (JR/W)	Fort Macon	Morehead City/Carteret
NC SP-2	2410 (V/W)	Mount Mitchell	Black Mountain/Yancey
NC SP-2	5487 (JR/W)	Mount Mitchell	Black Mountain/Yancey
NC SP-3	3421 (JR/W)	Doughton	Albemarle/Stanly
NC SP-4	1499 (JR/W)	Doughton	Albemarle/Stanly
NC SP-5	3422 (JR/W)	Mountain View	Danbury/Stokes
NC SP-6	3423 (JR/W)	Diamond Shoals	Buxton/Dare
NC SP-7	(Not recorded)		
NC SP-8	1499 (JR/W)	Not recorded	Albemarle/Stanly

STATE-FOREST CAMPS

CAMP NUMBER	COMPANY NUMBER	CAMP NAME	CAMP LOCATION (POST OFFICE/COUNTY)
NC SF-65	430 (JR/W)	Hofmann	Maysville/Jones
NC SF-65	5424 (JR/C)	Hofmann	Jacksonville/Onslow
NC SF-68	4482 (JR/W)	White Lake	Elizabethtown/Bladen
NC SF-76	3448 (JR/W)	Honeycutt	Hoffman/Richmond

FISH AND WILDLIFE SERVICE CAMPS (Renamed Biological Survey Camps)

CAMP NUMBER	COMPANY NUMBER	CAMP NAME	CAMP LOCATION (POST OFFICE/COUNTY)
NC FWS-2	436 (JR/W)	Virginia Dare	Manteo/Dare
NC FWS-3	424 (JR/W)	Mattamuskeet	New Holland/Hyde

BIOLOGICAL SURVEY CAMPS

CAMP NUMBER	COMPANY NUMBER	CAMP NAME	CAMP LOCATION (POST OFFICE/COUNTY)
NC BF-1	424 (JR/W)	Redington	Swan Quarter/Hyde
NC BF-2	436 (JR/W)	Virginia Dare	Manteo/Dare
NC BF-3	424 (JR/W)	Mattamuskeet	New Holland/Hyde
NC BF-7	424 (JR/W)	Not recorded	Belhaven/Beaufort

PRIVATE-LANDS CAMPS

CAMP NUMBER	COMPANY NUMBER	CAMP NAME	CAMP LOCATION (POST OFFICE/COUNTY)
NC P-51	2412 (V/W)	Not recorded	Jackson Springs/Moore
NC P-52	437 (JR/W)	Not recorded	Lake Waccamaw/Columbus
NC P-53	429 (JR/C)	Knapp	Fort Bragg/Cumberland
NC P-54	434 (JR/W)	Not recorded	Walnut Cove/Stokes
NC P-55	438 (JR/W)	James	North Wilkesboro/Wilkes
NC P-56	436 (JR/W)	Not recorded	Durham/Durham
NC P-57	433 (JR/W)	Dyer	Morganton/Burke
NC P-58	432 (JR/W)	Not recorded	Stantonsburg/Wilson
NC P-59	430 (JR/W)	Winston	Windsor/Bertie

NC P-60	2411 (V/C)	Young	Hollister/Halifax
NC P-61	2410 (V/W)	Not recorded	Lake Lure/Rutherford
NC P-62	427 (JR/W)	Sapona	Southport/Brunswick
NC P-63	436 (JR/W)	Virginia Dare	Manteo/Dare
NC P-64	1221 (JR/W)	William H. McLaurin	Laurinburg/Scotland
NC P-65	5420 (JR/C)	Not recorded	North Wilkesboro/Wilkes
NC P-66	3448 (JR/W)	Sledge	Brevard/Transylvania
NC P-67	3403 (JR/W)	Warren	Washington/Beaufort
NC P-68	4482 (JR/W)	White Lake	Elizabethtown/Bladen
NC P-69	3404 (JR/C)	Butters	Butters/Bladen
NC P-70	Not recorded		
NC P-71	Not recorded		
NC P-72	Not recorded		
NC P-73	5424 (JR/C)	Young	Bolton/Brunswick
NC P-74	5420 (JR/C)	Pender	Maple Hill/Pender
NC P-75	433 (JR/W)	Defiance	Buffalo Cove/Caldwell

MILITARY-LANDS CAMPS

CAMP NUMBER	COMPANY NUMBER	CAMP NAME	CAMP LOCATION (POST OFFICE/COUNTY)
NC Army-1	410 (JR/C)	Not recorded	Fort Bragg/Cumberland
NC Army-2	1496 (JR/C)	Puppy Creek	Fort Bragg/Cumberland
NC Army-3	1497 (JR/C)	Finlayson	Raeford/Hoke
NC Army-4	410 (JR/C)	Black Jack	Aberdeen/Moore
NC Army-4	5425 (JR/C)	John J. McSwain	Fort Bragg/Cumberland
NC Army-5	1499 (JR/W)	Alex Fields	Southern Pines/Moore
NC NP-A-1	6447 (JR/W)	Devers	Fort Bragg/Cumberland
NC NP-A-2	3423 (JR/W)	Black Jack	Raeford/Hoke
NC NP-A-3	426 (JR/W)	Honeycutt	Raeford/Hoke
NC NP-A-4	6462 (JR/C)	Not recorded	Holly Ridge/Onslow
NC NP-A-5	6468 (JR/C)	Knox	Jacksonville/Onslow
NC NP-A-6	6469 (JR/C)	Broaddus	Jacksonville/Onslow
NC NP (D)-1	6447 (JR/W)	Devers	Fort Bragg/Cumberland
NC NP (D)-2	3423 (JR/W)	Black Jack	Raeford/Hoke
NC NP (D)-3	426 (JR/W)	Honeycutt	Raeford/Hoke
NC NP (D)-4	6462 (JR/C)	Not recorded	Holly Ridge/Onslow
NC NP (D)-5	6468 (JR/C)	Knox	Jacksonville/Onslow
NC NP (D)-6	6649 (JR/C)	Broaddus	Jacksonville/Onslow
NC NP (D)-7	5424 (JR/C)	Not recorded	Fort Bragg/Cumberland
NC NP (D)-8	1497 (JR/C)	Not recorded	Fort Bragg/Cumberland
NC NP (D)-9	4487 (JR/C)	Not recorded	Jacksonville/Onslow
NC NP (D)-10	5420 (JR/C)	Not recorded	Jacksonville/Onslow
NC NP (D)-11	3404 (JR/C)	Not recorded	Jacksonville/Onslow
NC NP (D)-12	433 (JR/W)	Not recorded	Fort Bragg/Cumberland
NC NP (D)-13	497 (JR/W)	Not recorded	Fort Bragg/Cumberland
NC NP (D)-14	Not recorded		
NC NP (D)-15	4465 (JR/C)	Not recorded	Holly Ridge/Onslow

Notes

Chapter 1

1. Fiftieth anniversary program, CCC Camp F-24, Robbinsville, N.C. (Robbinsville: United States Forest Service, 1983), quoting Charles Lathrop Pack.

2. Kenneth Wayne Baldridge, "Nine Years of Achievement: The Civilian Conservation Corps in Utah" (Ph.D. diss., Brigham Young University, 1971), 3; Conrad L. Wirth, *Parks, Politics, and the People* (Norman: University of Oklahoma Press, 1980), 156.

3. H. L. Laubach, "A General Tests the CCC Boys," *Literary Digest* 121 (January 25, 1936): 17.

4. Thomas Wolfe, "The Great Schism," in *The Hills Beyond* (New York: New American Library, 1935), 183.

5. Stuart Chase, "When the Crop Lands Go," *Harper's* 173 (August 1936): 226.

6. Arthur M. Schlesinger Jr., *The Coming of the New Deal*, vol. 2 of *The Age of Roosevelt* (Boston: Houghton Mifflin Company, 1958), 341-342.

7. Quoted in *News-Sentinel* (Knoxville, Tennessee), October 30, 1989.

8. James West Davidson, *Nation of Nations: A Narrative History of the American Republic*, 2 vols. (New York: McGraw-Hill, 1990), 2:947; Arthur M. Schlesinger Jr., *The Crisis of the Old Order*, vol. 1 of *The Age of Roosevelt* (Boston: Houghton Mifflin Company, 1958), 248; Alan Brinkley et al., *American History: A Survey*, 8th ed., 2 vols. (New York: McGraw-Hill, 1991), 2:729 ff; William E. Leuchtenburg, *Franklin D. Roosevelt and the New Deal, 1932-1940* (New York: Harper and Row, 1963), 2.

9. J. S. Kirk et al., eds., *Emergency Relief in North Carolina: A Record of the Development and the Activities of the North Carolina Emergency Relief Administration, 1932-1935* (Raleigh: North Carolina Emergency Relief Commission, 1936), 2 (hereafter cited as *Emergency Relief in North Carolina*).

10. *Emergency Relief in North Carolina*, 2.

11. Leuchtenburg, *Franklin D. Roosevelt and the New Deal*, 3.

12. *Emergency Relief in North Carolina*, 9.

13. John A. Garraty and Robert A. McCaughey, *A Short History of the American Nation* (New York: Harper and Row, 1989), 346.

14. Schlesinger, *The Crisis of the Old Order*, 246.

15. Raymond Moley, *The First New Deal* (New York: Harcourt, Brace and World, 1966), 267.

16. Moley, *The First New Deal*, 266.

17. Samuel I. Rosenman, ed., *The Court Disapproves* (New York: Random House, 1935), 80.

18. *Public Papers and Addresses of Franklin D. Roosevelt*, 13 vols. (New York: Random House, 1938-1950), 4:80, hereafter cited as *Roosevelt Papers*.

19. Eleanor Roosevelt, *This I Remember* (New York: Harper and Brothers, 1949), 135.

20. Stewart L. Udall, *The Quiet Crisis* (New York: Rinehart and Winston, 1936), 143.

21. Edgar B. Nixon, *Franklin D. Roosevelt and Conservation, 1911-1945*, 2 vols. (Hyde Park, N.Y.: General Services Administration, National Archives and Records Service, Franklin D. Roosevelt Library, 1957), 1:10; Baldridge, "Nine Years of Achievement," 5.

22. Nixon, *Franklin D. Roosevelt and Conservation*, 1:35.

23. Ralph B. Perry, ed., *Essays on Faith and Morals by William James* (New York: World Publishing Company, 1962), 325; Moley, *The First New Deal*, 5.

24. Moley, *The First New Deal*, 5.

25. Nixon, *Franklin D. Roosevelt and Conservation*, 1:144.

26. Schlesinger, *The Coming of the New Deal*, 335-336.

27. *Roosevelt Papers*, 5:239.

28. *Roosevelt Papers*, 2:82, 3:198, 3:364.

29. Maren Stange, "Publicity, Husbandry, and Technocracy: Fact and Symbol in Civilian Conservation Corps Photography," in Pete Daniel et al., *Official Images: New Deal Photography* (Washington: Smithsonian Institution, 1987), 87.

30. Moley, *The First New Deal*, 268-269.

31. Moley, *The First New Deal*, 268-269.

32. Schlesinger, *The Coming of the New Deal*, 336.

33. John A. Salmond, *The Civilian Conservation Corps, 1933-1942: A New Deal Case Study* (Durham: Duke University Press, 1967), 15.

34. Salmond, *The Civilian Conservation Corps*, 22.

35. *Roosevelt Papers*, 2:82.

36. Nixon, *Franklin D. Roosevelt and Conservation*, 1:147.

37. Nixon, *Franklin D. Roosevelt and Conservation*, 1:151.

38. Wirth, *Parks, Politics, and the People*, 74.

Chapter 2

1. _____ (name withheld by request), interview with author, Madison County, N.C., 1985.

2. *Raleigh Times*, April 6, 1933; John A. Salmond, *The Civilian Conservation Corps, 1933-1942: A New Deal Case Study* (Durham: Duke University Press, 1967), 27.

3. *Charlotte Observer*, April 6, 1933.

4. U.S. Department of Labor, *Handbook for Agencies Selecting Men for Emergency Conservation Work, Emergency Conservation Work Bulletin No. 3* (Washington: Government Printing Office, 1933), 359 (hereafter cited as *ECW Bulletin No. 3*).

5. *ECW Bulletin No. 3*, 359.

6. Walker S. Buel, "The Army under the New Deal," *Literary Digest* 116 (August 26, 1933): 3.

7. Alison T. Otis et al., *The Forest Service and the Civilian Conservation Corps, 1933-1942* (Washington, D.C.: U.S. Department of Agriculture, August 1986), 9; Frank Ernest Hill, *The School in the Camps: The Educational Program of the Civilian Conservation Corps* (New York: American Association for Adult Education, 1935), frontispiece. Because North Carolina contained sizable tracts of federal land, such as Pisgah National Forest and the Great Smoky Mountains National Park, and thus possessed high potential for a variety of work projects, two additional corps—the Second and the Ninth—subsequently became involved in the state's conservation activities. Thus, some enrollees from the Second Corps (New York, New Jersey, and Delaware), each containing little or no federal lands, were dispatched to camps in North Carolina. Likewise, when North Carolina's lands were occupied with sufficient camps to carry out projected work projects, the state's surplus recruits were transported to work on understaffed projects in the Ninth Corps (Washington, Oregon, Idaho, Montana, Utah, Nevada, California, and Yellowstone Park). Information based on discharge data found in Civilian Conservation Corps Enrollment and Discharge Records, Emergency Relief Administration, State Administrative Records, Box 67, State Archives, Office of Archives and History, Raleigh.

8. "State of North Carolina: A Manual Concerning Regulations for Certifying of Applicants to the Civilian Conservation Corps," Record Group 35, National Archives, Washington, D.C.

9. *Salisbury Post*, July 14, 1933. A brief comparison of the army's mobilization of enrollees for the Civilian Conservation Corps with that for military service in World War I is enlightening. On April 7, 1917, the United States declared war on Germany and began mobilizing; three months later a total of 181,000 troops were in service. On April 3, 1933, a representative of President Roosevelt requested the army to initiate the enrollment of 25,000 men for civilian conservation work within three days. Three months later, the army had processed some "270,000 men, organized them into 1,330 companies, established that many forest camps on a front of 3,000 miles extending from the Atlantic to the Pacific, distributed in depth from Canada to Mexico, occupying every state . . . excepting Delaware, and moved 55,000 of them a distance of 2,200 miles from the east coast to the west coast." And, of course, North Carolina's Fort Bragg contributed its part.

10. *Charlotte Observer*, April 9, 1933.

11. *Mountaineer* (Waynesville), March 23, 1933.

12. *Mountaineer*, April 6, 1933.

13. *Asheville Citizen*, March 29, 1933.

14. *Charlotte Observer*, April 18, 1933.

15. *News-Herald* (Morganton), April 14, 1933.

16. Memorandum from Wilmington Chamber of Commerce to Sen. Robert R. Reynolds, undated (but probably just prior to September 25, 1933), J. C. B. Ehringhaus, Governor's Papers, Box 50, State Archives.

17. *Charlotte Observer*, April 5, 1933.

18. *Charlotte Observer*, April 5, 1933.

19. *Charlotte Observer*, April 6, 1933.

20. *Asheville Citizen*, April 6, 1933.

21. *Charlotte Observer*, April 7, 1933.

22. *Franklin Press*, April 27, 1933.

23. *Cleveland Star* (Shelby), April 28, 1933.

24. *Charlotte Observer*, April 16, 1933.

25. *ECW Bulletin No. 3*, 8.

26. *Asheville Citizen*, April 19, 1933.

27. J. S. Kirk et al., eds., *Emergency Relief in North Carolina: A Record of the Development and the Activities of the North Carolina Emergency Relief Administration, 1932-1935* (Raleigh: North Carolina Emergency Relief Commission, 1936); *ECW Bulletin No. 3*, 2.

28. *Winston-Salem Journal*, April 19, 1933; *Watauga Democrat* (Boone), April 27, 1933; *Marion Progress*, April 20, 1933; *Daily Times-News* (Burlington), April 26, 1933.

29. *Daily Times-News*, April 22, 1933.

30. *Journal-Patriot* (North Wilkesboro), May 4, 1933.

31. *Charlotte Observer*, April 25, 1933.

32. *Lenoir News-Topic*, April 20, 1933.

33. H. C. Pearce and wife to Mr. Oneal, Sept. 16[, 1934]. CCC Correspondence, 1933-1936, Emergency Relief Administration Records, Box 67, State Archives.

34. *Charlotte Observer*, April 20, 1933.

35. *Charlotte Observer*, May 5, 1933.

36. U.S. War Department, *Civilian Conservation Corps Regulations* (Washington, D.C.: Government Printing Office, 1933), Append. 2, 139 (hereafter cited as *CCC Regulations*).

37. *CCC Regulations*, Append. 2, 139.

38. *CCC Regulations*, 11, para. 19.

39. *Charlotte Observer*, April 20, 1933.

40. *ECW Bulletin No. 3*, 6.

41. *Cleveland Star*, April 28, 1933.

42. *Daily News-Times*, June 21, 1933.

43. *News-Herald*, May 26, 1933.

44. *News-Herald*, May 26, 1933.

45. *News and Observer* (Raleigh), June 9, 1933.

46. *Charlotte Observer*, June 4, 1933.

47. *News-Herald*, April 21, 1933.

48. *CCC Regulations*, 17, para. 28.

49. Samuel I. Rosenman, ed., *The Court Disapproves* (New York: Random House, 1935), 109.

Chapter 3

1. *Official Annual*, CCC, District B, Fourth Corps Area, 1934, 24. CCC annuals are truly endangered species, existing largely in the hands of former CCC enrollees or members of their families. Nevertheless, two repositories hold annuals relevant to this volume: the archives of *NACCCA Journal*, St. Louis, Missouri, hold *The Memories of District C, Fourth Corps Area, 1934, Civilian Conservation Corps*, published by Parke-Harper of Little Rock, Arkansas (the company no longer exists); and the archives of the Great Smoky Mountains National Park (GSMNP), Gatlinburg, Tennessee, hold the *Official Annual, Civilian Conservation Corps, C District, Fourth Corps Area*, 1937, published by Direct Advertising, Baton Rouge, Louisiana (likewise a nonexistent company). All CCC Official Annuals will hereafter be cited as *Official Annual*, CCC, with district and corps area, year, and page number.

2. *Official Annual*, CCC, District B, Fourth Corps Area, 1934, 24.

3. U.S. War Department, *Civilian Conservation Corps Regulations* (Washington, D.C.: Government Printing Office, 1933), 8, para. 14 c. (1), para. 16 (hereafter cited as *CCC Regulations*).

4. *CCC Regulations*, 8, para. 14 c. (10), para. 16.

5. Alison T. Otis et al., *The Forest Service and the Civilian Conservation Corps, 1933-1942* (Washington, D.C.: U.S. Department of Agriculture, August 1986), 12; Stan B. Cohen, *The Tree Army: A Pictorial History of the Civilian Conservation Corps, 1933-1942* (Missoula, Mont.: Pictorial Histories Publishing Company, 1980), 24.

6. *CCC Camp Directories*, 1933-1942, Record Group 35, National Archives, Washington, D.C.

7. *CCC Regulations*, 2, para. 3.

8. Conrad L. Wirth, *Parks, Politics, and the People* (Norman: University of Oklahoma Press, 1980), 87.

9. *Official Annual*, CCC, District B, Fourth Corps Area, 1934, 24.

10. *Franklin Press*, April 6, May 25, 1933.

11. *Franklin Press*, May 25, 1933.

12. *Marion Progress*, May 4, 1933.

13. *CCC Camp Directories*, 1933-1942. First Enrollment Period, Record Group 35, National Archives.

14. *Marion Progress*, May 25, 1933.

15. *Official Annual*, CCC, District A, Fourth Corps Area, 1936, 45. Fort Bragg continued to serve as the principal staging area for the conditioning of young recruits destined for conservation camps throughout the state. In June 1933 the national CCC newspaper reported that at Fort Bragg "5,980 boys have been received, examined, fed, clothed, vaccinated, inoculated, and put into top physical condition at [a] rate four times as fast as during the World War. By July 1st all of these boys, now well fed and happy, will be living next to nature in its wildest and most beautiful forms in the wonderful national and state forests of North Carolina and Tennessee." "General McCloskey Brags About His Camp at Fort Bragg," *Happy Days* 1 (June 24, 1933): n.p.

16. *Marion Progress*, May 25, 1933.

17. *Bryson City Times*, June 9, 1933.

18. *Bryson City Times*, June 23, 1933.

19. *Bryson City Times*, August 4, 1933.

20. *Official Annual*, CCC, District A, Fourth Corps Area, 1936, 50.

21. *Official Annual*, CCC, District A, Fourth Corps Area, 1936, 50.

22. *Official Annual*, CCC, District A, Fourth Corps Area, 1936, 123.

23. *News-Herald* (Morganton), July 14, 21, 1933.

24. *News-Record* (Marshall), June 1, 1933.

25. *Lenoir News-Topic*, April 10, 13, 1933.

26. *Lenoir News-Topic*, July 13, 1933.

27. Wirth, *Parks, Politics, and the People*, 193.

28. *Official Annual*, CCC, District C, Fourth Corps Area, 1937, 84. Not surprisingly, once the facility was established, it was christened "Camp Zeb Weaver" in honor of its chief political godfather, U.S. representative Zebulon Weaver. *CCC Camp Directories*, 1933-1942, Record Group 35, National Archives.

29. *News and Observer* (Raleigh), June 14, 1933.

30. *Asheboro Courier*, July 6, 1933.

31. *Official Annual*, CCC, District A, Fourth Corps Area, 1936, 83.

32. *CCC Camp Directories*, 1933-1942, Record Group 35, National Archives.

33. *Official Annual*, CCC, District B, Fourth Corps Area, 1934, 36.

34. *Asheville Citizen*, November 27, 1966.

35. *Asheville Citizen*, November 27, 1966.

36. *Mountaineer* (Waynesville), April 13, 1933.

37. *Mountaineer*, April 13, 1933.

38. *News and Observer*, March 31, 1935.

39. *News and Observer*, March 31, 1935.

40. *News and Observer*, March 31, 1935.

41. *CCC Camp Directories*, 1933-1942, Record Group 35, National Archives, passim; *Official Annual*, CCC, District A, Fourth Corps Area, 1936, 69, 105, 107, 113; *Official Annual*, CCC, District C, Fourth Corps Area, 1937, 80, 85; *Catawba News-Enterprise* (Newton), September 20, 1935; *News and Observer*, July 11, 1933; *Bryson City Times*, August 4, 1933.

Chapter 4

1. *Transylvania Times* (Brevard), August 31, 1939.

2. Address by Robert Fechner, director, CCC, to Thirteenth Women's Patriotic Conference on National Defense, January 26, 1938, Civilian Conservation Corps, Division of Selection, General Letter 13, Record Group 35, Box 1, National Archives, Washington, D.C.

3. Superintendent's Report for the First CCC Enrollment Period, November 15, 1933, Great Smoky Mountains National Park Archives, Gatlinburg, Tennessee, 1 (hereafter cited as Superintendent's Report for the First CCC Enrollment Period, GSMNP Archives).

4. *Bryson City Times*, June 30, 1933.

5. U.S. War Department, *Civilian Conservation Corps Regulations* (Washington, D.C.: Government Printing Office, 1933), 9, para. 15 (hereafter cited as *CCC Regulations*).

6. *CCC Regulations*, 18, para. 31. The eight-hour requirement did not apply to those in company overhead, who were required to work a sufficient number of hours to meet the administrative needs of the company commander.

7. *Franklin Press*, June 1, 1933. This schedule required two changes of command: at "work call," the commanding officer turned the work section over to the project superintendent, who then assumed command of the men and escorted them to the work assignment. Then, at 4:00 P.M., upon return to camp, the enrollees were re-consigned to the care of the commanding officer.

8. John C. Paige, *The Civilian Conservation Corps and the National Park Service, 1933-1942: An Administrative History* (Washington: U.S. Department of the Interior, National Park Service, 1985), 70.

9. Paige, *The Civilian Conservation Corps and the National Park Service*, 70.

10. Superintendent's Report for the First CCC Enrollment Period, GSMNP Archives.

11. *CCC Regulations*, 28, para. 41.

12. *CCC Regulations*, 29, para. 45.

13. Based on impromptu, unrecorded remarks by former enrollees at reunion of former CCC employees at Pigeon Forge, Tennessee, September 21, 1990.

14. *Transylvania Times*, August 31, 1939.

15. Col. George B. Buell, United States Army (Retired), quoted in Frank L. Bridges, "Daily Menus, 1937" (unpublished memoir, CCC Archives, Mars Hill College, Mars Hill, N.C.).

16. Col. George B. Buell, United States Army (Retired), quoted in Frank L. Bridges, "Daily Menus, 1937."

17. G. B. Maneval Collection (unpublished memoirs of a superintendent at a CCC camp in Globe, N.C., currently in possession of the author, awaiting transfer to Mars Hill College).

18. *Marion Progress*, May 25, 1933; *Bryson City Times*, June 30, 1933.

19. *CCC Regulations*, 127, para. 152.

20. *News-Herald* (Morganton), August 5, 1981. Griffith even offered Biggers a contract to play for the Senators, but the attack upon Pearl Harbor intervened and Biggers, like most of his CCC colleagues, went off to war instead.

21. *Bryson City Times*, June 30, 1933.

22. *Official Annual*, CCC, District C, Fourth Corps Area, 1934, 63.

23. *Official Annual*, CCC, District A, Fourth Corps Area, 1936, 95.

24. Fourth Corps Area, District B, "CCC Final Golden Gloves Boxing Bulletin, February 3, 1940" (unpublished flyer), in Frank L. Bridges, "Daily Menus, 1937" (unpublished memoir, CCC Archives, Mars Hill College).

25. *Franklin Press*, June 29, 1933.

26. *Transylvania Times*, October 29, 1933.

27. *Official Annual*, CCC, District A, Fourth Corps Area, 1936, 95, 143.

28. *High Tide* (annual compiled and edited by Camp Virginia Dare, [NC BF-2], Company 436, Manteo, 1936), 22.

29. "Welfare Activities Embrace a Number of Recreational Pursuits," *Happy Days* 4 (July 18, 1936): 3.

30. *Franklin Press*, August 19, 1937.

31. *News and Observer* (Raleigh), August 1, 1937.

32. *Bryson City Times*, July 28, 1933.

33. Personal memoir by G. B. Maneval, G. B. Maneval Collection.

34. "Alligator Pets Into Camp," *Happy Days* 4 (July 18, 1936): 10.

35. *Sand Spur* (newsletter published by CCC Camp NC P-62, Company 427, Southport) 2 (April 27, 1935): 6.

36. *Bryson City Times*, December 8, 1933.

37. *Transylvania Times*, January 27, 1937.

38. *Transylvania Times*, August 2, 1934.

39. *High Tide*, 22.

40. *CCC Regulations*, 129, para. 161.

41. "Nicknames Flourish in Camp," *Happy Days* 4 (July 25, 1936): 12.

42. "Nicknames Flourish in Camp," 22; Charlotte Pyle, "Civilian Conservation Corps: To Earn and Learn," in *Smoky Mountain Visitor Guide* (Gatlinburg, Tenn.: Smoky Mountain Visitor Guide, 1985), 32.

43. *News and Observer*, April 2, 1938.

44. Author's random analysis of various 1933 newspaper advertisements.

45. *News and Observer*, September 1, 1985.

46. Ronald B. Wilson, executive assistant to state administrator, to Lt. James B. Workman, personnel officer, 17th Field Artillery, Fort Bragg, N.C., North Carolina Emergency Relief Administration, CCC Correspondence, 1933, Box 3, State Archives, Office of Archives and History, Raleigh, N.C.

47. *Official Annual*, CCC, District A, Fourth Corps Area, 1936, 95, 149.

48. Federal Writers' Project, Works Progress Administration, *These Are Our Lives* (Chapel Hill: University of North Carolina Press, 1939), 412.

49. "Education Receives Heavy Emphasis," *Happy Days* 4 (July 18, 1936): 1, 4.

50. John A. Salmond, *The Civilian Conservation Corps, 1933-1942: A New Deal Case Study* (Durham: Duke University Press, 1967), 47-48.

51. Paige, *The Civilian Conservation Corps and the National Park Service*, 70.

52. Salmond, *The Civilian Conservation Corps*, 47-48.

53. *CCC Regulations*, 130, para. 162.

54. Paige, *The Civilian Conservation Corps and the National Park Service*, 85.

55. U.S. Department of the Interior, Office of Education, *CCC Camp Education: Guidance and Recreational Phases*, Bulletin No. 19 (Washington, D.C.: Government Printing Office, 1937), 3.

56. *Balsam Breeze* (monthly newspaper published by Camp NC F-14, Company 428), October 1937, 2.

57. *Official Annual*, CCC, District A, Fourth Corps Area, 1936, 149.

58. "Education Receives Heavy Emphasis," 1, 4.

59. Frank Ernest Hill, *The School in the Camps: The Educational Program of the Civilian Conservation Corps* (New York: American Association for Adult Education, 1935), 35.

60. "Education Receives Heavy Emphasis," 1, 4.

61. Hill, *The School in the Camps*, 35.

62. *Official Annual*, CCC, District A, Fourth Corps Area, 1936, 39.

63. "Education Receives Heavy Emphasis," 1, 4.

64. Author's random sampling of CCC camp newspapers in North Carolina.

65. *Transylvania Times*, September 21, 1933.

66. *Transylvania Times*, August 17, 1933.

67. *Transylvania Times*, September 21, 1933.

68. Huey Ray (now deceased), longtime resident of the Mars Hill community and well known for his services as public school administrator in Madison County, personal comment to author, July 10, 1983.

69. Frances Snelson to author, May 15, 1991; *Cleveland Star* (Shelby), March 23, 1935.

70. *Balsam Breeze*, October 1937, 1.

71. *Catawba News-Enterprise* (Newton), July 30, 1936.

72. Tennessee Valley Authority, "Report of Work Accomplished in T.V.A. C.C.C. Camps Administered by the U.S. Forest Service, July 1936-June 1937," unpublished report, Tennessee Valley Authority headquarters library, Knoxville, Tennessee, 17.

73. Civilian Conservation Corps, Enrollment and Discharge Records, Emergency Relief Administration Records, Box 67, State Archives.

74. Civilian Conservation Corps, Division of Selection, Record Group 35, Box 26, National Archives.

Chapter 5

1. "The CCC. What It Is and What It Does," General Letter Number 51, Office of the Director, March 11, 1939, Record Group 35, Box 3, National Archives, Washington, D.C.

2. Radio station WBRC, Birmingham, Alabama, interview of Robert Fechner, director, Civilian Conservation Corps, September 19, 1939, Division of Selection, Folder 2 (1939), Record Group 35, National Archives.

3. *Lenoir News-Topic,* July 17, 1933.

4. John C. Paige, *The Civilian Conservation Corps and the National Park Service, 1933-1942: An Administrative History* (Washington, D.C.: U.S. Department of the Interior, National Park Service, 1985), 40. A vital aspect of CCC mentoring activity was on-the-job training. At a camp situated in the Great Smoky Mountains National Park, it was reported in 1935, "Mr. T. L. Yon, in connection with his work, has been instructing ten men in stone cutting and building, blue print reading, and staking out structures for erection. Mr. T. K. Pease has given about forty men instructions in landscaping, transplanting trees and shrubs and nursery maintenance." Superintendent's Report for the Fifth CCC Enrollment Period, 1935, Great Smoky Mountains National Park Archives, Gatlinburg, Tennessee, n.p. (hereafter cited as Superintendent's Report for the Fifth CCC Enrollment Period, GSMNP Archives).

5. *CCC Camp Directories,* 1933-1942, Record Group 35, National Archives.

6. The fact that these career professionals were under constant performance surveillance and were subject to seemingly endless inspection, without prior notice, diminishes still further the notion that a dole mindset was in evidence. North Carolina Emergency Relief Administration, Civilian Conservation Corps Enrollment and Discharge Records, 1933, Box 67, State Archives, Office of Archives and History, Raleigh.

7. *CCC Camp Directories,* 1933-1942, Record Group 35.

8. Civilian Conservation Corps, Division of Selection, General Letter (unnumbered), August 25, 1938, 5, Record Group 35, National Archives.

9. Paige, *The Civilian Conservation Corps,* 40. The duration of these camps varied from eight years for NP-5 to six months for NP-20, and the life-span of each was directly subject to the needs of the park. Moreover, the number of enrollees in each camp was in constant flux, with turnovers a certainty at the beginning and end of each six-month enrollment period. Finally, as work projects reached into the higher peaks of the park, it became necessary to establish smaller units known as "side," "spike," or "spur" camps.

10. Superintendent's Report for the First CCC Enrollment Period, November 15, 1933, 9, Great Smoky Mountains National Park Archives, Gatlinburg, Tennessee, n.p. (hereafter cited as Superintendent's Report for the First CCC Enrollment Period, GSMNP Archives).

11. *Asheville Citizen-Times,* April 5, 1936.

12. "Thousands of Dead Chestnut Trees Felled in Great Smokies to Promote Growth of New Forest," *Happy Days* 3 (July 25, 1936): 10.

13. Superintendent's Report for the Fourth CCC Enrollment Period, 1934-1935, Great Smoky Mountains National Park Archives, Gatlinburg, Tennessee, n.p. (hereafter cited as Superintendent's Report for the Fourth CCC Enrollment Period, GSMNP Archives).

14. Superintendent's Report for the Fourth CCC Enrollment Period, GSMNP Archives; Superintendent's Report for the First CCC Enrollment Period, GSMNP Archives.

15. Superintendent's Report for the First CCC Enrollment Period, GSMNP Archives.

16. *Official Annual,* CCC, District A, Fourth Corps Area, 1937, 82, 202.

17. *Official Annual,* CCC, District A, Fourth Corps Area, 1937, 82, 202.

18. Superintendent's Report for the Fifth CCC Enrollment Period, GSMNP Archives.

19. Superintendent's Report for the Fifth CCC Enrollment Period, GSMNP Archives.

20. Superintendent's Report for the Fifth CCC Enrollment Period, GSMNP Archives.

21. Superintendent's Report for the Fourth CCC Enrollment Period, GSMNP Archives.

22. Superintendent's Report for the Fourth CCC Enrollment Period, GSMNP Archives.

23. Superintendent's Report for the Fourth CCC Enrollment Period, GSMNP Archives. A sister camp, NP-18, stationed at Ravensford, likewise razed a number of buildings and engaged in a general clean-up at a recently abandoned mill site.

24. Superintendent's Report for the Fifth CCC Enrollment Period, GSMNP Archives.

25. Superintendent's Report for the Fifth CCC Enrollment Period, GSMNP Archives.

26. James P. Jackson, "Living Legacy of the CCC," *American Forests* 94 (September-October 1988): 47.

27. Superintendent's Report for the First CCC Enrollment Period, GSMNP Archives.

28. Stanley W. Abbott to Thomas C. Vint, April 7, 1937, Resident Landscape Architect's Correspondence, Blue Ridge Parkway Archives, Asheville, N.C.

29. Superintendent's Annual Reports, 1938-1942, Blue Ridge Parkway Archives.

30. Resident Landscape Architect's Monthly Report, December 1941, Blue Ridge Parkway Archives.

31. Resident Landscape Architect's Monthly Report, April 1941, Blue Ridge Parkway Archives.

32. Paige, *The Civilian Conservation Corps*, 118.

33. Resident Landscape Architect's Annual Report, June 30, 1943, Blue Ridge Parkway Archives.

34. *Asheville Citizen*, April 4, 1933.

35. U.S. Department of Agriculture, *National Forests in the Southern Appalachians* (Washington, D.C.: Government Printing Office, 1940), passim.

36. *National Forests in the Southern Appalachians*, passim. Protection from forest fires was one of the highest priorities of forest management, and CCC regulations were quite specific as to the duties of enrollees in that regard: "Enrollees will be subject to emergency calls by the project superintendent of the work agency on any day at any hour of the day or night for the purpose of fighting forest fires, or in similar emergencies affecting life or property." U.S. War Department, *Civilian Conservation Corps Regulations* (Washington, D.C.: Government Printing Office, 1933), 18, para. 32.

37. *CCC Camp Directories*, 1933-1942, Record Group 35, National Archives. The fact that the first fourteen such camps were established during the first six months of the CCC program means that approximately 2,800 enrollees were immediately launched into a North Carolina adventure that would mean a new life for them and for the forests in which they worked.

38. Forest Service Inspection Reports, July 7-August 2, 1941, Record Group 35, Box 26, National Archives.

39. *Official Annual*, CCC, District A, Fourth Corps Area, 1936, 41.

40. *Marion Progress*, August 31, 1933.

41. *Transylvania Times* (Brevard), April 4, 1935, quoting editorial in *Charlotte Observer*.

42. *Skyland Post* (Jefferson, N.C.), November 3, 1938.

43. *Charlotte Observer*, May 5, 1934.

44. *Asheville Citizen-Times*, April 25, 1937.

45. *Transylvania Times*, January 2, 1940.

46. *Lenoir News-Topic*, August 31, 1933.

47. *Official Annual*, CCC, District A, Fourth Corps Area, 1937, 99. Members of Camp NC F-25, Company 3455, also reported that they had constructed a fire tower at an elevation of 5,300 feet, making it necessary for enrollees to "carry fifteen tons of material to the top of the mountain, a distance of four miles. . . ."

48. A. M. Deitz Collection, Daily Diaries, CCC Collection, Mars Hill College Archives, Mars Hill, N.C.

49. G. B. Maneval Collection (unpublished memoirs of a superintendent at a CCC camp in Globe, N.C., currently in possession of the author awaiting transfer to Mars Hill College).

50. Wesley M. Gewehr et al., *American Civilization: A History of the United States* (New York: McGraw-Hill, 1957), 447.

51. Tennessee Valley Authority, "A Peace Time Army: The Tennessee Valley Authority's Civilian Conservation Corps, 1933-1942" (unpublished report, TVA, Knoxville, Tennessee), 1.

52. Records of Occupancy, April 9, 1935-March 10, 1942, U.S. Forest Service, Record Group 95, Box 36, National Archives.

53. Tennessee Valley Authority, "Report of Work Accomplished in T.V.A. C.C.C. Camps Administered by the U.S. Forest Service, October, 1935-June, 1936" (unpublished report, Tennessee Valley Authority headquarters library, Knoxville, Tennessee), 1.

54. *Asheville Citizen*, April 2, 1936.

55. *Asheville Citizen*, March 13, 1938.

56. *Asheville Citizen*, March 13, 1938.

57. *Asheville Citizen*, April 2, 1936.

58. *Transylvania Times*, November 9, 1939.

59. Inspection Report, Pisgah Forest, 1940, Forest Service CCC, Record Group 95, National Archives.

60. Tennessee Valley Authority, "Report of Work Accomplished in T.V.A. C.C.C. Camps Administered by the U.S. Forest Service, July 1937 to June 1938" (unpublished report, Tennessee Valley Authority headquarters library, Knoxville, Tennessee), 14.

61. Tennessee Valley Authority, "A Peace Time Army," 19.

62. Tennessee Valley Authority, "A Peace Time Army," 19, 1.

63. *Charlotte Observer*, April 27, 1936.

64. *Daily Times-News* (Burlington), May 26, 1935.

65. *Winston-Salem Journal*, May 7, 1935.

66. North Carolina Emergency Relief Administration, CCC Correspondence, 1940, Box 3, State Archives.

67. *Winston-Salem Journal*, August 4, 1935. To Rep. W. B. Umstead of North Carolina's Sixth Congressional District went most of the credit for the appropriation. Umstead had taken the lead in handling the matter, working closely with Hugh H. Bennett, director of soil erosion control.

68. *Cleveland Star* (Shelby), July 10, 1935; *News and Observer* (Raleigh), July 10, 1935. The *News and Observer* listed the counties slated to receive the new camps: Mecklenburg, Guilford, Alamance, Durham, Surry, Caswell, Forsyth, Rockingham, Granville, Anson, Davidson, Union, Richmond, Rowan, Iredell, Gaston, Cleveland, Catawba, Franklin, Randolph, Harnett, and Rutherford. Prior to July 10, 1935, North Carolina had been allotted only three camps: NC SCS-1, Company 434, at High Point (Guilford

County); NC SCS-2, Company 437, at Polkton (Anson County); and NC SCS-3, likewise at High Point. *CCC Camp Directories*, 1933-1942, Record Group 35, National Archives.

69. *CCC Camp Directories*, 1933-1942, Record Group 35, National Archives.

70. *Randolph Tribune* (Asheboro), November 11, 1934.

71. *Cleveland Star*, July 10, 1935.

72. *Asheville Citizen*, March 20, 1939.

73. *Winston-Salem Journal*, October 8, 1935.

74. *Winston-Salem Journal*, August 25, 1935; "Soil Conservation in North Carolina," Department of Conservation and Development Reports, 1938, 40, Box 14, State Archives.

75. *Winston-Salem Journal*, October 15, 1935.

76. *Randolph Tribune*, November 11, 1934.

77. *Cleveland Star*, November 20, 1935.

78. *Official Annual*, CCC, District A, Fourth Corps Area, 1936, 93.

79. *Official Annual*, CCC, District A, Fourth Corps Area, 1936, 93.

80. *Official Annual*, CCC, District A, Fourth Corps Area, 1936, 93.

81. *Catawba News-Enterprise* (Newton), September 19, 1939. Considering that from 1934 to 1942 CCC camps labored to check soil erosion throughout North Carolina, the work accomplishments returned many times the federal dollars invested in establishing and administering those camps.

82. *Cleveland Star*, August 14, 1935.

83. Conrad L. Wirth, *Parks, Politics, and the People* (Norman: University of Oklahoma Press, 1980), 95.

84. Wirth, *Parks, Politics, and the People*, 105.

85. Wirth, *Parks, Politics, and the People*, 105.

86. Wirth, *Parks, Politics, and the People*, 113.

87. S. Kent Schwarzkopf, *A History of Mt. Mitchell and the Black Mountains: Exploration, Development, and Preservation* (Raleigh: Division of Archives and History, 1985), 90.

88. *Winston-Salem Journal*, May 25, 1935.

89. Department of Conservation and Development, report from Thomas W. Morse, assistant in charge of state parks, to J. S. Holmes, state forester, on state parks from January 1, 1936, to July 1, 1936, 1, Box 14, State Archives (hereafter cited as Department of Conservation and Development, report from Morse to Holmes).

90. Department of Conservation and Development, report from Morse to Holmes. Already in place atop Mount Mitchell were a number of buildings constructed prior to the arrival of the CCC: a caretaker's house and lodge, an observation tower, a temporary concession stand, and an open-pit latrine. Thus the CCC could concentrate on fire-hazard reduction, waterlines, trails, and support buildings. Department of Conservation and Development, State Park Reports, 1936-1941, Box 16, State Archives.

91. Department of Conservation and Development, State Park Reports, 1936-1941, Box 16, State Archives; *CCC Camp Directories*, 1933-1942, Record Group 35, National Archives.

92. Department of Conservation and Development, State Park Reports, 1936-1941, Box 16, State Archives. The work was likely halted as a result of a controversy involving a privately owned toll road that provided access to the park.

93. V. R. Ludgate to Stanley W. Abbott, May 21, 1938, Resident Landscape Architect's Correspondence, Blue Ridge Parkway Archives, Asheville, N.C.

94. *News and Observer*, January 17, 1940.

95. *CCC Camp Directories*, 1933-1942, Record Group 35, National Archives; Schwarzkopf, *A History of Mt. Mitchell*, 105.

96. Schwarzkopf, *A History of Mt. Mitchell*, 104.

97. Walter C. Biggs Jr. and James F. Parnell, *State Parks of North Carolina* (Winston-Salem: John F. Blair, 1989), 22-23.

98. R. Bruce Etheridge to Mayor, Beaufort, N.C., April 20, 1936, Department of Conservation and Development, Activities of the Department, Parks, 1936-1941, Box 16, State Archives.

99. Etheridge to Mayor, Beaufort, N.C., April 20, 1936.

100. *Shelby Star*, April 15, 1935.

101. *Shelby Star*, April 15, 1935.

102. Department of Conservation and Development, State Park Reports, 1936-1941, Box 14, State Archives.

103. *Stanly News and Press* (Albemarle), August 16, 1940.

104. *Salisbury Post*, March 31, 1935; *Official Annual*, CCC, District A, Fourth Corps Area, 1936, 87.

105. *Official Annual*, CCC, District A, Fourth Corps Area, 1936, 87.

106. *Stanly News and Press*, August 16, 1940.

107. Department of Natural Resources and Community Development, Master Planning Unit, Morrow Mountain State Park Plan, February 1979, 3, Department of Conservation and Development, Parks (State and National), Box 16, State Archives.

108. *Stanly News and Press*, August 16, 1940.

109. *Official Annual*, CCC, District A, Fourth Corps Area, 1936, 125.

110. State Park Reports, 1936, Department of Conservation and Development, Box 16, State Archives.

111. "Most Easterly CCC Camp in the Country Fights Shifting Sands," *Happy Days* 4 (July 25, 1936): 10.

112. Department of Conservation and Development, State Park Reports, 1936-1941, Box 14, State Archives.

113. "Most Easterly CCC Camp in the Country Fights Shifting Sands," 10.

114. Wirth, *Parks, Politics, and the People*, 193; Paige, *The Civilian Conservation Corps*, 123.

115. Biggs and Parnell, *State Parks of North Carolina*, 144.

116. *Winston-Salem Journal*, August 11, 1935.

117. Lawrence McRae to J. C. B. Ehringhaus, September 13, 1933, J. C. B. Ehringhaus, Governor's Papers, Federal Relief Program, Box 50, State Archives.

118. *Winston-Salem Journal*, August 11, 1935.

119. *Official Annual*, CCC, District A, Fourth Corps Area, 1936, 65; *Winston-Salem Journal*, August 11, 1935.

120. State Park Reports, 1936, Department of Conservation and Development, Box 14, State Archives.

121. *Winston-Salem Journal*, October 21, 1991.

122. Miscellaneous comments made by participants at Hanging Rock State Park reunion and dedication ceremony, October 26, 1991.

123. Biggs and Parnell, *State Parks of North Carolina*, 210.

124. Biggs and Parnell, *State Parks of North Carolina*, 210.

125. Biggs and Parnell, *State Parks of North Carolina*, 210.

126. *CCC Camp Directories*, 1933-1942, Record Group 35, National Archives.

127. Department of Conservation and Development, report from Morse to Holmes.

128. *News and Observer*, April 12, 1936.

129. *News and Observer*, April 12, 1936.

130. *CCC Camp Directories*, 1933-1942, Record Group 35, National Archives.

131. *High Tide* (annual compiled and edited by Camp Virginia Dare, [NC BF-2], Company 436, Manteo, 1936), 22.

132. *High Tide*, 8.

133. *High Tide*, 8. Another project of the camp was mosquito control, which involved the digging of many yards of ditches in the hope of promoting drainage and destroying breeding sites.

134. Morgan H. Harris, interview with author, Swan Quarter, N.C., September 1990; *News and Observer*, February 2, 1938.

135. Author's miscellaneous interviews with former CCC enrollees, alumni reunion, New Holland, N.C., September 19, 1990.

136. *News and Observer*, February 6, 1938.

137. As this book was going to press, a law was enacted whereby the N.C. Department of Cultural Resources would repair and renovate the lodge. The property will be transferred to and managed by the Wildlife Resources Commission. (SL2007-13)

Chapter 6

1. *Cleveland Daily Star* (Shelby), July 28, 1983.

2. T. L. Grier, North Carolina CCC Supervisor, to W. Frank Persons, Labor Department, Washington, D.C., August 8, 1940, Civilian Conservation Corps, Division of Selection, Record Group 35, Box 15, National Archives, Washington, D.C.

3. "CCC Camps to be Closed as Rapidly as Possible—House Sounds Death Knell in 230-120 Vote," *Happy Days* 10 (July 4, 1942): 1; *CCC Camp Directories*, 1933-1942, Record Group 35, National Archives.

4. Edgar B. Nixon, *Franklin D. Roosevelt and Conservation, 1911-1945*, 2 vols. (Hyde Park, N.Y.: General Services Administration, National Archives and Records Service, Franklin D. Roosevelt Library, 1957), 1:147; John A. Salmond, *The Civilian Conservation Corps, 1933-1942: A New Deal Case Study* (Durham: Duke University Press, 1967), 23.

5. Alison T. Otis et al., *The Forest Service and the Civilian Conservation Corps, 1933-1942* (Washington, D.C.: U.S. Department of Agriculture, 1986), 7; John C. Paige, *The Civilian Conservation Corps and the National Park Service, 1933-1942: An Administrative History* (Washington, D.C.: U.S. Department of the Interior, National Park Service, 1985), 93-94.

6. Paige, *The Civilian Conservation Corps and the National Park Service*, 93-94.

7. J. C. B. Ehringhaus, Governor's Papers, Federal Relief Program, Box 50, State Archives, Office of Archives and History, Raleigh.

8. Charles H. Taylor, Acting Director, CCC, to Senator Josiah W. Bailey, August 2, 1940, Civilian Conservation Corps, Division of Selection, Record Group 35, Box 15, National Archives.

9. *CCC Camp Directories*, 1933-1942, Record Group 35, National Archives.

10. *CCC Camp Directories*, 1933-1942, Record Group 35, National Archives.

11. *Official Annual*, CCC, District A, Fourth Corps Area, 1936, 137.

12. *Official Annual*, CCC, District A, Fourth Corps Area, 1936, 137.

13. *Official Annual*, CCC, District A, Fourth Corps Area, 1936, 133.

14. *Official Annual*, CCC, District A, Fourth Corps Area, 1936, 139.

15. *Official Annual*, CCC, District A, Fourth Corps Area, 1936, 143. The reporter added that the camp's educational program had produced favorable results, with numbers enrolled in illiteracy classes becoming fewer while educational and vocational classes expanded in size and attendance.

16. "Enrollee Activities, SCS-5 (C), Yanceyville, North Carolina," Records of the Division of Planning and Public Relations, Photographs, Record Group 35, Box 7, National Archives.

17. *Official Annual*, CCC, District A, Fourth Corps Area, 1936, 139.

18. *Official Annual*, CCC, District A, Fourth Corps Area, 1936, 133.

19. *Official Annual*, CCC, District A, Fourth Corps Area, 1936, 151.

20. *Official Annual*, CCC, District A, Fourth Corps Area, 1936, 149.

21. "Fourth Corps Negro Contingent, 12,000 Strong, Went from Plow Handle to Pencil and Grasped Opportunity's Hand," *Happy Days* 4 (July 18, 1936): 2. For many of the African American enrollees, life in the CCC camps meant better food and nutrition. The *Happy Days* article put the matter this way: "The meager fare of log cabins has given place to regular meals, nourishing food and good table manners. And how they have put on weight! In one camp in North Carolina these colored boys gained an average of twenty-four pounds each in five months."

22. "Fourth Corps Negro Contingent, 12,000 Strong," 2.

23. "Fourth Corps Negro Contingent, 12,000 Strong," 2.

24. "Fourth Corps Negro Contingent, 12,000 Strong," 2.

25. North Carolina Emergency Relief Administration, Miscellaneous Correspondence, 1934-1935, Box 3, State Archives.

26. North Carolina Emergency Relief Administration, General CCC Correspondence, June 20, 1934, Box 3, State Archives.

27. North Carolina Emergency Relief Administration, General CCC Correspondence, June 28, 1934, Box 3, State Archives.

28. Ronald B. Wilson, executive assistant to state administrator, to Col. Talbot Smith, U.S. Army Recruiting Office, Charlotte, March 25, 1935, Emergency Relief Administration, CCC Correspondence, 1935, Box 3, State Archives.

29. J. C. B. Ehringhaus, Governor's Papers, Federal Relief Program, Box 50, State Archives.

30. J. C. B. Ehringhaus, Governor's Papers, Federal Relief Program, Box 50, State Archives.

31. J. C. B. Ehringhaus, Governor's Papers, Federal Relief Program, Box 50, State Archives.

32. J. C. B. Ehringhaus, Governor's Papers, Federal Relief Program, Box 50, State Archives.

33. J. C. B. Ehringhaus, Governor's Papers, Federal Relief Program, Box 50, State Archives.

34. J. C. B. Ehringhaus, Governor's Papers, Federal Relief Program, Box 50, State Archives.

35. J. C. B. Ehringhaus, Governor's Papers, Federal Relief Program, Box 50, State Archives. This contrite letter to the contrary, the original protest did have a negative impact: the camp remained at Butters for less than a month and was then transferred to Ramseur in Randolph County, in the process having its official designation changed from "P-69" to "SCS-20."

36. All foregoing telegrams from Federal Relief Program, 1933-1937, J. C. B. Ehringhaus, Governor's Papers, Box 50, State Archives.

37. *Official Annual*, CCC, District A, Fourth Corps Area, 1936, 117.

38. *Official Annual*, CCC, District A, Fourth Corps Area, 1936, 75.

39. *News and Observer* (Raleigh), January 26, 1938.

40. Clyde R. Hoey, Governor's Papers, Box 64, State Archives.

41. All foregoing correspondence from Clyde R. Hoey, Governor's Papers, Box 64, State Archives.

42. Clyde R. Hoey, Governor's Papers, Box 64, State Archives.

43. All foregoing correspondence from Clyde R. Hoey, Governor's Papers, Box 64, State Archives.

44. *News and Observer*, August 2, 1938. Claims that Umstead was losing political sustainability were of questionable validity. He served for six years in the U.S. House of Representatives before receiving appointment to fill a vacant seat in the U.S. Senate in 1946. Although he lost his bid for reelection to the Senate in 1948, he successfully ran for governor in 1952.

45. *CCC Camp Directories*, 1933-1942, Record Group 35, National Archives.

46. *Monroe Enquirer*, May 29, 1939.

47. *Monroe Enquirer*, May 29, 1939.

48. *Monroe Enquirer*, May 29, 1939.

49. *Monroe Enquirer*, June 1, 1939.

50. *Monroe Enquirer*, June 1, 1939.

51. *Monroe Enquirer*, June 1, 1939.

52. *Monroe Enquirer*, editorial, June 1, 1939.

53. *Monroe Enquirer,* June 1, 1939.

54. *Monroe Enquirer,* June 8, 1939.

55. *Monroe Enquirer,* editorial, June 8, 1939.

56. *Monroe Enquirer,* June 15, 1939.

57. *Cleveland Star,* July 26, 1935.

58. *Cleveland Star,* August 2, 1935.

59. *Cleveland Star,* August 7, 1935.

60. *Cleveland Star,* August 9, 1935.

61. *News and Observer,* August 9, 1935.

62. *Cleveland Star,* August 12, 1935.

63. *Cleveland Star,* August 12, 1935.

64. A few months later an effort was made to move the camp from Shelby to Huntersville, but it failed—not only because Huntersville refused to accept an African American camp but also, and especially, because the people of Cleveland County vigorously lobbied their congressional delegation to keep the camp in their home county. Those efforts succeeded in keeping the facility in Cleveland County until October 1937, when it was moved (in good standing) to Monroe, where it undertook similar tasks. Two years later, however, an unfortunate racial incident made it necessary to remove the camp to Fort Bragg. *Official Annual,* CCC, District A, Fourth Corps Area, 1936, 151; *News and Observer,* June 25, 1939.

65. Forest Service Inspection Reports, "Side Camps," NC S-65, Company 430, Fiscal Years 1937-1942, Record Group 95, Box 26, National Archives.

66. Forest Service Inspection Reports, "Side Camps," NC S-65, Company 430, Fiscal Years 1937-1942, Record Group 95, Box 26, National Archives.

67. *Cleveland Daily Star* (Shelby), July 28, 1983.

Chapter 7

1. Ray Kinsland, CCC seminar sponsored by Appalachian Consortium, Greensboro Historical Museum, Greensboro, N.C., August 4, 1992.

2. Conrad L. Wirth, *Parks, Politics, and the People* (Norman: University of Oklahoma Press, 1980), 87. Originally, the title "Emergency Conservation Work" ("ECW") designated the national CCC program, and the phrase "Indian Emergency Conservation Work" (or "IEWC") identified Native American CCC endeavors. But as of July 1, 1937, legislation changed the title of the national program to "Civilian Conservation Corps" and the Native American operations to "Civilian Conservation Corps—Indian Division" ("CCC-ID"). Bureau of Indian Affairs, Cherokee Agency, Funds and Appropriations, 1937, Record Group 75, Box 18, National Archives, Washington, D.C. (hereafter cited as BIA, Cherokee

Agency, Funds and Appropriations, with appropriate year or years).

3. John A. Salmond, *The Civilian Conservation Corps, 1933-1942: A New Deal Case Study* (Durham: Duke University Press, 1967), 33.

4. BIA, Cherokee Agency, Funds and Appropriations, 1940-1942, Record Group 75, Box 18, National Archives.

5. BIA, Cherokee Agency, Statistical Information, Fiscal Year 1942, Record Group 75, Box 18, National Archives (hereafter cited as BIA, Cherokee Agency, Statistical Information, with appropriate year or years).

6. Letter from Cherokee Agency to Indian Affairs Office, Washington, D.C., March 31, 1942, Correspondence, 1942, Record Group 75, Box 18, National Archives.

7. BIA, Cherokee Agency, Statistical Information, Fiscal Year 1942. One of the group foremen, Jarrett B. Blythe, emerged from the program as one of the most respected and beloved Cherokee tribal chiefs. Blythe, highly respected both by fellow Indians and whites, distinguished himself by being elected to and serving as principal chief of the Eastern Band of Cherokee Indians on three separate occasions: October 1931 to October 1947, October 1951 to October 1959, and October 1963 to October 1967. He ably participated in and promoted the CCC program on his reservation.

8. BIA, Cherokee Agency, Projects Authorized, Fiscal Year 1938, Record Group 75, Box 18, National Archives (hereafter cited as BIA, Cherokee Agency, Projects Authorized, with appropriate year or years), Record Group 75, Box 18, National Archives.

9. BIA, Cherokee Agency, Funds and Appropriations, Fiscal Year 1942-1943, Record Group 75, Box 18, National Archives.

10. BIA, Cherokee Agency, Projects Authorized, Fiscal Year 1938, Record Group 75, Box 18, National Archives.

11. BIA, Cherokee Agency, Projects Authorized, Fiscal Year 1938, Record Group 75, Box 18, National Archives.

12. BIA, Cherokee Agency, Projects Authorized, Fiscal Year 1938, Record Group 75, Box 18, National Archives.

13. BIA, Cherokee Agency, Funds and Appropriations, Fiscal Years 1937-1939, Record Group 75, Box 18, National Archives.

14. BIA, Cherokee Agency, Funds and Appropriations, Fiscal Year 1940-1941, Record Group 75, Box 18, National Archives.

15. BIA, Cherokee Agency, Funds and Appropriations, Fiscal Years 1940-1942, Record Group 75, Box 18, National Archives.

16. BIA, Cherokee Agency, Funds and Appropriations, Fiscal Year 1940-1941, Record Group 75, Box 18, National Archives.

17. BIA, Cherokee Agency, Projects Authorized, Fiscal Year 1938, Record Group 75, Box 18, National Archives.

18. BIA, Cherokee Agency, Statistical Information, 1940-1942, Record Group 75, Box 18, National Archives.

Chapter 8

1. *Transylvania Times* (Brevard), May 11, 1933.

2. U.S. Department of Labor, *Handbook for Agencies Selecting Men for Emergency Conservation Work, Emergency Conservation Work Bulletin No. 3* (Washington, D.C.: Government Printing Office, 1933), 11.

3. U.S. War Department, *Civilian Conservation Corps Regulations* (Washington, D.C.: Government Printing Office, 1933), 9, para. 14 d.

4. Civilian Conservation Corps, Division of Publicity, Folder 2, Record Group 35, National Archives, Washington, D.C.

5. *CCC Camp Directories*, 1933-1942, Record Group 35, National Archives.

6. Civilian Conservation Corps, Division of Selection, Folder 2, 1939, Record Group 35, National Archives.

7. Ovid M. Butler, ed. *American Conservation in Picture and Story* (Washington, D.C.: American Forestry Association, 1941), 139.

8. U.S. Forest Service, General Information, 1941, Record Group 95, Box 26, National Archives.

9. U.S. Forest Service, General Information, 1941, Record Group 95, Box 26, National Archives.

10. Letter of appointment, A. M. Deitz Collection, CCC Archives, Mars Hill College, Mars Hill, N.C.

11. U.S. Forest Service, General Information, 1941, Record Group 95, Box 26, National Archives.

12. *Daily Mail* (Anderson, S.C.), April 24, 1941.

13. U.S. Forest Service, General Information, 1941, Record Group 95, Box 26, National Archives.

14. *News and Observer* (Raleigh), February 2, 1941.

15. *News and Observer*, August 17, 1941. CCC director McEntee attempted to put the best possible face on the drill order, saying: "The boys will not be given guns. This is not putting the Corps in the military establishment. The purpose of the instruction is to strengthen and broaden the basic health and PT programs provided all CCC enrollees. The Corps training will better fit the boys for service in the Army if they are inducted or volunteer, and likewise, will better equip them for jobs in defense industries. The whole idea of the drill is to spruce the boys up."

16. *News and Observer*, September 7, 1941.

17. *News and Observer*, October 28, 1941. The camp closings were an integral part of President Roosevelt's efforts to bolster national defense. "In view of the current world condition," Roosevelt said, "I feel that the War Department should be relieved from all activities which might in any way interfere with its main objective—preparation for defense."

18. John C. Paige, *The Civilian Conservation Corps and the National Park Service, 1933-1942: An Administrative History* (Washington, D.C.: U.S. Department of the Interior, 1985), 32.

19. Paige, *The Civilian Conservation Corps and the National Park Service*, 32.

20. *Congressional Record*, 77th Cong., 2nd sess., 1940, 88, pt. 4:4928.

21. *Congressional Record*, 77th Cong., 2nd sess., 1940, 88, pt. 4:4935.

22. *Congressional Record*, 77th Cong., 2nd sess., 1940, 88, pt. 4:5604.

23. *Congressional Record*, 77th Cong., 2nd sess., 1940, 88, pt. 4:4930.

24. *Congressional Record*, 77th Cong., 2nd sess., 1940, 88, pt. 4:5612. Sen. Josiah W. Bailey of North Carolina voted to liquidate the CCC. (North Carolina's other senator, Robert R. Reynolds, is recorded as "Not Voting" on the question.)

25. *Congressional Record*, 77th Cong., 2nd sess., 1940, 88, pt. 4:5940. Members of the House of Representatives from North Carolina who voted to liquidate the CCC included Graham A. Barden, Harold D. Cooley, Robert L. Doughton, and Alfred L. Bulwinkle; those voting against liquidation were Zebulon Weaver, Herbert C. Bonner, and William O. Burgin. *News and Observer*, July 1, 1942.

26. "CCC Camps to Be Closed as Rapidly as Possible," *Happy Days* 10 (July 4, 1942): 1.

27. "CCC Camps to Be Closed as Rapidly as Possible," 2.

28. "Long Live the CCC" (editorial), *Happy Days* 10 (July 4, 1942): 4. Concurrently, on July 3, 1942, the editor of the *Salt Lake Tribune* (Salt Lake City, Utah) expressed in a single sentence what might serve as a most appropriate epitaph for the corps: "The CCC may be dead but the whole country is covered with lasting monuments to its timely service." Quoted in Kenneth Wayne Baldridge, "Nine Years of Achievement: The Civilian Conservation Corps in Utah" (Ph.D. diss., Brigham Young University, 1971), 361.

29. *Forest Service Bulletin*, General Information, Vol. 23 (Washington, D.C.: U.S. Department of Agriculture, U.S. Forest Service, 1939), 8, Forest Service CCC, Record Group 95, Box 26, National Archives.

30. Civilian Conservation Corps, Division of Selection, 1935, Record Group 35, Box 26, National Archives.

31. Brief Summary, Work Accomplishments, North Carolina, 1933-1942, CCC Pictographs, Record Group 35, National Archives.

32. Mrs. Thomas O'Berry, director, Emergency Relief in North Carolina, to W. Frank Persons, Department of Labor, Washington, D.C., March 5, 1935, Civilian Conservation Corps, Division of Selection, Record Group 35, Box 26, National Archives.

33. O'Berry to Persons, March 5, 1935.

34. O'Berry to Persons, March 5, 1935.

35. O'Berry to Persons, March 5, 1935.

36. *News and Observer*, April 3, 1938.

37. Frank L. Bridges, alumnus of Camp NC F-14, Balsam Grove, N.C., speech delivered at annual reunion, September 1990.

Bibliography

Unpublished Documents

Blue Ridge Parkway Archives, Asheville, N.C.

CCC Photographs.
Superintendent/Resident Landscape Architect's Reports and Correspondence, 1938-1942.

Brigham Young University, Salt Lake City, Utah

Baldridge, Kenneth Wayne. "Nine Years of Achievement: The Civilian Conservation Corps in Utah." Ph.D. dissertation, 1971.

Great Smoky Mountains National Park Archives, Gatlinburg, Tennessee.

CCC Photographs.
Superintendent's Semiannual and Annual CCC Reports, 1933-1942.

Mars Hill College Archives, Mars Hill, N.C.

Bridges, Frank L. "Daily Menus, 1937." Unpublished memoir, CCC Collection
Deitz, A. M. Collection. Letters and Daily Diaries. CCC Collection
CCC Photographs.

National Archives, Washington, D.C.

Records of the Bureau of Indian Affairs [BIA] (Record Group 75)

Cherokee Agency, Funds and Appropriations.
Cherokee Agency, Statistical Information.
Cherokee Agency, Projects Authorized.
Correspondence.

Records of the Civilian Conservation Corps (Record Group 35)

Annual, Special, and Final Reports.
Bulletins, 1939-1942.
Camp Directories, 1933-1942.
Camp Inspection Reports, 1933-1942.
General Correspondence, 1933-1942.

General Photographic File, 1933-1940; 1940-1942.
Photographs of Black Enrollees.
Pictographs, 1933-1942.
Publicity File, 1940-1942.
Records Relating to the CCC Educational Program, 1933-1942.
Records Relating to the Organization and Operations of the Selection Work, 1933-1942.
State Procedural Manuals and Records, 1933-1942.

Records of the Forest Service (Record Group 95)

Fiftieth anniversary program, CCC Camp F-24, Robbinsville, NC. Robbinsville: U.S. Forest Service, 1983.
Forest Service Bulletins.
General Information.

Records of the National Park Service (Record Group 79)

Photographs.

North Carolina State Archives, Raleigh, N.C.

Barden, Albert, Collection.
CCC Activities, North Carolina State Parks and Forests, in Department of Conservation and Development Records, 1933 and afterward.
CCC Photographs.
Division of Forestry, Forest Resources, Photographs.
Emergency Relief Administration Records, 1933 and afterward.
Governor's CCC Correspondence, in various Governors' Papers, 1933-1942.

Southern Highlands Research Center, UNC-Asheville, Asheville, N.C.

Photographs.

Tennessee Valley Authority Archives, Knoxville, Tennessee

CCC Photographs.

"A Peace Time Army: The Tennessee Valley Authority's Civilian Conservation Corps, 1933-1942." Unpublished report.

"Report of Work Accomplished in T.V.A. C.C.C. Camps Administered by the U.S. Forest Service, October 1935-June, 1936." Unpublished report.

"Report of Work Accomplished in T.V.A. C.C.C. Camps Administered by the U.S. Forest Service, July 1936-June 1937." Unpublished report.

"Report of Work Accomplished in T.V.A. C.C.C. Camps Administered by the U.S. Forest Service, July 1937-June 1938." Unpublished report.

Personal Collections

Brooks, Charles, Correspondence. In possession of Becky Brooks Wallace, Lillington, N.C.

Maneval, G. B., Collection. In author's possession, awaiting transfer to Mars Hill College.

State and Federal CCC-related Publications

Congressional Record. 77th Congress, Second Session, Vol. 88, Part 4.

Kirk, J. S., et al., eds. *Emergency Relief in North Carolina: A Record of the Development and the Activities of the North Carolina Emergency Relief Administration, 1932-1935*. Raleigh: North Carolina Emergency Relief Commission, 1936.

Otis, Alison T., et al. *The Forest Service and the Civilian Conservation Corps, 1933-1942*. Washington, D.C.: U.S. Department of Agriculture, 1986.

Paige, John C. *The Civilian Conservation Corps and the National Park Service, 1933-1942: An Administrative History*. Washington, D.C.: U.S. Department of the Interior, National Park Service, 1985.

U.S. Department of Agriculture. *National Forests in the Southern Appalachians*. Washington, D.C.: Government Printing Office, 1940.

U.S. Department of the Interior, Office of Education. *CCC Camp Education: Guidance and Recreational Phases, Bulletin No. 19*. Washington, D.C.: Government Printing Office, 1937.

U.S. Department of Labor. *Handbook for Agencies Selecting Men for Emergency Conservation Work. Emergency Conservation Work Bulletin No. 3*. Washington, D.C.: Government Printing Office, 1933.

U.S. War Department. *Civilian Conservation Corps Regulations*. Washington, D.C.: Government Printing Office, 1933.

Newspapers

Asheboro Courier
Asheville Citizen
Asheville Citizen-Times
Boston (Mass.) *Traveler*
Bryson City Times
Catawba News-Enterprise (Newton)
Charlotte Observer
Cleveland Daily Star (Shelby)
Cleveland Star (Shelby)
Daily Mail (Anderson, S.C.)
Daily Times-News (Burlington)
Franklin Press
Happy Days (Washington, D.C.)
Journal-Patriot (North Wilkesboro)
Lenoir News-Topic
Lincoln County News (Lincolnton)
Marion Progress
Monroe Enquirer
Mountaineer (Waynesville)
New York Times
News and Observer (Raleigh)
News-Herald (Morganton)
News Record (Marshall)
News-Sentinel (Knoxville, Tenn.)
North Carolina Public Welfare News
Raleigh Times
Randolph Tribune (Asheboro)
Salisbury Post
Salt Lake Tribune
Shelby Star
Skyland Post (Jefferson, N.C.)
Stanly News and Press (Albemarle)
Transylvania Times (Brevard)
Watauga Democrat (Boone)
Winston-Salem Journal

CCC Camp Newspapers

Balsam Breeze. Issued by Camp NC F-14, Company 428.

Sand Spur. Issued by Camp NC P-62, Company 427.

CCC Camp Annuals

High Tide. Issued by Camp Virginia Dare (Camp NC BF-2, Company 436), Manteo (complete range of publication dates unavailable).

Official Annual. Issued by Fourth Corps Area, Districts "A," "B," "C," and "II." 1934, 1936, 1937.

General Published Works

Biggs, Walter C., Jr., and James F. Parnell. *State Parks of North Carolina.* Winston-Salem: John F. Blair, 1989.

Brinkley, Alan, et al. *American History: A Survey,* 8th ed. 2 vols. New York: McGraw-Hill, 1991.

Buchanan, George E. *My CCC Days.* Brevard: The author, 1935.

Butler, Ovid M., ed. *American Conservation in Picture and Story.* Washington, D.C.: American Forestry Association, 1941.

Buxton, Barry M., ed. *The Great Forest: An Appalachian Story.* Boone: Appalachian Consortium Press, 1985.

Cohen, Stan B. *The Tree Army: A Pictorial History of the Civilian Conservation Corps, 1933-1942.* Missoula, Mont.: Pictorial Histories Publishing Company, 1980.

Cole, Olen, Jr. *The African-American Experience in the Civilian Conservation Corps.* Gainesville: University of Florida, 1999.

Davidson, James West. *Nation of Nations: A Narrative History of the American Republic.* 2 vols. New York: McGraw-Hill, 1990.

Federal Writers' Project, Works Progress Administration. *These Are Our Lives.* Chapel Hill: University of North Carolina Press, 1939.

Garraty, John A., and Robert A. McCaughey. *A Short History of the American Nation.* New York: Harper and Row, 1989.

Gewehr, Wesley M., et al. *American Civilization: A History of the United States.* New York: McGraw-Hill, 1957.

Hill, Frank Ernest. *The School in the Camps: The Educational Program of the Civilian Conservation Corps.* New York: American Association for Adult Education, 1935.

Leake, Fred E., and Ray S. Carter. *Roosevelt's Tree Army: A Brief History of the Civilian Conservation Corps.* Arlington, Va.: National Association of CCC Alumni, 1983.

Leuchtenburg, William E. *Franklin D. Roosevelt and the New Deal, 1932-1940.* New York: Harper and Row, 1963.

Moley, Raymond. *The First New Deal.* New York: Harcourt, Brace and World, 1966.

Nixon, Edgar B. *Franklin D. Roosevelt and Conservation, 1911-1945.* 2 vols. Hyde Park, N.Y.: General Services Administration, National Archives and Records Service, Franklin D. Roosevelt Library, 1957.

Oliver, Alfred C., Jr., and Harold M. Dudley. *This New America: The Spirit of the Civilian Conservation Corps.* New York: Longmans, Green and Company, 1937.

Perry, Ralph B., ed. *Essays on Faith and Morals by William James.* New York: World Publishing Company, 1962.

Public Papers and Addresses of Franklin D. Roosevelt. 13 vols. New York: Random House, 1938-1950.

Roosevelt, Eleanor. *This I Remember.* New York: Harper and Brothers, 1949.

Rosenman, Samuel I., ed. *The Court Disapproves.* New York: Random House, 1935.

Salmond, John A. *The Civilian Conservation Corps, 1933-1942: A New Deal Case Study.* Durham: Duke University Press, 1967.

Schlesinger, Arthur M., Jr. *The Age of Roosevelt.* 2 vols. Boston: Houghton Mifflin, 1957-1958.

Schwarzkopf, S. Kent. *A History of Mt. Mitchell and the Black Mountains: Exploration, Development, and Preservation.* Raleigh: Division of Archives and History, 1985.

Udall, Stewart L. *The Quiet Crisis.* New York: Rinehart and Winston, 1936.

Wirth, Conrad L. *Parks, Politics, and the People.* Norman: University of Oklahoma Press, 1980.

Wolfe, Thomas. *The Hills Beyond.* New York: New American Library, 1935.

Articles

Buel, Walker S. "The Army under the New Deal." *Literary Digest* 116 (August 26, 1933).

Chase, Stuart. "When the Crop Lands Go." *Harper's* 173 (August 1936).

Douglas, John Aubrey. "The Forest Service, the Depression, and Vermont Political Culture: Implementing New Deal Conservation and Relief Policy." *Forest and Conservation* 34 (October 1990).

Farley, Yvonne Snyder. "A Good Part of Life: Remembering the Civilian Conservation Corps." *Golden Seal* 7 (January-March 1981).

Jackson, James P. "Living Legacy of the CCC." *American Forests* 94 (September-October 1988).

Laubach, H. L. "A General Tests the CCC Boys." *Literary Digest* 121 (January 25, 1936).

Pulliam, Raymond. "Destroying Mt. Mitchell." *American Forestry* 21 (February 1915): 85.

Pyle, Charlotte. "Civilian Conservation Corps: To Earn and Learn." In *Smoky Mountain Visitor Guide,* August 1985.

Stange, Maren. "Publicity, Husbandry, and Technocracy: Fact and Symbol in Civilian Conservation Corps Photography." In Pete Daniel, et al., *Official Images: New Deal Photography.* Washington, D.C.: Smithsonian Institution, 1987.

Interviews

Harris, Morgan H. Swan Quarter, N.C. September 1990.

Ray, Huey. Madison County. July 10, 1983.

Snelson, Frances. N.p. May 15, 1991.

Unidentified interviewee. Madison County, N.C. 1985.

Speaking Engagements

Bridges, Frank L. Speech delivered at annual reunion. N.p. September 1990.

Kinsland, Ray. CCC seminar sponsored by Appalachian Consortium. Greensboro Historical Museum, Greensboro, N.C. August 4, 1992.

CCC Alumni Reunions

Hanging Rock State Park. October 26, 1991.

New Holland, N.C. September 19, 1990.

Pigeon Forge, Tenn. September 21, 1990.

Index